Applied Theatre: Creative Ageing

The **Applied Theatre** series is a major innovation in applied theatre scholarship, bringing together leading international scholars that engage with and advance the field of applied theatre. Each book presents new ways of seeing and critically reflecting on this dynamic and vibrant field. Volumes offer a theoretical framework and introductory survey of the field addresses, combined with a range of case studies illustrating and critically engaging with practice.

Series Editors
Michael Balfour (Griffith University, Australia)
Sheila Preston (University of East London, UK)

Applied Theatre: Creative Ageing

Sheila McCormick

Series Editors

Michael Balfour and Sheila Preston

Bloomsbury Methuen Drama
An imprint of Bloomsbury Publishing Plc

B L O O M S B U R Y
LONDON · OXFORD · NEW YORK · NEW DELHI · SYDNEY

Bloomsbury Methuen Drama

An imprint of Bloomsbury Publishing Plc

Imprint previously known as Methuen Drama

50 Bedford Square	1385 Broadway
London	New York
WC1B 3DP	NY 10018
UK	USA

www.bloomsbury.com

BLOOMSBURY, METHUEN DRAMA and the Diana logo are trademarks of Bloomsbury Publishing Plc

First published 2017

© Sheila McCormick and contributors, 2017

Sheila McCormick has asserted her right under the Copyright, Designs and Patents Act, 1988, to be identified as author of this work.

British Library Cataloguing-in-Publication Data

A catalogue record for this book is available from the British Library.

ISBN: HB: 978-1-474-23383-5
ePDF: 978-1-474-23385-9
eBook: 978-1-474-23384-2

Library of Congress Cataloging-in-Publication Data

A catalog record for this book is available from the Library of Congress.

Series: Applied Theatre

Cover design: Louis Dugdale
Cover image © Shuttershock

Typeset by Integra Software Services Pvt. Ltd.
Printed and bound in Great Britain

To find out more about our authors and books visit www.bloomsbury.com. Here you will find extracts, author interviews, details of forthcoming events and the option to sign up for our newsletters.

To Maeve and Hugh
My greatest supporters
Every day, you are missed

Contents

List of Figures

Acknowledgements

I wish to thank series editors Michael Balfour and Sheila Preston for all their advice and support as well as the contributors for their patience and generosity. I would like to give special thanks to my friend Fintan Walsh whose humour is a tonic and whose guidance is invaluable. Finally, thanks to my family especially the constant joy that are Maeve, Ellen, Mylo and Rubin. And to my best friend and partner in crime, Brian, thank you for your love and support and for making me laugh whatever the weather.

Notes on Contributors

Michael Balfour is inaugural Chair of Applied and Social Theatre at Griffith University, Brisbane, Australia. His area of research is focused on the social applications of theatre and performance. Professor Balfour has published three monographs, four edited books and more than twenty-six peer-reviewed papers in high impact journals and collections. He has won many awards for his research in arts and health, applied theatre as well as several prestigious National Teaching Awards. Recent research projects have included creative approaches to working with newly arrived refugees, verbatim theatre with returning veterans from Iraq and Afghanistan, mapping performing arts projects in Australian prisons and exploring the impact of playful work with people who have mid to late dementia.

Anne Davis Basting (PhD) is an educator, scholar and artist whose work focuses on the potential for the arts and humanities to improve our quality of life as communities and individuals. For over fifteen years, Basting has developed and researched methods for embedding the arts into long-term care, with a particular focus on people with cognitive disabilities like dementia. Basting is author of numerous articles and several books, including *Forget Memory: Creating Better Lives for People with Dementia* (2009) and *The Stages of Age: Performing Age in Contemporary American Culture*. Basting is the recipient of a Rockefeller Fellowship, a Brookdale National Fellowship and numerous major grants, including the MAP Fund and NEA Artworks. She is author and/ or producer of nearly a dozen plays and public performances, including *Slightly Bigger Women* (2015) and *Finding Penelope* (2011), a play inspired by a year of intergenerational conversations about the myth of Penelope from Homer's *Odyssey*, and professionally staged at a long-term care facility. Her latest book – *The Penelope Project: An Arts-based Odyssey to Change Elder-Care* (2016) co-edited with Maureen Towey and Ellie Rose – tells the story of that remarkable collaboration. Basting is founder and president of the award-winning non-profit TimeSlips

Creative Storytelling, which brings creativity into care relationships to transform aging. She is Professor of Theatre at the University of Wisconsin-Milwaukee, where she teaches engaged arts practices.

Marie Cooke is Professor of Nursing within Menzies Health Institute Queensland, Griffith University and Deputy Head of School (Research) in the School of Nursing and Midwifery, Griffith University. She has a strong client-focused clinical research profile as well as educational research with clinicians to implement evidence into practice. Her research is in relation to clinical trials and symptom management. She has a substantial track record in projects that involve an intervention and pre- and post-testing, including randomized controlled trials (RCTs). She has led RCTs, involving multi-disciplinary teams, which have focused on symptom management (e.g. agitation, mood, anxiety, pain, nausea and vomiting) across a range of clinical settings and populations.

Julie Dunn's research work focuses on play, playfulness and drama. She has published widely in these areas, with a specific area of interest being their points of intersection. With research projects involving participants as varied as young children, adult drama learners and people living with dementia, the contexts for Julie's research work are highly diverse. Recent work has focused on the role of emotion and how the different emotions provoked within play and drama influence the engagement and meaning making of participants. Julie was the 2005 winner of the American Alliance for Theatre and Education Distinguished Dissertation Award and her book *Pretending to Learn* (co-authored with John O'Toole) was winner of a 2003 Excellence in Educational Publishing Award.

Jayne Lloyd is a practice-based PhD student at Royal Holloway, University of London. Her research explores the use of reminiscence and interdisciplinary arts practices (theatre, music, fine art and dance) with care home residents, including those living with dementia. It focuses on Reminiscence Arts and Dementia – Impact on Quality of Life (Age Exchange, RADIQL), a three-year programme created by Age Exchange and funded by Guy's and St Thomas Charity. Her research draws together her practice as an installation artist and over ten years' experience of working in community engagement, development and facilitation roles.

Beth Luxmoore works for the Alzheimer's Society as Programme Development Manager. Beth was awarded her PhD in Biomedical Engineering in 2013. Shortly after, she made a career change to follow her interest and passion in supporting older people and people with dementia to live well. Beth joined the Alzheimer's Society to lead a project to deliver arts-based activity groups for people with dementia and carers and to work with researchers to understand how the impact of these services could be measured. Since 2014, she has led the Salford Involvement Project, aiming to put into practice innovative approaches to involving people affected by dementia in the work of the Alzheimer's Society, and continues to work closely with people affected by dementia, researchers and commissioners to make services more person-centred, to understand communication approaches for people with more advanced dementia and the implementation of co-production approaches.

Wendy Moyle is Program Director, Menzies Health Institute QLD, Griffith University, Brisbane, Australia. Wendy's research expertise is in the areas of dementia, depression and delirium. Her research focus has been on understanding and interventions to improve quality of life and emotional engagement in people with dementia and their carers. She has a keen interest in technologies and her research over the last five years has been testing assistive technologies/social robots and complementary and alternative medicine interventions with people with dementia.

Helen Nicholson is Professor of Theatre and Performance at Royal Holloway, University of London. Helen has been co-editor of *RiDE: The*

Journal of Applied Theatre and Performance since 2004, and author of several books in the field, including *Applied Drama: The Gift of Theatre* (2005, second edition 2014), *Theatre & Education* (2009) and *Theatre, Education and Performance: The Map and the Story* (2011), for which she was awarded the Distinguished Book Award by the American Alliance for Theatre and Education in 2012. She has recently led a research project on the role of the arts in dementia care, funded by Guys and St Thomas' Charitable Trust.

Clive Parkinson is the Director of Arts for Health at Manchester Metropolitan University, a specialist research unit that explores the relationship between creativity, culture, the arts and health. He is a founding member of the National Alliance for Arts, Health and Wellbeing, and is currently a co-investigator on the Dementia & Imagination project in the UK, which is exploring the links between the visual arts, well-being and sense of community. Clive has worked for the National Health Service and voluntary sector supporting people from diverse backgrounds and, where possible, putting culture and the arts at the forefront of his work – which focuses on people and their possibilities – not illness and deficit. He is interested in the unexpected outcomes of arts engagement and is currently working with partnerships in Australia, Italy, France, Lithuania and Turkey. Working with people in recovery from substance addiction, he has developed a Recoverist Manifesto and he regularly blogs at: http://artsforhealthmmu.blogspot.co.uk/

Mike Pearson is Emeritus Professor of Performance Studies in the Department of Theatre, Film and Television Studies at Aberystwyth University. He creates theatre as a solo artist; with artist/designer Mike Brookes in Pearson/Brookes; with National Theatre Wales; and with senior performers' group Good News From The Future. He is co-author with Michael Shanks of *Theatre/Archaeology* (2001) and author of *In Comes I: Performance, Memory and Landscape* (2006), *Site-Specific Performance* (2010), *MickeryTheater: An Imperfect Archaeology* (2011) and *Marking Time: Performance, Archaeology and the City* (2013).

Introduction

'Of all realities [old age] is perhaps that of which we retain a purely abstract notion longest in our lives', says Proust with great accuracy. All men are mortal: they reflect upon this fact. A great many of them become old: almost none ever foresees this state before it is upon him. Nothing should be more expected than old age: nothing is more unforeseen.

De Beauvoir, 1970: 10

Human beings are no different from any other cellular organism. At the point of conception a process of cellular division occurs; foetal development, birth, growth and eventual maturation follow. Once achieved, physical maturation, including sexual maturation, assures that the cycle continues. Physical harm aside, the conclusion of human growth heralds the move towards degeneration, which continues to an inevitable end point; the death of the cellular organism/older adult. Despite this inevitability, as De Beauvoir points out, ageing appears to have the potential to surprise; it is the unwelcome guest who wasn't invited but who turns up regardless. The inability to accept and pre-empt its arrival means the natural process of ageing is often met with distain, paranoia and even fear.

Applied Theatre: Creative Ageing aims to consider the human reluctance to accept ageing as a natural part of life and to consider what can be done to lessen the naivety with which it is approached. It does so not to prescribe a methodology for ageing but rather to consider how applied theatre practices might engage with the topic of ageing in ways that make it more visible and more considered. To this end, Part I of the book examines biological and sociological viewpoints that surround ageing before moving on to outline and define specific forms and movements within the applied theatre field. In the second section, a range of chapters from practitioners and theorists considers the role of creative practice with, for and by older adults. These chapters demonstrate the breadth of practice occurring internationally in this area while simultaneously displaying the diversity of critical analysis currently being undertaken. *Applied Theatre: Creative Ageing* chooses to engage with the subject from a Western perspective with the knowledge that further research into multi- and cross-cultural work is needed. Throughout, creative methodologies and issues that surround the practice of applied theatre with, for and by older adults are considered. Also examined are the claims of increased wellness and/or quality of life that accompany the practice. These claims are observed along with an acknowledgement of the growing importance of practice in this area and the arguments (implicit or explicit) that exist for that practice to be acknowledged and developed as a specific and individual entity within applied theatre.

Contexts of ageing

To consider the process of ageing, and suggest a specific origin point, either in biological or in social terms, would be impossible; instead this section acknowledges the role society and culture have in defining age. Ageing, this book argues, is an individual experience that does not occur in a biological bubble. Rates of ageing of course respond to physiological cellular and molecular change, but they are also dependent on individual factors that include environment and behaviour, as well as social, cultural and political circumstances. In Part I of this book, the biology of ageing is considered, not in isolation but in conversation with changes that have occurred (longitudinal and social) in relation to the process in order to consider how arts practice might respond to these changes.

There appears to be no definitive point where adulthood begins. While bone growth and skeletal development curtails towards the end of teenage years, brain development continues into the late twenties. Last to develop is the prefrontal cortex, a structure found at the front of the brain just behind the forehead. This part of the brain is reserved for high cognitive functions such as planning and decision making. It is where an understanding of social behaviour and awareness is processed and where personality, empathy and the ability to interact with others are formed (Starratt, 2016). The prefrontal cortex provides the traits that distinguish us as human. It is interesting then that this part of the human body is the last to fully develop and that this development occurs closer to middle age than childhood.

All of the above is mentioned not to challenge the agreed point where adulthood begins but to acknowledge that this moment is unfixed and depends on a society's understanding (both scientific and cultural) of ageing at the time. Now in my forty-first year, I am loath to acknowledge that 200 years ago the average human was considered to have lived a long life if he or she had managed to reach my age. In equal measure, I am delighted with the findings regarding my frontal cortex, not least because they explain and potentially excuse some of the folly of my twenties, but because they also challenge the notion that forty was ever old age at all, or even middle age as our present understanding would have it. On the contrary, the findings mentioned above appear to suggest that, at this point in my life cycle, I am, in fact, only a short distance into adulthood.

The physical toll of everyday life, prevalence of infectious disease and high child mortality in our recent history have meant that for the average human in existence 200 years ago, reaching adulthood at all would have been a steep statistical challenge. Public Health England evidences that 'over the last 30 years there has been an upward trend in life expectancy at older ages in England' (2016). In England, men can now expect to live for a further nineteen years at age sixty-five, twelve years at seventy-five, six years at eighty-five and three years at ninety-five, while women should expect to live a further twenty-one years at sixty-five, thirteen years at seventy-five and seven years at eighty-five (Public Health England, 2016). In fact, the data shows that while there are differences between countries, 'in the EU as a whole there has been an overall upward trend in life expectancy at older ages' (Public Health England, 2016). Kirkwood (2001) argues that the previous fifty years have seen life expectancy increase by two years each decade, suggesting those who lived over the course of those fifty years had, for every decade they had lived, gained an 'extra twenty percent free' (2001: 5). Further research in 2015 by the Department of Epidemiology and Biostatistics supports these claims suggesting that while women have long since enjoyed a few more adult years than their male counterparts, between 1981 and 2012, life expectancy increased by an average of eight years three months for men and six years for women, closing the female–male gap. The study also suggested that by 2030, the national life expectancy in Britain may rise to reach eighty-five – an increase of seven years – for men, and eighty-seven – an increase of six years – for women, further reducing the female advantage (Bennett et al., 2015).

Poverty and its associated factors remains an overriding influence on how a society ages. In the United States, recent data from the National Centre for Health Statistics (2016) showed that while life expectancy might be rising, it is the poor who are losing ground in both income and life span. Commenting on the data, Travernise notes that in the 1970s, a sixty-year-old man in the top half of the earnings ladder could expect to live one year three months longer than a man of the same age in the bottom half. By 2001 he could expect to live five years nine months longer than his poorer counterpart (Tavernise, 2016). In 2015 the World Health Organization (WHO), ranking countries in terms of life expectancy, placed the average life expectancy at birth at 71.4. With Japan, Korea, Australia, New Zealand, Scandinavia and parts of Europe and North America ranking among the highest with a life expectancy of over eighty years, several other countries exhibited expectancies decades lower (WHO, Life Expectancy at Birth, 2015). In countries with higher rates of poverty such as Chad, Somalia and Angola, the average life expectancy is greatly reduced. Here individuals live on average less than fifty-five years (WHO, Life Expectancy at Birth, 2015).

Even if the average human manages to avoid accidental death or one of the five diseases that cause premature death (diseases associated with the liver, cardiovascular and respiratory system, as well as cancer and stroke) (NHS, 2015) and lives to reach the point of being an octogenarian and beyond, will he or she think of himself or herself lucky or, indeed, old? As De Beauvoir notes, 'when we are young and in our prime we do not think of ourselves as already being in the dwelling-place of our own future old age. Age is removed from us by an extent of time so great that it merges with eternity: such a remote future seems unreal' (1970: 10).

The public–private continuum

These observations are offered as a positive position from which to frame what follows. Yes, ageing can be viewed negatively and yes, ageism and age-related bias remain imbedded in our culture. However, considering the findings of neuroscience, advancements that have occurred both in society and in the field of medicine, and the changes in demographics that have occurred as a result of these advancements, we must acknowledge that in our lifetime the notion of age itself has changed. My fortieth year does not signify in the same way as it did for my parent's generation or their parent's; its meaning has altered and, if the associations attached to my particular age can change and be redefined, then surely so too can attitudes towards ageing itself change. This cannot happen unassisted however and what follows in the upcoming chapters suggest applied theatre might have a role to play in responding to the changing demographic of our society. The chapters acknowledge the ability of artists to use creative strategies and practices to support the needs of older adults, both physical and emotional, while also, at times, attempting to shift attitudes in relation to ageing. Encouraging and supporting more practice in this area might go some way towards allowing the changes that have occurred in relation to ageing to be explored and, potentially, to encourage a reconsideration of how they might be embraced so that individuals might live well while living longer.

Applied theatre and creative practice with older adults occurs along a public–private continuum and, as a form, is varied. Like its counterparts, theatre and creative practice with older adults is made with, for and by a particular group, in diverse spaces for diverse reasons, occurring both in public within community venues and in private in residential care settings. Applied theatre with, for and by older adults addresses issues (physical, pathophysiological, social and mental) associated with ageing such as reduced mobility and cognition, reduced independence, marginalization, social isolation, loneliness and depression. Practice in this area is undertaken for a number of reasons from encouraging participation and engagement to facilitating professional artists or older performers to engage politically with issues associated with ageing (such as ageism and marginalization) and in doing so to challenge those issues.

Along the public/ private continuum are varying levels of interaction, creativity and ability. The 'public' may refer to work that exists in the public domain and whose remit is to engage both the community in which it is placed and society more generally. Often public-orientated artistic work is focused on product and on the principles of creative exchange, those that occur between performer, performance and audience. Work that sits at the other end of the continuum occurs in settings that are private. While work that is public can have a rich affective process, this might be only one of its intentions. Private work however often focuses heavily on what happens in the moment of interaction. It is based around concepts of experience, affect and process. In other words, it focuses on the experience of arts practice and on the atmosphere and relationships that develop as a result of that practice.

Applied Theatre: Creative Ageing explores practice, both public and private, in an attempt to understand the form and its implications. Each example included in the forthcoming chapters can be positioned along that continuum, with that position dictating different kinds of practice with different kinds of concerns. In the sections that follow, the importance of creativity as well as the relevance of ability is considered in relation to notions of the private and the public and the spaces in between. Some examples of practice will be easier to position along the continuum than others. The work of practitioners such as Mike Pearson and Lois Weaver discussed in Chapter 2 exemplifies practice that engages with the themes of ageing and is public facing. Private or more intimate practice is also explored in the second chapter in examples such as Small Things: Creative Project while the spaces in between the private and public are examined in the same chapter in relation to festivals, networks and theatre companies specifically developed with, for and by elderly actors, artists and participants. These practices are considered in relation to their intimate or public-facing nature.

Later in the contributed chapters by Clive Parkinson, Helen Nicholson and Jayne Lloyd, as well as Michael Balfour, Julie Dunn, Wendy Moyle and Marie Cook, the private, hidden quality of the practice is examined further allowing concepts of creativity and care to be explored. Beth Luxmoore's chapter allows spaces between the public and private to be analysed in her examination of the Alzheimer's Society's Non-Pharmaceutical Intervention (NPI) project. Thus, these contributions reveal the varying levels of sociality, autonomy and creative capacity found along the public–private continuum.

Throughout this volume, several recurring themes emerge. Firstly, that the medical model of care seems absent from applied theatre with, for and by older adults. Although practice in applied theatre with older adults may have beneficial medical outcomes, such practice embraces person-centred and relational models. Nicholson and Lloyd, along with Balfour et al., discuss the benefit of this embrace. Person-centred practice does not generalize; it takes into account the individual and their response to the world. Personal capacity to create and engage in arts practice is not predicated on a diagnosis.

Indeed, the individual is taken into account away from generalized ideas regarding disease diagnosis and associated symptoms. Similarly, stereotypes regarding ability in relation to age are avoided. The relational module considers the person-centred approach while also taking into account the interaction that is occurring between the participant and the facilitator.

Secondly, unlike other examples of applied theatre, practice that considers ageing is not necessarily explicitly concerned with education or development. Instead, it is built on a shared understanding of the benefits of social engagement. Whether based in a care home or a reparatory theatre, arts practice in this area allows sociality and the experience of being present and sharing a space/experience with another person to take precedence. This other person might be a fellow participant, a facilitator, a family member, a friend or a carer.

While some examples of applied practice may prioritize the potential of that practice to evoke change, or to have a positive effect, thus focusing on outcome, relational applied theatre with older adults considers the importance of the moment of interaction and the affect communally experienced in that moment.

Finally, while not always educational in intention, practice with, for and by older adults that occurs at the public end of the continuum can potentially highlight the position of older adults in society, and where that is marginal, call for action and potentially facilitate change.

The structure of this book

Part one: Ageing and applied theatre

Section one of the book frames understandings of ageing from a Western context. Chapter 1 introduces the current cultural, sociological and political debates that surround around ageing. It highlights changes in demographics and the challenges these present for individuals and society more broadly. The material gathered here is intended to provide a discussion of what it means, and will mean, to age in contemporary society. For the most part, the chapter focuses on the struggle to understand and embrace ageing and offers some considerations on how our approach to ageing might be improved. Here, some examples of applied practice are introduced that will be discussed in more detail in Chapter 2. The intention behind offering this material is to provide a foundation for the theoretical questions that echo throughout the book regarding applied theatre with, for and by older adults.

In Chapter 2, specific examples of practice are explored in order to develop a theoretical framework through which to view applied theatre and ageing, this chapter aims to contextualize the practice in order to consider how specific arts forms have been translated by artists and practitioners to best serve the needs of the older adult in whatever setting they are encountered. Using specific examples, the chapter examines the rationale behind arts practice with, for and by older adults, along with the inherent artfulness and potential positive outcomes attached to the practice.

All applied theatre with older adults is not the same; it is not conceived in the same way and does not have the same intentions. The case studies included in Chapter 2 exist along the continuum discussed. Using the continuum as a framing device allows the unique characteristics of applied theatre with, for and by older adults to be acknowledged and explored. It also provides a space where specific issues that relate to the practice can be analysed in detail.

The chapter begins with a consideration of the community theatre origins of applied theatre and ageing. This historical context allows for a demarcation of the practice beyond the fields of education or development usually associated with applied theatre. The separate sections that follow provide a number of interesting perspectives on practice that can be attached at different points along the continuum. From public-facing activities (such as festivals) at one end to individual one-to-one work at the other, these examples of practice highlight the continuum and the varying levels of ability and creativity that exist on it. Out of these discussions, the first section concludes with a set of reflections on applied theatre practice with, for and by older adults and offers some suggestion as to what the future might hold for this specific and unique area of theatre practice.

Part two: Contributions

The second section presents a series of contributions from scholars and practitioners working in the area of applied theatre and ageing. Their work is positioned at different points along the continuum from public to private and is curated as such. The earlier chapters address more intimate examples of practice, engaging with debates that consider the importance of relationality and affect, while the latter chapters move from the private and intimate to consider more public-facing activities that occur in the area of applied theatre and ageing.

In Chapter 3, Balfour, Dunn, Moyle and Cooke consider relational clowning and approaches to arts practice that consider the work of practitioners such as Lecoq, Gaulier and Pagneux. Examining concepts such as play, complicite and Le Jeu, the authors analyse a multi-disciplinary project entitled Playful Engagement that engaged nursing and applied theatre academics, staff and residents of five residential care facilities and two relational clowns. Their intention within the project being to identify the potential interactions relational clowning might encourage for individuals with a diagnosis of dementia.

In their use of play, complicite and Le Jeu, 'relational clowns' responded to intuition and feelings felt in moments of interaction. By exploring two specific moments of practice, the authors consider relational clown practice and these concepts in detail. Understanding the need to observe and consider the multifaceted and layered realities that occurred in those moments, as well as a need to consistently and continuously gauge the atmosphere, feeds into the authors' consideration of play and complicite in relation to the practice. Their reading of Le Jeu in this instance was developed by play and complicite as it related to the clown's ability to respond in the moment and exist in relation to everything else, material and immaterial, in that moment.

Balfour and his fellow authors argue complicite was found to occur both between performers and between performers and participants and that realization highlights the importance of pleasure in the interaction for both the performer and participant. This pleasure, they suggest, might encourage play and as a result, joy. Thus, Balfour and his colleagues stress the importance of understanding moments of affect and for 'connection and relatedness' which as they note, 'provided opportunities for residents and artists to engage in ways that privilege temporary and ephemeral moments of pleasure, play, silence and indulgence, recognizing that every encounter requires renegotiation and adaptation as situations, moods, and conditions change' (this volume: 123).

In Chapter 4, Nicholson and Lloyd also consider affect opening their discussion with the observation that it is often the immeasurable, unquantifiable 'feel' of a care home that is commented on by those who experience it. Despite this, they go on to note, 'the well-being and quality of life of residents is only recognised when individuals can be measured, this means that the more communal, affective and sensory qualities of a residential care settings are often overlooked' (125). Following Lloyd's work with residents in a care home, both authors acknowledge this potential inequity and consider ways residents within a care home setting with a diagnosis of dementia can engage with artists to re-imagine the care home as a creative space. In order to do so, they examine the ways home and home-making are considered and experienced in everyday life. Also considering relational rather than patient-centred interactions, the authors note the connection that concepts of home have to both the spatial and temporal imaginaries and the materiality of everyday routines and objects. They point to the opportunities this connection affords for artists, whose work, according to Nicholson and Lloyd, 'necessarily involves encounters between material and imaginative elements, and who are thus well placed to encourage creative engagements with different imaginaries of home and to foster new social relationships in the material present of a residential setting' (126).

In Chapter 5, Clive Parkinson provides a discussion of the subjective reality and dominance of medical science. Pointing to the benefits of arts practice in health and well-being, he argues that the evaluative, scientific language of medicine might not be best equipped to understand these benefits and instead argues for the development of a different language through which one could examine arts practice that occurs with individuals in poor health. While evidence of the impact of arts on health and well-being is growing, this chapter suggests that an understanding of its cultural value might not be best understood through the lens of medicine, but through its own language. For Parkinson, medical knowledge is unassuming in its need for completeness whereas arts practice exists in the less absolute spaces, somewhere between, as he puts it, 'knowledge and imagination' (162). He suggests 'bringing people up close and personal with artistic revelation, cultural engagement and participation offers a more ambiguous and nuanced conversation about what it is to be human' (162) and argues against the idea that arts practice in this area is 'some instrumental "high quality" cultural tool, meted out to the poor and uneducated and dispensed by a nanny-state' (162). Instead, he suggests it is something more essential than that and claims, arts practice, with its immeasurable, ambiguous and uncertain nature can do more than simply, 'ameliorating against disease' (162). In his words, it may enable a 'deeper understanding of the subjective realities and diverse lived experiences of others' (162).

Both Chapters 6 and 7 engage with practice that is public and concerned with ideas of engagement, sociality and community. Written by Anne Davis Basting, Chapter 6 examines her highly successful Timeslips practice and its development leading to the creation of The Islands of Milwaukee project. Doing so, Basting argues applied theatre can be a force to foster expression in marginalized members of society. Thus potentially, she maintains, offering re-imaginings of the systems of support offered to these members that might encourage inclusivity and sustainability.

With an understanding of the challenges associated with collaborations between older adults and support agencies, Basting explores such intentions reflecting on a project that was both intimate (occurring in individuals' homes) and outward facing (culminating in a large-scale public installation). Through the experience of publicly sharing the stories that emerge from her intimate Timeslips workshops, Basting developed multiple play productions which she claims educate audiences 'about the expressive strengths of people with dementia and the promise that improvisation holds for transforming care relationships' (166). In her chapter, she discusses practice which moves from the private, hidden space of the care home to practice developed out in the community, first addressing people in their own homes and then engaging the wider community through public performance. Throughout, what is celebrated is the improvizational root of the practice, its sustainable and accessible nature and its positive impact on relationships between older adults and those who might care for them.

In Chapter 7, an interview with eminent scholar and theatre practitioner Mike Pearson again considers practice that is public facing but that still considers ageing in personal and intimate ways. Here the distinguished theatre maker discusses his practice, particularly his 2014 (and 1974) performance *Lessons of Anatomy*, as well as his work with theatre group Good News from the Future, to consider how artists might continue to make work as they age and how that work might encourage an audience to consider ageing in new ways.

Finally, Chapter 8 exists somewhere between the public and private and so provides an interesting final chapter through which to consider the framework presented in section one. Here Beth Luxmoore explores work that is designed to occur in a workshop setting and is thus neither private nor public facing. In this chapter she includes her analysis of the Alzheimer's Society's NPI project, a project including workshops of six types of creative activity for people living with dementia and their families over an eighteen-month period. The project was commissioned in the hope that it might accrue a basis of evidence for the efficacy of such interventions in managing behavioural and psychological symptoms of dementia in a community setting, which in turn might ultimately reduce reliance on health services and anti-psychotic medications. As a result, it provides an interesting and valuable counterpoint to earlier discussions regarding the issues that exist in relation to arts practice and evaluation.

Throughout all of the chapters, what is fore grounded is the level of diversity existing within applied practice with, for and by older adults. This diversity is driven by the complex nature of a practice that resides along a continuum, one which factors in degrees of ability and creativity. In the sections that follow, the range of practice that exists in the area of applied theatre and ageing is explored in more detail and in relation to current research in ageing. The framework that comes out of this discussion introduces paradigms that can be adopted for further study of such practice.

Applied Theatre: Creative Ageing opens up a discussion, one that explores our relationship to ageing and questions how applied theatre practice might help us reconsider that relationship. An historical analysis of society and ageing shows that attitudes towards this natural process have changed over time. There is no reason, therefore, that our attitude to ageing as a society might not change for the better in the future. What follows here considers the role of applied theatre practice in that change. *Applied Theatre: Creative Ageing* offers examples of how the form of arts practice can relate both to an individual's experience of ageing and to broader themes and issues that surround ageing as a heterogeneous, yet universal, fact of life. Including a diversity of practice in the survey and later through the contributions, this book serves to highlight the complex nature of the form, its intentions and, most importantly, the communities it attempts to serve.

Part One

Ageing, the Individual and Society

Sheila McCormick

This chapter provides a framework for a discussion regarding the nature of ageing, the cultural and social significance of considerable demographic change and the challenges this change presents. The material gathered here is intended to provoke further dialogue around what it means, and will mean, to age in Western society. Focusing on the struggles associated with ageing and considering the notion that we might be able to age better, the chapter does so with the intention to provide a foundation for the theoretical questions on applied theatre, with, for and by older adults, which resonate throughout the book.

The chapter is structured under the following headings: 'Historial Perspectives on Ageing'; 'What Is Ageing?'; 'The Individual and Ageing'; 'Society and Ageing'; 'Living Longer Better'; 'The Quality of Life Debate'; and 'Positive Steps: An Age-inclusive Society'. As such, it moves from an analysis of ageing and its impact on the individual and society more generally to a consideration of how it might be better approached and a consideration of quality of life (QoL) in an effort to produce a more age-inclusive society. By introducing current cultural, sociological and political debates, these sections allow the changes in demographics and the challenges these changes present to be highlighted and examined. This examination then provides a discussion of what it means, and will mean, to age in contemporary society, focusing on understanding and embracing ageing while considering approaches that might improve its impact. At points throughout the chapter, examples of applied practice are alluded to that will be discussed in more detail in Chapter 2. The intention behind offering this material is to provide a foundation for the theoretical questions that recur throughout this book regarding applied theatre with, for and by older adults.

Historical perspectives on ageing

Just over 100 years ago, the father of geriatrics, Ignaz Leo Nascer, lamented the degeneration of perfect physical organs and tissues to the point that they could no longer function to the level necessary for life. Thus, the shift from the perfect organism with the ability to renew itself to one imperfect, unable to repair itself, has baffled scientists for a century. As early as 1914, Nascher argued that ageing is not a process of becoming worn out like an engine but rather something that occurs as a manifestation of life. It is not wear and tear or overuse that accounts for the ageing process. Misuse has its implications for ageing but the body left unused at any age will fall into disrepair. Immobility, for example, in any human body will inevitably lead to muscle wasting and impaired skin integrity, not to mention reduced cardiovascular and respiratory capacity. That being said, renewal through use is not eternal; it continues only to a point.

The word 'geriatrics' has its root in the Greek *geron* meaning 'old man' and *iatros* meaning 'healer'. Fundamentally, the medical specialism (much like its counterpart, paediatrics) has been concerned with diseases associated with a specific group, in this case older adults. As a specific area of interest, geriatrics did not exist before the beginning of the twentieth century and it was not until 1914 that Nascher (1863–1944) produced his seminal work *Geriatrics*. It would be another thirty years before the British Geriatrics Society was founded with the intention to relieve the 'suffering and distress amongst the aged and infirm by the improvement of standards of medical care for such persons[…] and [through] the publication and distribution of the results of research' (British Geriatrics Society, 2016).

Nascher's book considers both the cause of ageing and the physiological and patho-physiological needs of the older population but it does so with an attitude of inevitability. As a branch of medical care, geriatrics researched the causes and attempted to alleviate the effects of diseases associated with ageing, but it was not until the advent of its counterpart, gerontology, that both the specific medical and social aspects of ageing (both as outcomes and intrinsic factors) were considered in a holistic way. Gerontology considers the social, environmental and individual factors that older adults experience as they move into the latter stages of the human lifespan. According to Putney et al. (2005), as the population of older adults increased, gerontology evolved as an area of interest to diverse groups including social science, psychology and public health. It is this area of medical and social science that informs much of the current research into ageing and innovations that offer opportunities to consider how the experience of ageing might be improved.

Gerontology research has shown that if reconsidered, the process of ageing might allow for approaches to be developed that achieve the best possible outcome for older adults. In other words, with further understanding of the process of ageing might come a shift in culture that impacts positively on the experience of ageing. It might encourage individuals to endeavour to renew for as long as possible and as a result to live better for longer. As Kirkwood puts it, if the idea of a programmed death is relinquished then better sense can be made of ageing (2001: 12). For current homo sapiens (in the West at least), rather than marking ageing as a mechanism for decline and ultimate death, it may be possible to consider it more as a gradual build-up of unrepaired faults in the human biological make-up. From a medical point of view, this could allow a reconsideration of the nature and cause of these faults, potentially slowing their accrual. From a sociological point of view, reconsidering why ageing occurs and what it actually means might in turn alter the negative connotations associated with this natural occurrence. In the West, a relatively comfortable existence (in comparison to previous generations) has already had a measurable impact on the health and survival of older adults. Humans know how to live longer; it is the ability to live better that remains a challenge.

What is ageing?

It is generally accepted that better sanitation (Riley, 2001), disease prevention through vaccination (Ehteth, 2003) and advancements in disease detection (Eyre et al., 2008) mean individuals no longer die from the same causes as their forbearers. Missing out on one set of diseases does not mean eternal life, however. In the twenty-first century, adult humans die more from degenerative rather than infectious disease. For example, in 2013 there were 506,790 deaths in England and Wales. Of those deaths,

> Ischemic heart disease was the leading cause of death for males in 2013, which accounted for 15.4% of male deaths. The leading cause of death for females was dementia and Alzheimer's disease, which accounted for 12.2% of female deaths during 2013. The second leading cause of death in 2013 was lung cancer (malignant neoplasm of trachea, bronchus and lung) for males and ischemic heart disease for females. (Office for National Statistics, 2015)

In the wake of vaccination, cancer, diseases of the major organs, dementia-related illnesses, stroke and diabetes make up the main causes of death in the West. They form the bases for what Kirkwood terms 'mortality substitution', which bluntly put means every living thing must die from something (2001: 8). Thus, while vaccination means that the majority of individuals are spared early deaths from tuberculosis and typhoid, humans now live long enough to fall prey to heart disease, cancer and stroke. Ageing makes each of these diseases more likely while also increasing the probability that the average adult might experience two or more conditions at the same time. Alongside disease linked to the ageing process itself (e.g. cardiovascular disease) are issues relating to degeneration, both of the body and of the mind. Thinning bones, weakening muscles and diminished senses all have the potential to increased frailty as we age. However, the rate at which degeneration occurs and the impact that degeneration has on general health depend on a range of factors, including lifestyle (exercise, diet, socialization) and our genetic predisposition.

With this in mind, the argument could be made (without seeming ungrateful) that science and medicine have propelled Western society at least to a point where death is more often than not linked to an increase in the amount of time spent on earth. Rather than through accident or exposure to a particular pathogen, death now comes from a gradual assault (that occurs through the accumulation of years) on the organism which post maturation falls short in its ability to renew itself.

Later in this section, ageism is examined and its unique position explored. As a prejudice, ageism is exceptional in that it encourages the prejudice of the individual to be projected on a group that the individual will one day be part of. Despite the Equality Act 2010, ageism persists and one must wonder if its prevalence and lack of monitoring through political correctness are related to the positioning of old people in society as material reminders of ageing and death. In the past, victims of diseases such as smallpox, leprosy and typhoid were shunned lest their disease be contracted and deaths ensue. Perhaps age now provides a modern equivalent where the old adult (much like the typhoid sufferer) makes plain our mortality simply by existing.

Defining ageing is difficult. One definition might refer to the notion of growing older, with that growth predicated on the passage of time. For some scholars, however, the measurement of years as a marker of ageing is increasingly meaningless (Ferraro, 2007; Maddox and Lawton, 1998). Considering a person's age is a way to mark particular experiences and according to Morgan and Kunkel (2016), it is these experiences that matter, not time itself. They argue, 'time's passing is of concern only because it is connected, however loosely, with other changes: physical, psychological and social' (Morgan and Kunkel, 2016: 2). As is discussed here, examining these three areas of change allows for a fuller understanding of ageing in general.

Physical ageing has been linked to pathology and the body's decreased function. Certain outcomes such as wrinkles, grey hair and decreased immune, reproductive and cardiovascular function have all been linked to age, but scholarship questions whether these changes are inevitable or whether they are, in fact, more predicated on lifestyle and environmental factors and are therefore preventable (Morgan and Kunkel, 2016). Considering this position and its influence on understandings as to why individuals age at different rates and in different ways, researchers such as Rowe and Kahn (1998) developed the concept of *successful* ageing, which delineated the process into three categories: optimal, pathological and usual. 'Optimal', as the word suggests, sees an individual age with little change to his or her physical health. 'Pathological' ageing, on the other hand, is characterized as being accompanied by chronic disease. Finally, 'usual' ageing is positioned somewhere between the two, referring to typical experiences of ageing with some loss of function but enduring physical health.

The second area of change used to define ageing is *psychological*. Several important features need to be considered in relation to this category. First, Cohen (2006) argues that human development is something that occurs from birth to death. It does not cease once we reach adulthood but continues as we age. Second, according to Morgan and Kunkel, 'personality does not undergo profound changes in later life; most personality traits, self-concept and self-esteem remain fairly stable from midlife onwards' (2016: 4). As they continue, 'although the developmental challenges and opportunities vary through life, the strategies people use to adopt to change, to refine and reinforce a sense of self, to work towards realising full human potential are practiced throughout adulthood. The simple passage of time seldom requires or causes fundamental changes to these basic personality structures and strategies' (2016).

If physical and psychological changes provide no universally inevitable outcome for the ageing adult, if an analysis of their impact only serves to highlight the diverse and hegemonic experience of ageing and the uselessness of chronological age as a marker, then we must look to third and final area of change, the *social*, and consider its influence on the experience of ageing.

To quote Morgan and Kunkel again:

> If age brings only small universal and inevitable changes in physical and cognitive functioning, and in the trajectory of adult development, why does it matter in people's lives? [...] age is significant because of

the social meanings, structures, and processes attached to it. Grey hair, wrinkles, longer reaction time, and even some short-term memory loss matter only because the social world in which we live has defined those characteristics as meaningful. Much of social meaning of ageing is tied to erroneous beliefs about the effects of ageing on physical and mental capacities. (2016: 4)

Regardless of their erroneous nature, these beliefs assign a position for older adults, to dictate what they can and cannot, should and should not do. *Social* ageing refers to the assumptions and expectations that are placed on older adults as they age and the impact these have on the experience of ageing, both on a personal and universal level.

Strehler (1962: 13–16) offers four criteria for ageing: universality, intrinsicality, progressiveness and deleteriousness. He argues that ageing is progressive and made up of a series of gradual changes; ageing is universal; unlike specific disease, ageing occurs in all members of the population, that ageing is accumulative and continuous; it does not end and gets worse the longer it occurs, and ageing is intrinsic to the organism; it is part of its very nature that changes occur regardless of the environment. Finally, unlike other periods of change or development in the human life cycle (such as maturation), ageing is degenerative as opposed to developmental. Age is therefore deleterious and causes change that compromises rather than improves biological function.

Each of us, in our own unique way, will age according to Strehler's criteria. We will not, however, age as a result of the misconception outlined by Kirkwood that 'in some fundamental sense we cannot survive for longer, or [...] are programmed to die because this is necessary to make way for the next generation' (2001: 10). This notion is tenuous at best because the human body is programmed more for survival than decline.

Having attempted to produce some historical context and discussion regarding the nature of ageing, I examine in the following sections first the personal impact ageing has on the individual before moving on to a discussion regarding the relationship between society and ageing.

The individual and ageing

Contemporary gerontology acknowledges the need for a multi-disciplinary approach, one as concerned with the psycho/social implications of ageing as it is with its physical consequences. For that reason, the writing throughout this book is holistic; it considers the older adult individually, as a member of society, and as a marker for others to imagine their own future. Social, cultural, psychological and philosophical considerations ensure that the subject of ageing is examined beyond the physical and, as a result, throughout this book are threaded observations and analysis regarding the politics of ageing and the political position/power of older adults in contemporary society. In order to examine how society deals with ageing, it is important to understand the philosophical and psychological responses of the individual to the process. For that reason, these next section considers society and ageing in tandem with observations on ageing as a personal, lived experience.

De Beauvoir notes the difficulty associated with assuming an aged self (1970: 10). She argues this is because in youth being old is something alien, something that happens to someone else. In De Beauvoir's words, 'in the old person that we must become, we refuse to recognise ourselves' (1970: 10). This dual quality of at once knowing and at the same time being unable to accept the changes age brings ties to the notion that, while most humans regularly acknowledge death throughout their lives and accept its inevitability, old age seems beyond comprehension.

According to Segal, 'as we age, most of us are still trying to hold on to some sense of who and what we are, however hard this may become for those who start to feel increasingly invisible' (2013: 1). Old age can be doubly traumatic, not only bringing with it inevitable changes that make our own bodies seem strange, but also (and unlike other stages of human development) ensuing a sense of invisibility, of either not being seen or somehow being seen as less than one once was. Engaging in a conversation with De Beauvoir, Segal recounts her own reluctance to accept her age despite her 'repeated insistence that "old age" is an "Other" which lives within everyone, whatever your age' (2013: 10). Unless struck by a premature terminal illness or an unfortunate deadly accident, that 'Other' will inhibit the lives of most men and women. Rather than rejecting this inevitable presence, perhaps recognizing it 'could help us all to re-conceptualise our responsibilities towards those we are so often inclined to reject' (Segal, 2013: 10–11). Accepting that old age is not something that happens outside of the confines of oneself and the moment one inhabits but is something that occurs across a life cycle may normalize the process. As both Segal and De Beauvoir suggest, with this acceptance may come increased empathy and accountability from younger members of society for older adults.

De Beauvoir reflects on her own experiences of ageing, explaining:

> When I was a little girl I was amazed and indeed deeply distressed when I realised that one day I should turn into a grown-up. But when one is young the real advantages of adult status usually counterbalance the wish to remain oneself, unchanged. Whereas old age looms ahead like a calamity: even among those who are thought well preserved, age brings with it a very obvious decline. (1970: 11)

No one becomes old in a single instant and yet often individuals discussing their own ageing do so with a tone of disbelief. It is as if their ageing happened without their knowledge and is something to be ashamed of. Noting that 'already, we can use scientific insights to overturn many preconceptions – or, should I say, misconceptions – about why and how we age' (2001: 10), Kirkwood heralds the positive impact of scientific advancements on ageing, which not only alleviate some of the physiological and patho-physiological suffering associated with process but also encourage changes in the social, cultural and political ideologies that surround it, often oppressive and marginalizing in nature. For Kirkwood, demographic change is something to be celebrated not commiserated as for him it marks 'the greatest triumph that our species has achieved' (2001: 5).

Society and ageing

Kirkwood's sentiment goes against the all-too-prevalent attitudes which prophesize doom and gloom in relation to the recent changes in human longevity. Describing society's fear of what she calls 'grey aliens', Karpf writes that the popular language that surrounds ageing forebodes 'an "agequake", a "demographic time bomb "or even "a grey tsunami"' (2014: 30). As she continues, 'We're no longer at risk of an invasion of triffids or Martians but of old people – invariably portrayed as a major social problem and a drain on resources, rather than a resource themselves' (2014: 30). Instead of embracing recent demographic change and its potential to open up new possibilities, there are those who decry a future where older adults provide little more than a drain on services. However, as this book argues, while the demographic change that sees more older adults living for longer might have the ability to instil panic in some, in others it provides opportunities to embrace ageing with a sense of excitement and anticipation. Put plainly, ageing and the fact that people are, on average, living longer than at any time in human history might become something to celebrate.

In the West, by comparison to any previous historical period, human populations live longer lives and it is because of this, rather than in spite of it, that it is important to learn how to live as fully as possible. For ageing to happen well, an emphasis on living must become intrinsic to the process. But a note of caution, first what must be considered is what is meant by 'well' and whether, in a neo-liberal society, the anxiety to age 'better' might develop a situation where an inability to do so (through illness or environment) is vilified. As Segal comments, focusing on notions of ageing well may encourage the binary between the two narratives of ageing, between the 'stories of progress and stories of decline; of ageing well and ageing badly' (2013: 17). Indeed, she suggests that the 'uncritical promotion of positive active ageing' can have the following effect:

> This narrative of ageing well, ageing healthily, can itself be
> problematic, even contradictory [...] as if we could all live into
> old age unburdened by actual signs of ageing. This scenario is thus
> itself partially complicit with the disparagement of old age, refusing
> to accept much that ageing entails, including facing up to greater
> dependence, fragility and loss, as well as the sadness, resentment or
> anger that accrue along with life itself. (2013: 18)

Segal warns against notions of ageing that tie with neo-liberal, anti-
welfare agendas, ones which refuse to acknowledge the needs of older
adults and to provide for those needs. She also suggests that notions
of 'ageing badly' are often attached to those who need care (2013: 18).
This, she continues, produces a situation where the concept of 'ageing
badly' reinforces the notion that actual signs of ageing, natural though
they may be, are somehow 'anomalous' (2013: 18). Understanding the
process of ageing, both for its universality and individuality, as well as
its inevitability allows for a focus on QoL that is applicable to different
states of being.

As we age we accrue the stuff of life. This stuff can be both
material and immaterial (Nicholson, 2011). It consists of things and
of experiences which, in later life, can often be of loss. The longer an
individual lives, the more likely he or she is to experience the loss of
loved ones, of independence, of power and of status. But as social,
political and cultural capital wanes, perhaps it is the loss of self, a
loss that must be continually faced, that has the potential to be the
most disturbing. The test of time cannot be held back, however, nor
should it be. Instead, ageing can be reclaimed as a natural part of the
life cycle, one which need not remove agency. There are many reasons
for contemporary responses to ageing; however, all of these can be
challenged and the status quo potentially altered with arts practice
providing one of many agents for change.

Segal interprets old age as an 'other' that lives within us,
suggesting that the loss of our 'self' is not only felt as such, but
is doubly traumatizing as it comes as a replacement. This 'other'

is recognizable in all the negative stereotypes implanted in our consciousness from an early age and is reinforced by insidious ageism all too prevalent in our society. So as age ensues, the individual is replaced, as Segal puts it, by 'The affect-laden symbolic apparatus of fantasies, metaphor, condensation, accompanying our encounters with those witches of folktales, ghouls of horror movie, and the countless other versions of crones or dementing oldies, both male and – far more savagely – female' (2014: 19). This replacement, this 'uncanny' visitor with all his or her affect-laden symbolism, is something at once both strange and familiar. It arouses (in us and in others) an anxiety that is more about death than ageing. As was suggested earlier, the ageing 'other' reminds us of our mortality and must be repelled. Segal continues, 'a living person can appear uncanny, and weirdly frightening, if they trigger thoughts of extinction, reminding us of our mortality, when thoughts of death always hover somewhere in the presence of life' (2014: 21).

Anxiety at the prospect of ageing and relentless attempts to remain young or, for a time at least, younger, come from the foreboding associated with the process, the existential understanding that as the stages of life are ticked off, infant, child, teenager, adult, oblivion follows. It is no wonder then that old age as a state of being is one to be rejected, pitied, ignored or worse, attacked. Consider this along with the pervasive nature of ageism and one would be forgiven for feeling concern for one's future self. How arresting contemporary examples of ageism would be if they were applied to gender, sexuality, race or nationality. Our child self is no less so than our teenage self. Similarly, our aged self is no less 'self' than the one inhabited up to that point. Ageing is a state of human existence; it is part of a life cycle. Yet how many of us would, without second thought, use the word 'old' in colloquial language to denote some form of negativity. Take examples such as 'dirty old', 'silly old', 'angry old' and see how the adjective is doubly accusatory, as though being silly is bad, but being silly *and* old is much worse.

It can be argued that the rhetoric of the so-called 'demographic time bomb' (2014: 29) outlined by Karpf is based on false assumptions. One of these assumptions, that the growing number of older adults will be a financial drain on society, is challenged by the author who notes, 'In reality, increasing numbers of us of "working age" are unemployed, while growing number continue to work beyond state – pension age, so you can no longer neatly correlate age with economic activity' (2014: 30). Similarly, Karpf points to the disproportion between the care received by older adults and the care they are provided in society, either as carers to their partners or other older family members or indeed, in the provision of essential childcare supplied by many grandparents. As she continues, 'does either point to older adults being "economically inactive"?' (2014: 30). For Mullan, this positioning of older adults as a 'drain' is explained as deliberately exaggerated, developed in a neoliberal effort to shift society from 'collective provision towards personal responsibility' (2002: 164), which in turn moves a duty of care from the state to the individual themselves and onto private profit-making care providers. This all presents a bizarre paradox where the burden model is being peddled by the very individuals who will themselves constitute members of this large cohort of older adults. As Mullan notes, 'These commentators – the majority young adults or middle-aged – are peddling the frightening prospect of an invasion of old people draining public finances, seemingly oblivious of the fact that they're describing themselves!' (2014: 30). Again, this is the peculiar nature of ageism, one that separates it from other forms of prejudice. It is delivered and proliferated by those who will themselves one day form the very demographic they choose to oppress.

Andrews offers the following statement in relation to this peculiarity:

> Fighting against ageism would on the face of it seem to be in every person's self-interest, or at least every person who hopes to live a long life. Why is this not so? The key lies in the ability of people to see old people not as an extension of their future (or even present) selves, but rather as totally apart from themselves. (1999: 303)

Ageism exists because on some level we are able to disassociate our present selves from our future selves. This produces, as Bytheway argues, 'a set of beliefs originated in the biological variation between and relating to the ageing process' (1995: 14). The consequence of this, Bytheway continues, is that

> Ageism generates and reinforces a fear and denigration of the ageing process, as stereotyping presumptions regarding competence and the need for protection [and in] particular, ageism legitimates the use of chronological age to mark out a class of people who are systematically denied resources and opportunities that others enjoy, and who suffer the consequences of such denigration, ranging from well-meaning patronage to unambiguous vilification. (1995: 14)

An acknowledgement that ageing is not the resting place of a particular group but something we experienced throughout our lives at different rates and in different ways might challenge this separation. Similarly, an understanding that age is not a homogenous state, along with a refusal to caricaturize the older adult, might offer a detoxification of our relationship to the ageing process which could, in turn, enable us to age better. An example of this potential can be seen in the 2010 Equality Act.

Andrews suggests that in recent years researchers in the study of ageing have 'adopted a terminology of "agelessness". They argue that old age is nothing more than a social construct and that until it is eliminated as a conceptual category, ageism will continue to flourish' (1999). However, Andrews disputes this position, arguing that the trend towards agelessness is itself a form of ageism which deprives older adults of their most hard-earned resource: their age. Old age is a unique phase of the lifecycle replete with continued developmental possibilities but for Andrews, the rhetoric that 'you are as old as you feel' is dangerous. Importantly she argues, 'One of the more successful and subtle mechanisms through which ageism operates in our culture is in our redefinition of certain – desirable – types of old age as "young"' (1999). We are not as old as we feel; we are as old as we are. Encouraging old age to disappear creates an 'artificial dissection' which

Andrews states, 'causes us to cut ourselves off from ourselves' (1999). One consequence of endemic ageism is its ability to encourage older adults to assimilate and internalize their devalued appraisal by society (Bengston et al., 1985). As Andrews explains,

> Internalization of self-hatred – in this case the ageism of the old – is a response commonly adopted by members of an oppressed group, and it is this which leads people to try to pass as being of another group [...] But this strategy is limited because it is built on pretence: one is required to deny who and what one is, which is ultimately disempowering. Moreover, while such a strategy may in a limited sense be affirming for the person who employs it, fundamentally it is at the expense of others. At best, one has made an exception for oneself which is based on an illusion, and which leaves fully intact the larger structure of oppression. (1999: 311)

Given the unpleasant nature of ageism, choosing to hide behind someone older in order to 'pass' as someone younger is not surprising. However, when one attempts to pass as younger, one attempts to disassociate oneself from the category of older adult, thereby suggesting that membership of that category is to be maligned. With this comes the understanding that one can never truly belong. The attempt at 'passing' ultimately, as Healey notes, participates in one's own 'erasure' (1994: 83).

It is not all gloom, however. As Andrews (1999) explains, in some instances, old age allows the individual to grow into his or her self. Still the same person, this growing allows the individual to become even more so. This is not agelessness in the negative connotation of the word, rather a radical reconstruction of the notion of successful ageing. The continuity theory of ageing embodies some of these principles. As Atchley (1993) explains, 'Continuity theory is evolutionary. It assumes that the patterns of ideas and skills, which people use to adapt and act, develop and persist over time; that a course of developmental direction can usually be identified; and that the individual's orientation is not to remain personally unchanged but rather consistent with the individual's past' (1993: 5, 6). Thus, the theory argues that to grow old is but one facet of ongoing personhood. It suggests that one does not cease to grow or develop just as one does not transform into an unknown other simply through the passage of time.

Living longer better

Having examined the individual and society in relation to responses to ageing, the previous section outlined some potentially positive aspects to Western society's changing demographics. There also exist, however, numerous challenges for ageing individuals. The following passages allow a consideration of how we might address these challenges and in doing so attempt to live better for longer.

The proliferation of negative stereotypes associated with ageing is formidable in its insidious nature. This proliferation is alarming because, if anything, extraordinarily negative stereotypes of the ageing process have grown more negative as life expectancy has increased. Unlike previous generations, survival to old age in the twenty-first century seems to be received less as an achievement and more as an affront. One source of negativity towards older adults might come from the assertion that on some level, the old should make way for the younger generation, releasing limited resources of which the old have taken more than their fair share. This concept exists, however, in a world where ageing has, up to the relatively recent past, been a rarity. Thus, it seems redundant to make such assertions with such a limited understanding of what the future might hold. We do not know how recent demographic changes will affect society. By normalizing our ability to age for longer, we can begin to make better sense of our ageing and consider its positives rather than negatives.

Segal notes that confronting ageing is both daunting and complicated. Acknowledging her own reticence on the subject, she suggests it points to the bigotries which underlie issues of ageing, noting that 'my very hesitation, of course, tells me just how much needs to change before we can start to face up to the fearful disparagement of old AGE, including our own prejudices' (Segal, 2013: 1). Perhaps self-preservation motivates the prejudices held for older adults. In a similar way to the attempts at passing mentioned above, if there is always someone older, then there is someone closer to the abyss. But if the struggle is always to remain closer to the young than the old, then the possibilities for what Segal calls 'staying alive to life itself' might be missed (2013: 4).

Again, from a Western context, issues relating to ageing are compounded by two things: the growth in numbers of older adults and our changing socio-economic norms. Alterations in family size and structure, for example, have had an impact on the amount of familial support available to some of our oldest adults. A decrease in child mortality towards the end of the twentieth century in turn impacted on the birth rates meaning fewer children were born to the current older population. Similarly, according to Coleman et al. (1991), an increase in geographical mobility has meant that more children are living at a distance from their parents and original family home. More women in the work force and an increase in the prevalence of divorce has also had an impact, removing the traditional role of the daughter or daughter-in-law as carer. All of the above, according to Coleman et al., have led to the 'weakening of connections between the generations, where complex patterns of family relationships have often taken the place of simple ties' (1991: 9). As the authors go on to explain, these changes in social structure do not diminish the individual bonds of affection and responsibility felt by children towards their parents but they do require other forms of intimate relationships to be formed, suggesting that 'contacts with other than family members are likely to be relatively more important nowadays – especially contact between peer groups, people of the same age and position in life who also often share similar interests' (1991: 9).

Historically, it was not the poor but the wealthy that aged. For many, this is no longer the case, but for some older adults poverty and its implications for physical and mental ill health are still issues. According to Bowling, 'In Britain, the largest source of income for people of state pension age is state benefits, including the state retirement pension' (2005: 174). She estimates that poverty affects around a fifth of all people of pensionable age (Bowling, 2005) and quotes the results of a 2004 UK Help the Aged survey which found that in 10,000 people aged over sixty, 'fifty eight percent dreaded the onset of winter because of fears about money, illness and isolation. One in three of those questioned expressed fears about winter heating bills. Just over half said that they managed on less than 8,000 pounds a year, and only twelve percent said they had annual incomes in excess of 18,000 pounds a year' (Bowling, 2005: 175). If one considers the rate of inflation since 2004, that lower figure equates to £11,400 a year in 2016. A more recent study, the 'Annual Fuel Poverty Statistics Report', published by the British government in 2015 showed that 'there is no clear pattern in the proportion of households which are fuel poor in progressively older occupants. There is, however, a clear pattern of increasing depth of fuel poverty in older households. Those where the oldest occupant is aged less than 34, for example, have a mean fuel poverty gap of approximately £260, whereas those aged over 60 have a gap of around £450' (Department for Energy and Climate Change, 2015).

According to Fischer, pre-industrial society was 'non-literate in its culture, agrarian in its economy, extended in its family structure, and rural in residence. The old were few in number but their authority was very great. Within the extended family the aged monopolised power, within an agrarian economy they controlled the land' (1978: 20–21). As Fischer continues, modernization 'shattered this "traditional" society and transformed the status of the aged in four ways' (1978: 21). Firstly, he argues the development of modern health technology has multiplied the number of the elderly and contributed to the ageing of the population and its workforce. This, in turn, has created a pressure towards retirement, forcing older adults out of the most valued and highly regarded roles, depriving them of utility, curtailing their income and lowering their status. Secondly, modern economic technology has created new occupations and transformed most of the old ones, which has also meant the loss of jobs, incomes and status for this group. Thirdly, urbanization has attracted younger people from rural communities to the cities, thus breaking up the extended family and producing a more nuclear conjugal unit. Finally, the growth of mass education and literacy means that 'there can be no mystique of age'; in other words, older adults have lost their status as providers of knowledge and wisdom gleamed through extended experience (1978: 20, 21). All of this, along with a growing obsession with youth, has led to the erosion of the power and autonomy of older adults. The following section explores how a consideration of QoL might attempt to address some of these issues and relate to social and cultural practice that attempts to redress the often marginal position of older adults in society.

The quality of life debate

The Constitution of the World Health Organization (WHO) defines health as 'a state of complete physical, mental, and social well-being not merely the absence of disease' and QoL as an 'individuals' perception of their position in life in the context of the culture and value systems in which they live and in relation to their goals, expectations, standards and concerns' (WHO, 1997). QoL is a broad concept that includes a range of complex interlinked factors, including people's physical and psychological health, their level of independence, their social relationships, personal beliefs and relationship to the surrounding environment. Thus, in order to measurement QoL, a holistic examination of human life is needed. Bowling argues the increased interest in QoL and ageing lies not just in an attempt to manage illness but in an interest to move, 'away from a negative paradigm [...] towards a positive view of old age as a natural component of the life span – as a period of life in which one is free from many structured roles, able to explore areas of personal fulfilment and social activity in good health' (2005: 2). He goes on to note that, while 'in reality, limited resources, opportunity and ill health can be restrictive, there is still an overall focus on demolishing stereotypes of older age' (2005: 2). Thus in order for QoL to be increased for these members of society, work within society needs to be done to rebalance the negative position of older adults.

Early social and clinical research into QoL and ageing has tended to focus mainly on the pathology model with issues of dependency, poverty, service use and care needs, as well declining physical and mental health taking precedent. Such a focus, as Roos and Havens (1991) argue, has been at the expense of enablement, rehabilitation, prevention and cure. For them, the positivist perspective of functionalism has also influenced the development of narrow QoL scales, which in turn reinforce a focus on physical over psychological functioning. Research based on this model has inevitably underestimated the QoL of older people.

From the point of view of arts practice, QoL has become an important element in developing strategies for the all too prevalent evaluation activity required of many projects and practitioners. It has been adopted as a methodology for measurement with which to show impact and thus secure future funding for similar practice. This is understandable with much funding for applied practice in this area coming from health or social science streams. Thus, the language of social science and health has been adopted to prove 'effect' when, as is argued in Chapter 2, the language of 'affect' (particularly for examples of applied practice that are based on an intention to increase sociality) might be more appropriate. In these examples, it is the moment of interaction and the feelings that interaction engenders that are paramount with any positive lateral effects coming from the quality of that interaction. Add to this the understanding that ageing occurs in different ways and at different rates for different people and one begins to understand that arts practitioners who engage with QoL measurements as a means to manage and leverage funding need to be aware of the complexities of such measurements, as well as their limitations.

As was previously mentioned, there is no clear consensus as to what constitutes 'old' or indeed 'ageing'. Thus, any attempt to develop a unanimous definition for ageing ignores the diversity that exists within the group. That is not to say that QoL cannot be measured but individuality and differences between biological ageing and chronological ageing must remain in focus. In order for this to occur, an adequate sociological theory of age needs to distinguish between three different meanings: a person's chronological age, that person's social age and that person's physiological age. According to Arber and Ginn (1995) chronological ageing, which is essentially biological, needs to be distinguished from physiological age. It is a medical construct that refers to the physical ageing of the body and manifests itself in measured levels of functional impairment. The physiological status of two similar aged older adults might in fact be very different so to categorize them medically according to chronological age is misleading. Similarly, social age refers to the social attitudes and behaviour seen as appropriate for a particular chronological age, which again, viewed singularly, disregards the heterogeneous nature of older adults.

The great diversity among older people is often hidden by population figures and projections. Similarly, there is an increased awareness that physical and mental decline are not an inevitable part of ageing. As has been argued, there is no clear consensus regarding what constitutes 'old' and, as Bowling (2005) notes, any categorization by age obscures the psychological, social and physical diversity of older people. She concludes that 'while social structures may threaten well-being, individual experiences are derived from interrelation levels of social structure, such as social stratification (including age stratification), social institutions and interpersonal relationships, together with individual personality and psychological influences' (2005: 6). Continuity theory suggests that 'individuals make adaptations to enable them to feel the continuity between the past and present, which preserves their psychological well-being' (Atchley, quoted in Bowling, 2005: 3). So while such social theories may appear at first helpful, models of ageing need to be flexible and broad and working across disciplines.

Continuity theory calls for 'internal (self-concept) and external (social roles, activities, relationships and so on) consistency in people's lives, and a process of continuous development and adaptations throughout life in response to life events and changes' (Bowling, 1993: 4). Applied theatre with, for and by older adults might offer a means to engender these consistencies while simultaneously contributing opportunities for development and adaptation. However, in doing so, it must not ignore the diversity of experience and inequity (particularly in relation to wealth and health) experienced by older adults. That being said, as is discussed in the next chapter and indeed throughout the book, work in applied theatre may provide a vehicle through which continuation theory can be considered or at least supported.

Positive steps: An age-inclusive society

It may at first appear that the future of ageing is more negative than positive. That is not necessarily the case, however. For many years, activist groups such as the Grey Panthers and Better Government for Older People have been fighting to promote equality among generations and battle ageism. In Britain, Age Concern and the National Federation of Retirement Pensions Association campaign for the equal rights of older adults and initiatives have been developed internationally to address the needs of this diverse section of society. The following paragraph outlines one such example, global enterprise Age-friendly Cities, which works to promote consideration for older adults across cultural, social and civic platforms as a means to address their needs in urban environments.

The WHO's Global Network of Age-friendly Cities was established to encourage 'active ageing by optimizing opportunities for health, participation and security in order to enhance quality of life as people age' (WHO, 2007). The network spans the globe and includes cities such as New York, Dundalk, Stockholm and Tokyo to name but a few. The history of the initiative includes several key moments such as the adoption of the United Nations Principles for Older Persons by the UN Member States based on the International Plan of Action on Ageing in 1991. This plan encouraged governments to incorporate the principles of independence (participation, care, self-fulfilment and dignity) into their national programmes. The principles then became the foundation for the Age-friendly Cities approach.

The International Plan of Action was followed in 2002 with a policy framework entitled Active Ageing, developed by the WHO's Ageing and Life Course Programme. Out of that framework came the concept of the Age-friendly City, which was developed to encourage active ageing.

In its ideal state, the Age-friendly City is a place that enables older adults to remain connected to those around them. It recognizes the individuality of members of this demographic group and their range of capacities. It protects the vulnerable while promoting the ability of older adults to contribute to society. It is flexible in its anticipation of age-related needs and, finally, it is respectful of the resources among older people and their lifestyle choices (WHO, 2016). If supporting independence, individuality and health is the goal of the initiative than in order for it to be successful, an Age-friendly City must adapt its structures and services to provide full inclusivity. The WHO suggests focusing on specific domains that help identify barriers to inclusivity, including community and health care, transportation, housing, social participation, outdoor spaces and buildings, respect and social inclusion, civic participation and employment, communication and information. These domains speak to each other and overlap because they relate to the everyday life of any resident of a city. From an arts practice point of view, they call into question issues around accessibility and participation. They also highlight areas of good practice, outlined in the ensuing chapters, where arts practice can be seen to make a positive impact on several, if not all the domains. Indeed, the case study in Chapter 2 that includes Small Things: Creative Project shows the impact Manchester's status as an Age-friendly City has had on the company's opportunities to make work with older adults.

According to the Manchester Institute for Collaborative Research on Ageing (MICRA) at the University of Manchester, 'in fifteen years, a quarter of the world's population living in cities will be over sixty, as more and more people choose to grow old there' (MICRA, 2015). A 2015 film made by the research centre notes that demographic changes and the rise in urbanization are the two biggest changes society will face in the coming years in relation to growing older. Working with older co-researchers (aged from fifty-eight to seventy-four), the institute examined the life of older adults in cities to consider how older adults interact with their city. These co-researchers worked with hard to reach and socially excluded older adults to gain a deeper insight into their needs and into the factors that can help create an Age-friendly City.

Manchester is Britain's first Age-friendly City. Work associated with this initiative (as well as the work done by MICRA) means there are numerous examples of projects undertaken to encourage social inclusion and civic participation in some of the city's main arts venues. From the Coffee, Cake and Culture project, which provided a vehicle for older adults in residential care settings to experience the Whitworth Art Gallery and Manchester Museum, to the Elders Company, which was set up and runs under the auspices of the Royal Exchange Theatre for members aged sixty-five and over, to the Story Box project initially produced by the Library Theatre (now Home), which brings creative practice into residential care settings, Manchester's age-friendly status appears to have had a definite impact in terms of the amount of practice undertaken. Some of this practice will be explored in more detail in Chapter 2; but before that, it is important to acknowledge that innovations such as Age-friendly Cities can have a positive impact on creative practice that occurs with, for and by older adults.

The aim of this chapter has been to examine perspectives on ageing and the impact ageing has on the individual and society more generally so as to consider how we might embrace current changes in demographics and work to become a more age-inclusive society. There is a lot to be concerned about regarding ageing in the twenty-first century. There are specific criteria for ageing but these cannot undermine the unique and individual nature of the ageing experience. While problems in relation to how to approach the experience of ageing and the ways society treat older adults exist, what this chapter suggests is that there is evidence that it is possible to age better.

As the rest of *Applied Theatre: Creative Ageing* details, creative practice and applied theatre continues to respond to the needs of older adults with the intention to promote creativity, well-being and social capital while combating marginalization and social exclusion. In Chapter 2 particularly, a number of interesting examples of practice are included to allow these intentions to be examined in more detail. In order to consider the practice, the opening sections of the chapter outline the community theatre origins of applied theatre with, for and by older adults suggesting intentions in this area lean towards sociality, development and politicization. The chapter then outlines different perspectives of practice that it argues occur along a continuum from the public to the private. It does so while exploring the theoretical positions and considerations specific to each of these perspectives.

Perspectives on Practice: Applied Theatre and Ageing

Sheila McCormick

This chapter aims to discuss a number of interesting examples of applied theatre with, for and by older adults. In doing so, it considers a theoretical framework through which to view applied theatre and ageing. It allows for a contextualization of practice which considers specific methodologies and the use of those methodologies to best serve the older adult in a multitude of settings. Providing perspectives on practice, the chapter examines the rationale behind arts practice with older adults, along with the inherent artfulness and potentially beneficial outcomes attached to different forms of practice.

Research into the personal and societal benefits of applied arts practice and ageing has produced a number of claims. These claims include improved physical and mental health, as well as enhanced personal relationships and a growth in social capital. Indeed, according to a review of the impact of participatory arts on older people undertaken by the Mental Health Foundation, UK, eleven studies suggested that 'there are a variety of health benefits to be gained for older adults from participating in creative and performance arts programmes' (2011: 16). For example, Cohen et al. (2007) found evidence that engaging in creative acts had a positive effect on participants' health, a reduction in their use of medication and the incidence of falls. Similarly, Noice et al. (2009) found evidence that participating in theatre training improved cognitive skills in several populations of older adults, while Pyman et al. (2006) found similar benefits for mental health with participants who engaged in performance-based activities expressing increased confidence and an ability to make social connections. In relation to social capital, one study (Johnson, 2011) looked at the theatre production *On Ageing* by London-based theatre company Fevered Sleep. Examining the company's practice of devising work jointly with older adults and children (with the support of professional artists), the study highlighted the value of intergenerational creativity as something that encourages more positive impressions in children of old people.

This chapter acknowledges applied theatre with, for and by older adults and its community theatre origins. The historical contextualization included here recognizes a practice that has emerged from the fields of education and development, one that, at times, embraces its origins and, at others, focuses solely on sociality as an intended outcome. The discussion then explores how applied theatre with older adults facilitates varying levels of creativity and ability. The analogy of a continuum from the public to the private is used through which to explore in more detail the examples of practice. These instances of applied theatre with, for and by older adults are grouped together and positioned at different points along the continuum with private practice (e.g. work created within residential care settings) at one end and practice that is more public facing (e.g. work occurring in producing theatres) at the other. At different points, particular areas of practice with specific theoretical considerations are examined, while throughout, the universal importance of affect and sociality in relation to applied theatre and ageing is placed at the forefront. Out of these discussions, the chapter provides a survey of the field of applied theatre practice with, for and by older adults, upon which further conversations might develop regarding the future of this specific and unique area of theatre practice.

The chapter is structured in the following way. The opening section provides a historical context for applied theatre with, for and by older adults before moving on to introduce areas of theoretical interest including inclusivity, sociality and affect. The chapter is then broken up into three sections which explore these concepts (inclusivity, sociality and affect) in more depth through perspectives on practice in three distinct categories: work that is based in public, work that occurs in private and work that is created somewhere between. At points throughout the chapter, reference is made to my previous career as a general nurse. This career has allowed me to work with older adults in a variety of settings for more than a decade. It has, therefore, provided me an opportunity to witness changes first hand that have occurred in health provision and the care of older adults. The experience has also provided me with personal philosophical quandaries, particularly in relation to the challenges associated with the care of an individual with a diagnosis of dementia.

History and context – reminiscence

In relation to health and well-being, applied theatre with and for older adults has traditionally focused on reminiscence. Reminiscence work incorporates a communal exploration of past experiences and has been adopted in diverse areas from primary care settings such as care homes and community and cultural organizations including museums and art galleries. The work focuses on a participatory process of enhancing well-being by engaging a communal experience of remembering a shared past. As a practice, reminiscence has been used specifically in work with individuals with a diagnosis of dementia. In the UK, examples of the practice include the work of theatre company Age Exchange, one of the longest-running theatre companies working in this area.

Set up in 1983, Age Exchange works specifically with older adults. The company engages in both reminiscence and intergenerational arts and claims that the creative exploration of memories places 'reminiscence arts at the cutting edge of dementia support building bridges between the past, the present and the future' (Age Exchange, 2015a). Out of their practice, the company has created the Reminiscence Arts and Dementia Impact on Quality of Life (RADIQL) project, which supports people with dementia through person-centred reminiscence art practice. Working within a residential care setting and with the support of two major hospitals in London, the project delivers a combination of weekly group and one-to-one interventions using 'creativity and personal history in order to enrich caring relationships in the present' (Age Exchange, 2015b). Thus, their aim is to provide training and mentoring in reminiscence practice for staff working within these care facilities as a means to supporting ongoing practice in this area after the project ends.

Age Exchange provides an example of reminiscence practice that maintains an established position in the area of applied theatre with older adults. This practice is varied and innovative in its attempt to address issues associated with a diagnosis of dementia; it also has the ability to allow for moments of communal remembrance which have the potential to engender a sense of community and belonging. Material for reminiscence work can come from historical sources, allowing participants to share experiences of a specific event or from more general sources allowing for inclusivity and focusing on a range of experiences rather than specific memories. Age Exchange's *Stories of My Life,* for instance, focused on what life was like across England and Ireland for a group of women from the outbreak of the Second World War until the 1970s. Similarly, more generic communal experiences are considered just as valid and effective within the practice; everyone has undertaken a journey, for example, and most have experienced the seaside.

Reminiscence work can also happen spontaneously, as was found when examining reflective material from an outreach project developed by the Whitworth Gallery and Manchester Museum entitled the Coffee, Cake and Culture project (Roe et al., 2016). This project facilitated visits to both cultural venues by older adults from a local residential care home. The material that was examined for research purposes came in the form of anecdotal observations of the visits by Professor of Health Research Brenda Roe. One event within the project (a visit to the Manchester Museum) provided observations on the interactions between the older adults and a particular exhibit within the museum. In this material was an example which highlighted the spontaneous nature of communal reminiscence and its impact.

Set up to allow access to the cultural spaces, the Coffee, Cake and Culture project invited individuals with a diagnosis of dementia to visit the museum and gallery with the support of arts venues' community outreach teams. Both the museum and gallery have a vast array of artefacts and pieces of art housed within their walls but it was one particular artefact, the bones of an elephant named Maharajah, that prompted the moment of communal reminiscence in question. In 1875, Maharajah walked 220 miles from Edinburgh to the (long since closed) Bell Vue Zoological Gardens in Manchester. Although none of the visitors were alive at that time, so affiliated with Manchester and its residents is the story that it allowed a moment of communal reminiscence to occur when the group, silent up to that point, came upon the exhibit. In that moment, spurred on by memories, individuals in the group shared their personal experiences of the zoo and the Manchester of their youth. This allowed the experience of the museum to move from an individual to a communal one which, in turn, encouraged the group to engage further with the material in the museum and, more importantly, with each other.

As this example suggests, there are benefits to practice that engages with reminiscence. There are some academics and practitioners, however, who challenge its orthodoxy and suggest that its basis in cognition and focus on past experiences might make it less appropriate and accessible than other more imaginative forms of creative arts practice. As Nicholson comments,

> Reminiscence theatre is also undoubtedly enriched by insights from gerontology and the empathetic practices of person-centred care. But not everyone in residential care wants to be reminded of the past and reminiscence theatre necessarily focuses on what is absent, remembered or imagined – this means that theatre-makers can unwittingly collude with 'normalising' people with dementia by

> presenting memories in dramatic forms that construct an illusion that these stories are being enacted as the 'really were'. (2011: 54)

For Nicholson, of utmost importance is the acknowledgement of the person in the present for who they are now, not what they were, providing a focus on what the person has rather than what he or she has lost. She argues: 'Defining dementia – or indeed ageing – without focusing primarily on narratives of loss or decline requires a significant cultural change' (2011: 55). Nicholson acknowledges the painful process of loss individuals with a diagnosis with dementia, along with their family and friends, must go through, but argues that acknowledging their irreparably altered persona is vital to being able to accept the individual with a diagnosis of dementia in the here and now, for the person he or she is in the present. Continually looking for something that is no longer there through the process of reminiscence can be distressing; it can also potentially hinder relationships in the present and may ignore the potential for creativity still present and part of in the individual with a diagnosis of dementia. For Nicholson,

> Reminiscence with people with dementia is often predicated on the view that remembering the past will recover the 'real' person who has been lost but, when transformed into theatre, the process of 'normalising' the language and non-verbal gestures of people with dementia shows that it risks missing the richness of their imaginative lives in the present. (2011: 60)

She advocates finding 'ways to value incoherence, forgetfulness and inattention as well as the narratives of reminiscence' (2011: 54) so that this richness of imagination can be embraced and supported.

One mode of creative practice that acknowledges the creative capacity of individuals with a diagnosis of dementia is Anne Basting's TimeSlips. Rather than focusing on reminiscence, Basting advocates placing creativity and imagination at the centre of applied practice with older adults who have a diagnosis of dementia. Her practice of group storytelling acknowledges the incoherence, forgetfulness and inattention mentioned by Nicholson. For her, 'Creative storytelling supplies a social role, one with value, that allows for the integration of past and present, and that acknowledges the strengths and potential of the present lives of people with Alzheimer's disease and related dementia' (Basting, 2006: 193). As she argues, 'it offers storytellers an avenue for self-expression that frees them from the demands of memory' (Basting, 2006: 193). The practice strategizes to maintain inclusion despite breaks in memory and temporal understanding. Basting outlines the practice of TimeSlips herself in Chapter 6, but suffice to say the creative storytelling practice adopts a methodology that allows incoherence and temporal shifts supporting each storytellers' journey through the story. Rather than correct or re-orientate, TimeSlips embraces inconsistencies, acknowledging the relational aspect of memory and how much it is linked to our experience in the world.

According to Basting, 'Memory and story, and the selves we build with them, are crafted in relation to the world around us – the people, the places, the cultural influences. The world around us significantly encodes our experiences, how (and if) we retrieve them and how we make meaning of them' (Basting, 2006: 18). Thus, she acknowledges the need to continually master relational language in order for memory to be effective and highlights the demands placed on the individual with dementia in reminiscence arts practice and the struggles those demands incur. As she explains in her chapter in this book, rather than force a mode of memory retrieval not accessible to individuals with a diagnosis of dementia, a strategy similar to the 'yes and' technique found in improvisational performance practice can be adopted. This 'yes and' strategy is inclusive, nothing offered is ever considered incorrect and disregarded; on the contrary, every offering is embraced and built upon.

While the practice of reminiscence has been particularly relevant to the history and development of applied theatre with, for and by older adults, it is important to acknowledge the variety of practice that occurs in this area. Reminiscence as a practice remains popular, however other applied theatre practitioners working with elders choose to focus on engagement with the present rather than the past.

Inclusivity

Contemporary arts practice with older adults is global in its innovation, is varied in its practice and has an intention to provide opportunities for social inclusion. In 2012, the International Longevity Centre and Age UK published a report written by Dylan Kneale entitled 'Is exclusion still important for older people?' While the title might appear incongruous (when would social exclusion not be important?), the report is helpful, not least because it points to potential precipitating factors in relation to the social exclusion of individual social groups. The findings expressed in a survey like this might differ; of course, depending on the socio-economic groups included. At the very least, it appears to suggest that health and well-being factors are rated slightly higher than monetary factors in the exclusion of older adults.

According to Kneale, there are seven domains of social exclusion for older adults and while these include the exclusion from financial products and common consumer goods, they also incorporate social and cultural factors, with exclusion from decent housing and public transport, civic activities, local amenities, cultural activities and social relationships factoring heavily. Thus, in comparison to other marginalized groups, for some older adults, social and cultural exclusion is a chronic feature of their daily lives. Finally, if we agree with Duffy that individuals are excluded when there exists an 'inability to participate effectively in the economic, social, political and cultural life, alienation and distance from the mainstream' (1995: 241) then we must consider the causes of this inability and the role social stratification and more included members of society with better social capital play in precipitating this situation.

Innovative arts practice may have the ability to mitigate the social exclusion of the older members of our society. By its nature theatre requires communication and interaction. Indeed, Organ argues as follows:

> The advent and continued re-inventions of community arts/ participatory arts/ collaborative arts is a vital force in the opportunities

for older people in our increasingly ageing society to make themselves heard and understood and to enjoy discovering their own creativity through the medium of theatre and drama. The connection between older age and isolation make this inherently sociable art form a powerful medium for combating that isolation. (2016: 2)

In order to examine this force in detail, specific questions need to be asked. Any exploration of these practices aimed at developing social inclusion must first examine what makes social exclusion different for older adults. The social, cultural and political requirements of older adults should be considered along with their complex health and well-being needs.

In her survey of the field, Organ found arts practice with older adults growing in its diversity. She also pointed to several routes now taken by older adults interested in engaging with theatre, drama and performance. These include the following:

- Producing and Presenting Theatres with explicit offers for old people; including specific attention to the needs of people living with dementia and connecting to audiences in residential care
- Theatres with a strong inter-generational offer, complementing their youth theatres with an inclusive community theatre for all generations
- Professional arts companies with strong or dedicated interests in theatre by, for and with old people, including greater involvement by old people in the governance and direction of the company's work
- Professional theatre companies of old professional theatre makers
- Companies of older people – some of which are established standing groups and many more which are assembled for a specific production or project
- Play-reading groups in theatres and libraries
- Involvement in the traditional amateur theatre sector by significant numbers of older people as creatives as well as board members and organisers

- Volunteer and audience engagement programmes including involvement in archiving, education, front-of-house and fund-raising
- A Dementia Friendly theatre movement (Organ, 2016: 3)

Considering the diversity of these routes and the proliferation of arts practice in this area, it is important to acknowledge what each arts practice offers and how these individual offerings can be analysed in relation to the form as a whole.

Ways of understanding: Sociality, affect and applied theatre and ageing

The intentions behind engaging in these forms of arts practice vary; for some it is an opportunity to feel more included; for others to achieve a level of artistry. From a relational point of view, through the practice, moments of connection might occur between the older adult and their carer/family member outside of the remit of care. Agendas for applied theatre in this area might be 'development' or 'learning' focused. More likely, what links them is an interest in sociality, a human connection and an opportunity to interact and to be seen. An arts-based activity differs from other activities in that it has the potential to foster a sense of achievement, mastery and escapism as well as provide opportunities for sociality, a renewed sense of individuality and the development of social capital. Artfulness and its position within applied theatre with, for and by older adults is important because it can foster that level of achievement and mastery.

If closeness with others and process rather than product are valued in arts practice with older adults, then the suitability of traditional evaluation methods (one's outcome based) must be examined. An exploration of affect over effect should be considered when analysing and theorizing creative practice in this area.

In relation to evaluation, work with older adults often relies on support from philanthropic, social science and health funding streams. In 2015, the Baring Foundation, UK, provided over 300,000 pounds to fund national and international arts practice with, for and by older adults with companies such as the National Theatre Wales, the Australian Centre for Arts and Health and the West Yorkshire Playhouse. In the last two decades, these avenues for funding have proved vital to the development of arts practice in this area. However, to engage with these funding streams might mean to engage with quantitative evaluation methodologies which, in turn, might struggle to sufficiently articulate the experience of the interaction between artist and older adult.

Nicholson notes that 'the perception that the arts represent vernacular, subjective know-how and scientific knowledge is objective, empirical and "evidence-based" remains rooted in the popular imagination and embedded in much health policy' (2011: 49). However, as she points out, along with their skills, artists bring with them their understanding of the social and cultural significance of arts practice to healthcare settings. As she argues, 'their presence [...] draws attention to forms of knowledge not captured by paradigms of performance management' (2011: 48). Acknowledging that these other forms of knowledge are accessible through writing on affect in relation to applied and none-applied practice, Thompson suggests, 'art is understood to have a role in the present, as a protective force with an 'in spite of' quality that enables people to tolerate suffering, not so that they can become immune to it, but so that they have the energy to continue to resist' (2009: 2).

Applied theatre with older adults does not always fit within the conceived categories of the form. It is sometimes educational, and it is sometimes undertaken to encourage development; but more often than not, the remit of applied theatre with this heterogeneous group occurs to encourage sociality and interaction. The effect of the practice, what happens as a result of the creative intervention is often not as important as the affect that occurs in the moment of interaction and creation, what Thompson describes as 'the automatic, embodied responses that occur in relation to something else – be it object of observation, recall of a memory or practical activity' (2009: 119). By its nature, applied theatre with older adults is heavily invested in affect over effect, and embodied responses occur when moments of connection are privileged over an emphasis on other outcomes. As Thompson argues, research in the area is limited if it does not observe these responses, if it considers only the 'identifiable social outcomes, messages and impacts – and forgets the radical potential of the freedom to enjoy beautiful *radiant things*' (Thompson, 2009: 6).

Affect is of course difficult to measure but as Nicholson points out, paradigms of performance that prioritize measurable outcomes offer a restricted view of the world and also 'perpetuate particular ways of thinking and knowing that have been legitimized by those who hold cultural or political power' (2011: 49). There is no reason why both an ontological and an empirical focus cannot be valued, and why the artist cannot be trusted to understand his or her own practice, recognizing moments of affect when they occur and registering them as being of value, however difficult to document.

Artists working with older adults are regularly required to consider the impact of their practice and how its efficacy can be measured. These requirements have the potential to encourage artists to develop, as Nicholson notes, 'an internalised perception that only discourses assumed to be "scientific" or "objective" hold value, it also implies a belief that their own insights and interpretations have less authority' (2011: 49). Scientific or objective ways of knowing do not fully account for what Nicholson calls the 'intuition of empathetic and compassionate carers' (2011: 49). Equally, validating one form of knowledge over another prevents opportunities for a deeper understanding of the fundamentals of applied theatre with, for and by older adults. What Nicholson suggests as needed is a recognition and legitimization of different ways of knowing, an understanding that the 'tacit of knowledge of caters, the vernacular know-how of older adults and the creative insights of artists, are as valuable to the formation of knowledge as paradigms of performance that value measured outcomes and empirical data' (2011: 49). What follows in this chapter attempts to embrace these different ways of knowing including both quantitative and qualitative data as well as first-hand experience. The perspective on practice adopts an affect register through which to articulate first- and second-hand experience. Similarly, the chapters in Part Two of the book articulate epistemology gathered using mainly ontological means. Some also choose to inhabit a space somewhere between that binary where, as Nicholson notes, 'distinctions of knowledge between material and ephemeral (or fact and value) might be challenged (or subverted)' (2011: 49).

Situated along the continuum from the public to the private (discussed in the section on perspectives of practice) are areas of particular focus such as engagement, visibility and care. The term 'visibility' is used in relation to practices that are deliberately and necessarily hidden and those that choose a public platform to consider ageing. Also regarded are those practices which lie somewhere between these two positions. Engagement relates to sociality and the levels at which it occurs as a result of the practice. Care can be positioned on either end of the spectrum, from practice that is specific to care environments developed to engender an ethos of care to practice that encourages sociality and the care of others through the development of a community. Engagement, sociality and care are not mutually exclusive; throughout what follows, intersections between all three occur at regular intervals.

Offered here is not an exhaustive list of practice, nor a definitive analysis of the form. Instead, throughout this chapter, examples (both local and global) are introduced to encourage a survey of the field and an introduction to critical perspectives applicable to the practice of applied theatre with, for and by older adults.

Perspectives on practice

Public: Visibility, applied theatre and ageing

This section considers examples of practice that encourage the visibility of older adults in society. While some prioritize sociality, others embrace a political agenda, one that exposes particular inequities, stereotypes and prejudices experienced by older adults. Looking first at work that can be described as local, in other words, work that is produced with, for and by the community in which it is situated, the section briefly examines the work of Liverpool-based theatre company Collective Encounters and their work with their Third Age company. It then moves on to explore the work of the New Dynamics of Ageing project at the University of Sheffield as an example of practice occurring at a national level. Finally, it concludes with a section that examines the international work of Lois Weaver as Tammy WhyNot in *What Tammy Needs to Know about Getting Old and Having Sex*.

Collective Encounters

Collective Encounters is a Liverpool-based theatre company that has a well-being agenda as well as a remit that is both political and educational. Established in 2004, the company has been described as one focused on 'using theatre as a tool for social change' which seeks 'interesting ways of bringing people together in creative, collective encounters to explore some of the key issues of our time' (Thornton, 2013: 24). This bringing together of individuals occurs at a local level with the company continually responding to issues pertinent to the community in which it is embedded.

Collective Encounters developed Third Age Company in 2011, a group of older performers who attempt to be a voice for social change for their community. To that end, they have worked with writer Sarah Thornton to explore different political issues relevant to them and their peers. Notably, they produced *Health Is Wealth* (2015), which highlighted concerns relating to inequalities in health care. The play was performed at the Arts and Health Symposium in Liverpool before touring to health centres and libraries throughout Liverpool and the surrounding area.

Examining directly the experience of health care and ageing is just one area of interest for the company. In her 2015 article, Thornton suggests that the work of Collective Encounters is situated within a strand of applied practice known as Theatre for Social Change. For the company, this practice, according to Thornton (2015), is rooted in a call for the radicalization and re-politicization of the participatory arts sector so as to address social injustices in the context of British austerity. As such, it asks how theatre can 'challenge the ubiquitous neo-liberal narrative and what kinds of participatory arts practices might aid the global movement for radical change' (Thornton, 2015: 33). This interest in exposing the effect of neo-liberal rhetoric on the marginalized, more vulnerable members of society can be seen in *Health Is Wealth* as well as the work undertaken by the company to encourage more and better care for people living with a diagnosis of dementia or caring for such an individual. In 2013, working locally again with the Liverpool Museum, Collective Encounters produced a piece aimed at home-based carers. Commissioned by the museum to assist with their dementia awareness programme House of Memories, the company used materials from within the museum to provide social care staff with creative skills and resources to use when working with individuals with a diagnosis of dementia.

Considering *Health Is Wealth* and the company's work with House of Memories, Creative Encounters provides an example of practice grounded in politics that moves across the categories of engagement, visibility and care. Its work has impact at a national level but it seeks, first and foremost, to operate locally, deliberately engaging directly with the community it serves.

New Dynamics of Ageing project

Also in the UK, at a national level, the innovative New Dynamics of Ageing project is a multidisciplinary, cross-research council initiative whose practices, in a similar way to Creative Encounters, can be argued to similarly cross categories of engagement, visibility and care. Based in the Department of Sociology at the University of Sheffield, the eight-year programme aims to explore different areas of research and practice with an intention to potentially improve the quality of life of older people. As its website explains, the collaboration between a number of research groups has been undertaken to

> Develop practical policy and implementation guidance and novel scientific, technological and design responses to help older people enjoy better quality lives as they age. This requires integrating understandings of the changing meanings, representations and experiences of ageing and the key factors shaping them (including behavioural, biological, clinical, cultural, historical, social, economic and technological), through direct engagement with older people and user organisations. (University of Sheffield, 2016a)

The project suggests that interdisciplinary research into the technological, cultural, societal and physical world of older adults might present ways to combating issues for those adults on a local, national and global level and that these can be considered in order to potentially improve quality of life. The programme therefore considers forces that influence ageing and how these forces might be managed to ensure the best experience of ageing possible.

The central objectives of the programme appear to cover several areas. According to their mission statement, they wish to develop an understanding of the biological determinants and influence of social and environmental factors on healthy ageing. There is also an intention to understand the diverse ways ageing is considered, experienced and represented in contemporary society and that this representation often differs across a range of cultures. Finally, the agenda to incorporate innovative multidisciplinary research is undertaken as a means to provide an evidence base for policy making and practice, and as a result, contribute to well-being and quality of life (University of Sheffield, 2016a).

Included in the programme are projects concerned with arts and humanities, global ageing, health and well-being, mobility and independence, nutrition, statistics and technology. Often these themes cross paths. For example, the two projects discussed here have consequences for arts and humanities as well as health and well-being. The first, Representing Self – Representing Ageing, focuses heavily on the visibility remit discussed in this section.

Supported by the New Dynamics of Ageing, Representing Self – Representing Ageing involved researchers from the University of Sheffield, University of Auckland and University of Derby working with older female participants to consider the relationship between cultural representations of older people in the media and certain ideas and expectations regarding ageing and gender. The study argued that older women are more often negatively stereotyped than older men and are the target of a rapidly expanding anti-ageing industry. Thus, the study suggested the social status of older women is often attached to physical attractiveness and a youthful, sexualized ideal of beauty. In order to counteract these representations and their negative impact, the study involved older women in the production of counter images that, once produced, influence positive expectations of ageing. The findings of the project then argued that public access to alternative images has the potentiality to counteract ageist assumptions around ageing and women.

While not specifically applied 'theatre', the aims of the Representing Self – Representing Ageing are relevant because they encourage and enable older women (from a variety of communities) to be visible in counter images that subvert traditional and often negative images of female ageing. By producing these images, the participants were able to activate different cultural representations while also exploring the relationship between creative activity and well-being in later life. Thus, according to the researchers, the project was undertaken as a means to demonstrating how arts practice can impact on critical gerontology and how through such undertakings, the 'authority, wisdom and productivity' (University of Sheffield, 2016c) of older women can be better understood both publically and at a level of policy making.

In their discussion of 'active ageing', Warren and Clarke suggest the term came about due to an economic desire 'to limit the social protection costs associated with the trend towards early retirement of the labour force of most developed countries as the post war baby boom generation headed towards retirement' (2009: 234). However, they also point out the humanist intentions behind the term adopted by organizations such as the European Union, World Health Organization and the UK's Better Government for Older People, all of which suggest factors such as life-long learning, citizenship and community involvement as vital to active ageing. In 2010, out of the Representing Self – Representing Ageing project came a series of workshops undertaken with a range of women aged from forty-three to ninety-six from across Sheffield in the north of England. Initially, the workshops explored participants' experience of ageing and representations of ageing in the media in general. Later, the workshops moved into a creative phase, culminating in the women reclaiming their images through their own representations. Having encouraged access to an artistic medium unfamiliar to many of the participants, the project developed life-long learning through the mastery of a new skill. Similarly, by exhibiting the images publically in Sheffield from 2011 to 2013 before touring nationally to the Royal College of Art, Plymouth University and the City Screen York, the project encouraged community involvement and citizenship for its participants, providing an impetus for discussions directly related to their lives as older adults. To date, two permanent exhibitions of the work remain on display in Sheffield at the Age UK offices and at the Centre for Innovative Ageing in Swansea University.

As a result of the project, several interesting findings emerged (Warren et al., 2012). These related to assumptions made regarding the experience of ageing (that it is homogenous in nature) and the preoccupations that supposedly accompany it, as well as the general public's response to images that relate to ageing. For example, in comparison to their fellow participants in their eighties and nineties, women in their fifties and sixties felt more pressure from media and advertising. A range of experiences, both positive and negative, was captured by the participants but in the majority these challenged stereotypes of ageing and rarely represented the stereotyped emotional dimensions of ageing: grief and loss. Eighty-eight per cent of visitors to the exhibitions claimed they wanted to see more similar images of older women displayed in public and visitors expressed a particular wish to see 'ordinary' older women and those who were still 'making a contribution' represented. Unsurprisingly, corporeal changes were examined in the work with the body being identified as the main site for the experience of ageing. This was evident in the representations produced by several participants who incorporated signifiers of ageing such as wrinkles and greying hair in their images. Considering all of these finding, the researchers argue that the types of participatory visual methods used in the project had the potential to give women a sense of solidarity and ownership in the research process, which was read as having a positive impact on the participants (Warren et al., 2012).

Addressing the 88 per cent of visitors to the original exhibition who expressed a wish to see more positive representations of older women in the public domain, the project, led by Warren, made a daring move in November 2014. Over two nights, as part of the Economic and Social Research Council Festival of Social Science, two of Sheffield's most famous buildings were lit up with huge images of older women. The city's Town Hall and Library in Tudor Square were covered with images created by participants Kathleen, Eleanor, Jill and Shirley, not only counteracting the fact that images of older women are rarely seen in contemporary society but also the ways in which they are seen. As Warren explained,

> Women aged 50 and over make up over a quarter (27.4%) of Sheffield's population, yet we rarely see any representations of them or their lives when we are out and about in Sheffield [...] I thought it would be a

great idea to project images that have been created by older women from Sheffield onto the side of buildings that symbolise public life in the city, to encourage the general public to think about the diversity of women's lives as [they] grow older. (University of Sheffield, 2016c)

Discussing the issues attached to the project as well as capturing peoples' reactions to the images as they passed, BBC Radio Sheffield produced a programme after the event further highlighting the potential of such work to bring issues of ageing into the public domain for debate.

Representing Self – Representing Ageing shows how arts practices can reclaim representations of ageing, something which is similarly addressed in Ages and Stages, a research project from Keele University also supported by the New Dynamics of Ageing programme. Here, changing artistic and social representations of ageing were examined along with their interconnectedness to performing arts and a local community, in this case the Potteries in North Staffordshire.

Over the course of four years (2009–2012) primary investigator Miriam Bernard worked with a team from Keele University along with Jill Rezzano and partners New Vic Theatre, Newcastle-under-Lyme, the Victoria Theatre Archive, Staffordshire University, the Beth Johnston Foundation/Centre for Intergenerational Practice and Stoke-on-Trent Primary Care Trust. Through an exploration of representations of ageing in the Victoria/New Vic's pioneering social documentaries, along with interviews with older people about the Victoria/New Vic theatre and its place in their lives, the project aimed to provide an understanding of lives and histories of older adults in area. Members of the project first examined the archive of the New Victoria Theatre to focus on a literary and cultural analysis of historical representations of age in the Potteries. Following that, they used qualitative research in the form of interviews with individuals attached to the theatre (as performers, volunteers or audience members) to consider contemporary representations of ageing. These two strands were then brought together to produce a new intergenerational social documentary entitled *Our Age, Our Stage*, which involved an intergenerational group of performers and was produced in conjunction with an exhibition of archival material and the development of subsequent educational material for schools in the area.

The aims of the researchers (Bernard et al., 2012) are outlined in this statement below and included on the website for the project:

> Through the lens of older people's recollections and involvements in a particular place (The Potteries), linked with a particular artistic institution and its ground-breaking social documentary work (the New Victoria Theatre), and from the 1960s to the present day, we aim to explore how people, place and theatre come together to co-construct, represent and reflect on ageing and old age within the continuing struggles of this unique industrial community. (University of Sheffield, 2016b)

The rationale for the project states, 'Contemporary gerontology has highlighted the value of engaging older people in a variety of artistic activities, and the importance of the arts in constructing, perpetuating and challenging models and stereotypes of older people and the ageing process' (University of Sheffield, 2016b). Noting that together both literary and cultural scholars have been increasingly interested in representations of ageing and the artistic output of older people, the researchers attached to Ages and Stages questioned the fact that there were few UK studies that brought both of these areas of scholarship together. For them, the theatre is a 'particularly fruitful context for such investigations since it has historically been a cultural arena in which older people are particularly active participants, as audience members, employees and volunteers' (University of Sheffield, 2016b). The Victoria Theatre has a rich history of documentary theatre that tackles social, political and cultural issues. Because of this, it provides a primary source with which to chart the image of older adults throughout recent history. Once accessed by the researchers, it allowed them to consider how ageing had been constructed, represented and understood in the Potteries from the 1960s to present day and to 'illustrate the roles and positions of different generations within the community' (University of Sheffield, 2016b). Subsequently it allowed for an understanding of how institutions such as theatres, and the

Victoria Theatre in particular, can act as catalysts for the construction of identities, both of the individual and of a community and also what role that institution has in 'preserving community memory' (University of Sheffield, 2016b).

Finally, in a similar way to the Representing Self – Representing Ageing project, Ages and Stages wished to consider what impact its findings might have following the completion of the project on the lives of older adults, the 'practical and policy implications for involving the theatre, and the arts in general, in promoting active ageing and intergenerational understanding' (University of Sheffield, 2016b). Thus, as well as increasing the visibility of older adults and the representations of ageing that exist in the public domain, both projects had an intention to impact on policy relevant to older adults in a way that is beneficial and can be sustained.

The outcomes of Ages and Stages were designed to be practical, cultural and scholarly in nature. The project allowed for the development of a range of academic outputs that examined and developed methodological and theoretical research in the area of ageing and arts practice with older adults. Practically and culturally, it allowed for the development of an interdisciplinary documentary theatre performance and exhibition and the production of educational workshop material for primary and secondary schools. In *Our Age, Our Stage*, the company worked inter-generationally, bringing together older participants from the project and members of the New Vic's Youth Theatre in a documentary theatre production that retold some of the stories shared with researchers about community member's experiences of the theatre in general and the Victoria specifically, as well as their experience of ageing and creativity. This production was accompanied by the exhibition displayed in the New Vic Theatre that commemorated the fifty-year relationship between the theatre and its community in North Staffordshire. The project also allowed for an intergenerational theatre company to be established. To date, the Ages and Stages Theatre Company have developed two productions, the aforementioned *Our Age, Our Stage* and *Happy Returns*, both of which have played at the New Vic as well as touring the North Staffordshire area and beyond.

Creative Encounters, Representing Self – Representing Ageing, and Ages and Stages all operate at both the local and national level. In relation to research, they have impact beyond that but for the most part produce work to encourage visibility and understanding for the communities in which they are based. Their practice can be considered to align with the active ageing model as well as the continuity theory as all three encourage participants to use existing skills and abilities (as well as mastering new ones) to actively engage in, comment on and make visible their experience of the world as older adults. Other work, such as that produced by performance artist Lois Weaver (as her alter ego Tammy WhyNot), can be viewed as having a deliberate international focus which comments on issues universally significant to older adults whatever their nationality.

Tammy WhyNot

For over thirty years Weaver has worked with the company Split Britches to produce work that addresses and challenges sexual and gender stereotypes. In recent years, the performance artist has begun to consider issues associated with ageing and health. The following section looks at Weaver's work that challenges the taboo of sex and ageing through her alter ego Tammy WhyNot in *What Tammy Needs to Know about Getting Old and Having Sex*. This work increases the visibility of older adults, positioning them and their lives (including sex lives) at the centre stage in public-facing, international performances. By doing so, Weaver challenges understandings of ageing and sexuality in ways that reaffirm the ideas discussed at the beginning of this chapter. These include the fact that ageing is a natural phenomenon, that the experience of ageing is heterogenic, that there need not be a limit to the continued enjoyment of life as we age and finally that ageing itself might present opportunities to be more creative in the way one approaches life.

On her website Public Address Systems: Strategies for Engaging the Public through Performance, Place and the Everyday, Weaver describes her work as using performance to 'address political issues from unexpected angles' and in doing so creating performances that 'avoid didactic lecturing and traditional narrative forms in favor of complex, welcoming and absolutely theatrical experiences' (Weaver, 2013a). In her latest work as Tammy WhyNot, Weaver does that while tackling the taboo that surrounds ageing and sexuality. Tammy WhyNot is Weaver's alter ego. She has accompanied her on many an exploratory journey. Described by Weaver as 'a former famous country music singer turned lesbian performance artist' (2013a) Tammy engages directly with community groups in order to get 'involved in advocacy for social and economic justice and [to test out] experimental forms of democracy' (Weaver, 2013a). On the Public Address System website, Weaver collects and curates a range of Tammy's interventions which pair theatricality with collaborative research and public dialogue.

Tackling complex issues ranging from gender and sexuality to ageing, Tammy facilitates public engagement and dialogue through a heightened theatricality which engages audiences and encourages a collaborative exploration of the subject. Tammy allows Weaver the freedom to transgress taboo and navigate discussions on ageing and sexuality. Through revelations of the character's 'personal' sexual experiences Weaver encourages her audience to be similarly revealing, a practice that also occurs in her collaborative workshop practice. In the United States, Britain, Croatia, Poland and Tasmania, Weaver facilitates workshops in different settings (some residential, some community based) with groups of older adults. Each of these adults creates his or her own Tammy alter ego complete with costume, wig and make-up. In doing so, they are invited to embrace the character and her uninhibited nature, thus encouraging a similar lack of reserve when discussing their own sex lives.

Interactions from the workshop have provided some of the material for the performance *What Tammy Needs to Know about Getting Old and Having Sex*, where Weaver articulates the different and similar experiences of ageing by older adults in different countries. These moments of recollection are positioned within the performance along with a number of original country and Western 'hits' which Weaver uses to contextualize Tammy's sexual relationships, both old and new. The subject of the songs embraces Tammy's sexuality and libido while providing a subtext that acknowledges the sometimes difficult coupling of sex and ageing. The collaboration between Tammy and the workshop participants creates a space where members of the audience might consider their own relationship to sex as older adults or as someone who wishes to continue to enjoy sex as they age. This is not always a private act, however, as often Tammy leaps into the audience congratulating anyone who, when asked, acknowledges his or her continued enjoyment of an active sex life, whatever the age.

In the performance, anecdotal material included from the workshops highlights that, for a number of participants at least, as older adults their relationship to sex is far from distant; a sentiment echoed in the conversations with audience members, who, when pushed by the faded star, expose the fallacy of the ageing adult with the reduced libido. This fallacy is similarly exposed by experts included in the performance, such as David Lee, an Age UK Research Fellow from the School of Social Sciences, University of Manchester. At the performance hosted by the Z Arts centre, Manchester, Lee discussed his research project on sex and ageing with Tammy and the audience, providing evidence of what we all suspect to be true: that older adults can, and in fact do, experience a healthy sex life.

Describing the work, Weaver states she 'collaborates with older adults through interviews, performance workshops and public presentations in order to research the effects of ageing on people's desire for and ability to obtain sexual pleasure and intimacy' (2013b). Collaboration with these groups allowed for the development of the piece and this ethos of collaboration continues in its performance. In whatever venue the performance occurs, Weaver as Tammy shares the stage with a group of older adults from a community partner local to the area. Thus, throughout the performance Weaver shares the stage, first with other older adults from her workshops through images and anecdotes, then in her conversation with the audience and finally, in the physical presence of the older adults community group performing alongside Tammy. In a strategy that draws on our familiarity with the trope of the talk show host, Tammy engages the audience through a series of interactions that coax even the most reticent of members to discuss their relationships and sexual habits. With the audience foregrounded (perhaps not as co-creators but as embedded in the rhetoric of the material) in the performance, Weavers demonstrates how, in her own words, 'performance can be a tool for addressing public issues through joyful, non-hierarchical and deeply engaged means' (2013b).

While Weaver's work as Tammy WhyNot continues to be produced publically (most recently at Lancaster's feminist Hear Me Roar festival in 2016), she is also keen to highlight its ability to produce more long-term impact through the relationships that develop from the practice. For example, Aglow with Desire was a series of performance workshops that were conducted in collaboration with Association of Greater London Older Women (AGLOW). This group of women, sixty years of age and over, work to raise awareness of ageism, homophobia and sexism. The workshops, devised by Weaver, included a multigenerational perspective with students and graduates of Queen Mary University London working in collaboration with the AGLOW members to explore multiple perspectives on the issues outlined above as a means to create future public performance on the subject.

As a result of these interactions, Weaver's work as Tammy WhyNot can be read as being explicitly political. The practice makes visible issues and misconceptions associated with ageing and sex. It involves participants in challenging stereotypes and engages them in both the creation and facilitation of arts practice that considers ageing and its impact on our understanding of gender and sexuality. Thus, much like Collective Encounters and the Third Age theatre company or the New Dynamics of Ageing project, Weaver produces practice that encourages the visibility of older adults in order to expose stereotypes and prejudices experienced by older adults.

Private: Care, applied theatre and ageing

Quoting Gubrium (1995), Philips suggests care is 'characterised by diversity and "multiple discourses" of caring' (2007: 3). She argues that the notion of care in the twenty-first century has been 'recast – from the perception of care as a set of tasks, burdensome to the caregiver, to a broader perspective that views care within the wider environment in which it takes place, from duty and obligation to rights to give and receive care' (2007: 3). In the section that follows we examine the practice situated at the private end of the continuum along with notions of care in relation to applied theatre and ageing.

Phillips (2007) notes that the language of care has changed. Discussions about care now consider the rights of the individual as well as their dependence. Similarly, as the chapters that follow show, relationships of care have changed and are now prioritized along with notions of personhood. As Phillips continues, while care relationships were once defined by dependency and, as such, viewed negatively, the promotion of 'active ageing' may allow for a counter position to be taken, one which rids the concept of care of its negative associations. My own interest in care comes from my experience as a former general nurse and some of what I offer here (particularly towards the end of this chapter) is a tentative semi-autoethnographic exploration of my experiences caring for older adults in this capacity. These experiences are included to allow for an analysis of care in relation to individuals with a diagnosis of dementia and with the argument that arts practice may improve care in this area. Also included in this section are examples of practice that align with changing concepts of care such as the Story Box project created by the British company Small Things: Creative Projects and Hogewey, an innovative residential care home developed in the Netherlands.

The Story Box project

As has been mentioned, Manchester has the distinction of being the WHO's first Age-friendly City in the UK. Coupled with other innovations, including the Manchester Reducing Social Isolation and Loneliness in Older People 2014–16 programme, set up by the NHS and Manchester Clinical Commissioning Group, the city has embraced the need for change in order to provide accessibility and inclusivity to its oldest inhabitants. In recent years, Manchester has been home to a number of arts-based projects for older adults, which have taken place within its community and cultural institutions. One such project, the Story Box project, began in the Library Theatre before transferring to an independent arts company, Small Things: Creative Projects.

Small Things: Creative Projects is an arts-based company whose practice is designed to open up spaces for communication. Whether that communication is between staff and clients in a residential setting or between older adults and their community, the company works from a mission to use 'creativity and critical engagement to fuel learning, change and development' (Small Things, n.d.). The company works to develop 'projects that create space for thinking and togetherness in a wider range of settings' (Small Things, n.d.).

In 2012, lead artist Lowri Evans in collaboration with Sara Cocker received the support of the Paul Hamlyn Foundation and Manchester City Council to develop and deliver creative story-telling workshops in a variety of non-acute settings, including day centres, sheltered accommodation schemes and hospital day units. Included in the project was a residency with the Library Theatre where sessions were developed and delivered over a ten-week period by two professional facilitators. As well as designing sessions around different themes using a variety of music, props and costume, Story Box also included a remit to provide staff training. Current director of Small Things Liz Postlethwaite explains the practice is 'at its most successful when it can be incorporated into everyday life' (2014). Thus, the inclusion and training of care staff to sustain the work produced by Story Box is vital.

Practice undertaken in Story Box uses an empathetic and responsive methodology. Much like the relational clowning discussed later in Chapter 3, the work of Small Things requires observation in order to allow for individualized spontaneous responses that focus on the needs of the client in the moment of interaction. Postlethwaite describes such observation and response as 'good practice' explaining that 'dementia is an individual experience so every group is different' (2014), which means every interaction is different and requires an ability on behalf of the facilitator to adapt as necessary.

The Story Box project includes the use of sensory stimuli and the creation of collaborative stories (developed through play) that, rather than draw from the past, focus on the moment of interaction in the present. Using a range of art forms, incorporating drama, storytelling, singing, poetry and crafts to cater to different interests, the process enables 'participation by people at varying stages of dementia and with different physical and linguistic abilities' (Harris, 2013: 7). While the company has a core group of facilitators, prior to becoming involved with the project, many of these had no previous experience of working with individuals with a diagnosis of dementia. For Postlethwaite, this lack of experience is not an issue; what is important is that all facilitators are good communicators. At the forefront of the practice is an understanding of the participants' aspiration to engage and the company's mission to encourage purposeful arts interaction that allows for a three-way collaboration between artist, participant and support worker, all of whom, the company suggests, are experts in their own areas.

Small Things encourages its participants to be autonomous, thus the workshops are often participant led. This has considerable effects on the relationships that develop as artists, participants and carers interact. The Story Box practice adopted by Small Things embraces collaboration and as a result produces an environment where the status and the power to direct creative activity is fluid and can be challenged. This latter point has particular significance in the practice undertaken by the company in care settings which traditionally place the individual with a diagnosis of dementia in a submissive role as the recipient of care.

The Story Box project was evaluated by Dr Bethan Harris from the Interdisciplinary Collaboration for Research on Ageing (MICRA) at the University of Manchester. She recognizes the arguments made by Kinney and Rentz (2005) that:

> Dementia illnesses are incurable, [and therefore] improvement to overall care must include non-clinical interventions to support psychological discomfort associated with these disorders and to maintain or improve general wellbeing through what can be a prolonged disease course. (Quoted in Harris, 2013: 5)

In her report, Harris argues that the method of practice adopted by the Story Box project has a positive effect on the lives and social experiences of those participating. She bases this argument on observations and reflections collected from contributing artists, participants and carers, along with supportive findings from organizations such as National Institute for Health and Clinical Excellence (NICE) (2006) and the Department of Health (2009). Both of these organizations, according to Harris, 'recommend non-pharmacological interventions to support health and care systems' (2013: 5). Story Box's work aims to develop the types of participatory and multisensory activities recommended by NICE (2006) and the Department of Health (2009). These include multisensory stimulation and the therapeutic use of music and/or dance for individuals with varying symptoms associated with their dementia diagnosis, particularly agitation. Similarly, it identifies with the Department of Health's 2007 recognition of the benefits of arts practices as something that should be considered as an integral component of routine health care.

As well as advocating for arts intervention with older adults with a diagnosis of dementia, Harris' evaluation provides a practical guide to the practice included in the Story Box project. This guide supports earlier discussion regarding the company's intention for their practice to become imbedded and delivered within the care environment by the careers themselves. This practice involves developing a series of workshops that speak to each other in order to develop creative skills through a series of activities centred in each session around a common theme. According to Harris,

> These themes are selected in order that everyone participating can relate to them in some way. Hence, shared experiences such as the market or funfair are used and more fanciful experiences of which there is a shared knowledge (Oscar ceremonies and weddings for example) are suggested. The experience is not prescribed however, thus allowing for different cultural interpretations. (2013: 15)

Allowing for different interpretations ensures inclusion which is vital to the practice. A broad range of activities is included that appeals to a range of participants while also having the added benefit of allowing each participant to experience a variety of creative approaches. So while a central theme is always present (e.g. the seaside) within each session, facilitators and participants approach that theme through a number of different but related arts practices.

In Story Box, painting, music and movement, as well as the spoken word, are used to create an experience for the participants. Varying practices and materials in this way encourage a communal engagement driven by multisensorial stimulation. Added to this, the range of selected activities ensures that the practice appeals to everyone; if a participant is not engaged by one arts practice he or she might be engaged by another. Similarly, the theme for each session is chosen to cross socio-economic, ethnic and gender barriers. All of these factors are considered in an effort to encourage inclusion and engagement.

The ultimate aim of Small Things: Creative Project for the Story Box project is for the work to eventually be taken over by carers and continued once the artists leave. The success of the projects, according to Postlethwaite, is often down to finding partners with the same ethos who want things to be better for the older adults in their care. In her words, 'artists are good at finding creative ideas; collaboration with carers can encourage a creative approach to the care of individuals with a diagnosis of dementia' (Postlethwaite, 2014). Out of this comes a drive to advocate for staff development and for the embedded use of the Story Box methodology in everyday care interactions.

The outcome of the practice of Small Things can be to re-invigorate existing relationships, particularly those which may have become institutionalized within the care setting. It also has the potential to encourage independence or reveal levels of independence perhaps hitherto lost for the individual with a diagnosis of dementia. Perhaps this is because the practice is based on a sense of capacity not loss. The process does not engage in achievement or failure, rather on the interaction between the three experts: the participant, the carer and the arts practitioner. Added to this, the practice always ensures no participant can fail more than the arts practitioner. Again, much like the relational clowns in Chapter 3, failure is something which the facilitators embrace and normalize. Thus, the practice becomes about communication and arts intervention and less about achievement and arts intervention.

The philosophy behind the Story Box project appears to be based on the established notion that creative participation can improve well-being and reduce social isolation for people with dementia. This belief has led to Small Things adapting Story Box so that it can be incorporated into the care of older people, allowing individuals with and without a diagnosis of dementia to have the opportunity to try new things and be culturally active on a daily basis. The notion of keeping the practice going after the project ends is important. This is facilitated through the practice which engages carers in the artist's intervention but also through a scheme created by Small Things: Creative Projects which allows carers to become associate artists of the company once the residency ends. Thus carers can continue to develop their creative practice skills with the company on a regular basis, bringing those skills back into the non-acute setting in their work with those they care for.

The company has also gone on to develop a way of working in acute settings that is being piloted in a new three-year project with Tameside Hospital, to develop the idea of an embedded arts practitioner working within a hospital both on the wards and in accident and emergency departments. If successful, this scheme has the potential to influence the culture of dementia care as it recognizes the benefit of arts practice beyond chronic symptom control and enhanced well-being. It is settings such as hospital wards and accident and emergency departments, often unfamiliar to the individual with the diagnosis of dementia, that can prove the most distressing. Introducing the practice of Small Things to these areas provides weight to the argument that arts practice can also be of benefit to the management of acute symptoms in acute setting.

The work of Small Things is based very much in the present. It recognizes the older adult's ability (regardless of diagnosis) to engage creatively. As Postlethwaite explains, reaffirming an individual's position in the present is important. This is perhaps why she and the company worked on the collaborative project *How Do You See Me?*, first produced at the London College of Fashion as part of their 2013 Mirror Mirror conference which celebrated 'fashion, culture, age and ageing' (University of Arts London, 2013). Framed as a performance lecture, the production included a number of older adults sharing their experiences of fashion, exploring how, as a mode of expression, those experiences changed as they got older. Sharing personal images and memories, the performance was as much about identity and ageing as it was fashion and ageing. The production encouraged a reconsideration of how we remember objects as well as ourselves. Discussing pictures from their past, the seven participants in the production revealed past experiences as a way to explore their individuality apart from the ageing process.

Considering both the Story Box project and *How Do You See Me?* one can argue that the work of Small Things: Creative Projects with older adults crosses the boundaries of engagement, visibility and care. The company works to bring arts practice to individuals living within residential care settings as a means to encourage well-being and is endeavouring to mirror that practice in more acute settings. Other creative methodologies are also being adopted internationally in residential care settings that influence the interaction between older adults, their carers and the environment in which they reside.

According to Tronto (1993), care is a normal part of life through a life course. Care involves reciprocity and interdependency; at some point, we all with will assume the role of receiver as well as provider of care. We should not, therefore, pathologize those who need care. For Philips, 'Care is about tasks and labour, both physical and emotional. It is a practice involving certain ability factors: time, material resources, knowledge and skill, social relationships and feelings. Care also has to be discussed as an ethic, attaching particular value to responsibility, responsiveness and integrity' (2007: 31). The next section examines a radical care environment that incorporates the elements outlined by Trono. This environment, through its innovations, aims to facilitate social relationships that are responsive to the needs of individuals in its care.

For Tronto, 'providing good quality of care involves "emotional labour", the giving of self within social relations' (2007: 35). The upcoming example of the Hogewey residential care home in the Netherlands highlights this emotional labour in the attempt to find appropriate methods of care, ones that interestingly adopt performance strategies in their provision of care. This section then examines the role of creativity in methodologies of care for individuals with a diagnosis of dementia. In doing so, it considers two different approaches used in the care of individuals with this diagnosis: re-orientation and validation.

A personal reflection

Earlier in the chapter, I mentioned I would introduce some personal anecdotal material related to my training and previous career as a general nurse. I do so now as a means to frame an analysis of re-orientation versus validation approaches before moving on to discuss Hogewey and its ethos of care.

In 1993, I began my nurse training and was immediately part of the workforce. As was the norm at the time, while I spent some time in the class room, the majority of my training came through practice, working as a paid member of an established workforce with an entrenched hierarchy in a way that was very much task orientated. As a result, outside of the scientific knowledge necessary to understand such things as infection control, pathophysiology and aseptic technique, my understanding of the role of the nurse and the emotional needs of those in my care developed through experience and a process of trial and (hopefully, not too much) error.

When learning how to fulfil the emotional needs of those in my care, the phrase 'reassure the patient' was often bandied around as a totem of practice. It was, however, never really explained. There were no lessons outlining different forms of reassurance or, indeed, how one should go about offering the appropriate reassurance to respond to the individual needs of any particular patient. But then, this was the medical model of training which bound the patient to his or her disease and which would later be overtaken by the emphasis on patient-centred care.

For a short period in 2002, I worked in the elderly care unit of Our Lady's hospice in Dublin, Ireland. Working at night, as a charge nurse responsible for a number of wards, one is presented with a range of issues and challenges. The residents within the unit were almost all living with the symptoms associated with end-stage dementia, so without a doubt the most pressing challenge was to find ways to care for each individual client in their confused state in a way that alleviated distress and prevented potential agitation and aggression. At times, these moments of distress, of agitation and of aggression happened without warning and could easily be exacerbated if handled in a way inappropriate for that particular resident. My main aim as the primary carer then was always to 'reassure the patient' but as my training never formally explained what form that reassurance should take, how did I decide?

Reality orientation versus validation therapy: Hogewey

Reality orientation approaches attempt to facilitate the person's reconnection with their present place and time. It has a factual focus; it confronts factual errors and is based in objective rather than subjective reality. Validation therapy does something different. It engages with the reality experienced only by that individual in that moment, accepting that reality and the personal truth of another's experience. So, depending on the context, by accepting the reality of the other's experience one agrees to the facts of that experience. In doing so, one agrees to engage in the reality of a confused individual, perhaps becoming his or her mother, sister, aunt, choosing to characterize a person and engage in a reality seen and experienced only by the individual in their confused state.

Pioneered by Naomi Feil in the 1960s, the approach classifies individuals with cognitive impairment and is based on the general principle of validation; it also incorporates a range of specific techniques. Although criticized by some, Feil argues for its effectiveness and advocates 'the process of communicating with a disoriented elderly person by validating and respecting their feelings in whatever time or place is real to them at the time, even though this may not correspond with our "here and now" reality' (Vanderslott, 1994: 151).

In his preface to the seminal *The Presentation of Self in EveryDay Life*, Goffman notes: 'The stage presents things that are make-believe; presumably real life presents things that are real and sometimes not well-rehearsed' (1959: preface). In the moments when for the individuals in my care, their dementia created a cycle of confusion, anxiety and potentially aggression, my objective was always to interrupt the cycle as quickly as possible, to prevent any further distress or escalation in agitation and therefore to ensure the individual's emotional and physical safety. Drawing from my experience and with the needs of the other residents in mind, often only two choices were immediately available. One was to attempt reality re-orientation, to ask the patient to accept his or her present time, place and person; the other was to engage in the alternate reality experienced by the resident in that moment, to attempt to facilitate the person's reconnection with his or her present place and time or to engage in the world experienced by the individual in that moment. This position was prefaced on an agreement to play a part in a withheld reality, only accessible to and accessed by the person in my care. What is interesting is the decision to re-orientate or validate came intuitively, through experience. What is also interesting is the outcome of the decision to facilitate rather than re-orientate and its ability to prevent distress, agitation and, at times, aggression.

Now a researcher of performance, I look at this choice in a new light and in relation to current trends in the care of individuals with a diagnosis of dementia that formally adopt a level of performance. The residential care home Hogewey in Holland (discussed in detail later) provides an interesting case study for this discussion as it embraces unique practices which create a safe world for its residents unfettered by locks or an emphasis on reality orientation. As nursing scholars Jenkins and Smythe argue, the ethos of Hogeway has been developed in an attempt to minimize disability and maximize 'wellbeing by providing a physical and social environment congruent with people's lifestyles' (2013: 14). In doing so, the potential for alternative strategies to engage positively with the alternative realities produced in the mind of the individual with dementia is explored.

I now have some understanding of validation therapy and reality orientation and the debates that surround both; in 2002 I had neither. My decisions to attempt re-orientation or to play along, often taken under pressure in moments of heightened emotion and distress, were based on two factors. Firstly, experience. I considered what had been successful on previous occasions when a similar severity of confusion had occurred. If re-orientation had been used on those occasions, I considered how effective it had been in preventing further distress. Second, intuition, what route did I intuitively know would cause less distress. If the decision was taken to engage in the reality of the individual with dementia (to use theatrical terms) to become the other 'character' in the 'scene' and thus provide the 'theatrical' device with which to change the action, it was taken through instinct, accessed and acted upon in the moment.

In health care environments, historically the presumption has been that valuable knowledge is knowledge that is 'scientific' and 'objective'. As mentioned earlier in this chapter, Nicholson challenges this presumption, arguing that it undermines what she terms as the 'intuition of empathetic and compassionate carers who work with older adults on a daily basis' (2011: 49). The value placed on rational knowledge and the insecurities this value engenders in artists who work in ways that cannot be thus measured presents some interesting common themes in relation to the choices mentioned above. Concerns regarding the appropriateness of 'playing along' are potentially not that dissimilar from concerns felt by artists regarding the evaluation of their work with adults with dementia. Both come from an inherent lack of appreciation for intangible states of empathy and intuition because, by their nature, these states are immeasurable. Knowing the work is beneficial though intuition and choosing to 'play along' come instinctually and are thus intangible states, which despite immeasurability, produce potentially positive outcomes in the lives of others.

Despite being a potentially positive intervention, however, choosing to play a part in an unseen world is not without its challenges and ethical dilemmas. Engaging in the world of the other in this context is a communal event, contingent on both individuals' involvement. It is not, however, an improvisation with equal status for both players. Goffman suggests that in any everyday interaction, 'Many crucial facts lie beyond the time and place of integration or lie concealed within it' (1956: 13). But what of the interaction contingent on entering into an alternative reality offered by the individual with dementia? How does one engage in a reality, even an imagined one, when one does not know the rules or structures that make up that reality? By choosing to engage in the unseen world, one accepts the lack of ownership over the structures of that reality. One can only take cues and offer reassuring responses to those cues; one cannot change the dynamics of relationships or the structure of the interaction. Indeed, one must accept the historical context in which the relationship is based and the narrative structure, however nonlinear, all of which begs the following question: what position does the carer take in the performance? Are they facilitators or a vice to provide distraction? And what ethical culpability is engendered through the choice to play along?

When working in a situation that incorporates an experience that only the individual with dementia can access, other ways of understanding, knowing and creating must be developed. Engaging in an alternate world asks the carer to move creatively across boundaries in the presentation of his or herself. While it is accepted that in all interactions levels of performance exist, as Goffman continues, in the service occupations an understanding of positions come from the specialist who 'maintains an image of disinterested involvement in the problem of the client, while the client responds with a show of respect of the competence and integrity of the specialists' (1956: 21). A carer does not assume the role of an individual offering a service in the traditional capitalist sense, although the 'client/service' rhetoric used by Western health care providers might hope to suggest otherwise. However, Goffman's point is interesting in the context of this discussion. What he implies might also be applicable to the carer engaging in the world of the person with dementia; doing so potentially calls into question any ability to maintain a show of 'disinterested involvement'. This point is compounded further when influenced by Goffman's later argument, which states:

> While in the presence of others, the individual typically infuses his acting with signs which dramatically highlight and portray confirmatory facts that might otherwise remain unapparent or obscure. For if the individual's activity is to become significant to others he must mobilize his activity so that it will express *during the interaction* what he wishes to convey. (Goffman, 1956: 40)

Consider this statement in relation to the role of the carer looking after an individual in a state of distressed confusion already maintaining several levels of performance.

While the carer observes and performs for the individual in his or her care, he or she must also maintain a level of professionalism for other patients and observing bystanders. Add to this the performance necessary for validation to occur and one wonders how performing on so many levels and with so many ethical quandaries is even possible. The aforementioned Hogewey, however, provides an example where these performances and associated ethical quandaries have been addressed to provide innovative ways of caring for individuals with a diagnosis of dementia.

Hogewey is a residential care home situated in the Dutch town of Weesp. Built in 2010, the village type complex is set on four acres; its communal spaces include wide boulevards, cosy side streets, court yards and gardens. Two-storey brick houses take up the rest of the space along with a café, theatre, hairdresser's shop and restaurant. Residents of Hogeway are free to go wherever they wish and there is only one external door to the outside world. Importantly, this is the only door that locks.

At Hogewey residents live in houses designed around specific lifestyles. There is an urban house for those residents used to living in city and a cultural house for those who enjoy art, music and theatre. There is an Indonesian house where residents from the former colony live in a home decorated with Indonesian art, eat Indonesian food and even enjoy two degrees more heating in winter. Perhaps the house which most exemplifies the beliefs of the Hogewey project is the Gooise or Dutch upper class house, where chandeliers and lace table cloths are the decoration of choice and where the residents are waited on by the carers who choose to perform as servants.

In this example carers know the rules. Unlike my earlier anecdote, these carers have a close relationship with the residents and are well trained to know when they should 're-orientate' or 'validate'. As Director of Innovation and co-founder Yvonne Van Amerongen explains, 'people with dementia can be disturbed by other people telling them "the truth" and the truth is something they cannot cope with and they cannot understand, so this is the truth they can live with' (Department of Health, 2009). In Hogeway individuals live their lives in a similar way to how it was lived outside the complex walls. They shop, socialize, engage in purposeful tasks and activities of daily living. There is no attempt at reminiscence, so, for example, the supermarket stocks contemporary items and while the concerts might include music from the 1950s there is a sense of enjoying that music in the present rather than remembering enjoying it in the past. That being said, if a resident believes he or she is in his or her own home, takes an item from the supermarket and eats it without paying there are no consequences as there would be in the 'real' world; the staff simply add the item to the resident's bill. In the outside world such an event could potentially cause great distress. Instead, facilitated by the proper training to 'play along' staff at Hogewey are able to pre-empt potential stressors.

The ethos is not infallible, however, as Isabel van Zuthem explains: 'The home is not completely normal, we pretend it is, but ultimately it is a nursing home, these are people with severe dementia. Sometimes the illusion falls down; they'll try to pay at the hairdresser's, and realise they have no money, and become confused' (Henley, 2012). The difference here, however, is that the staff are trained to pre-empt such an event and, if necessary, can engage in the individual's alternate reality and react accordingly.

As mentioned above, Hogewey residents live lives not dissimilar to the ones they lived before entering the complex. Residents continue to cohabitate with their pets, and they visit the pub, the hairdresser and the doctor. However, unlike traditional care homes where services are brought in, residents of Hogewey maintain independence by being able to go out (while still inside the village) to get their hair done or visit the health centre. The aim then is to maintain familiar activities of daily living in the safety of this enclosed world. This intention is also visible in the inclusion of arts practice at Hogewey. Just as residents might have done in their lives outside the village, here they attend concerts and performances produced in communal areas, open to residents and their family members alike. Arts practice also enables the village to develop its relationship with the local community with local artists displaying their work and schools using the theatre. Thus, as well as arts practice that fosters a particular individual's creative energy, cultural activities in Hogewey contribute to a sense of community, of going out and enjoying art communally in the way one might have done outside the village while simultaneously bringing the village out into the community.

For Nicholson there exists a 'relational aesthetic inherent in the performance of everyday life as participants move between material and imagined worlds, between attention and inattention, between memories of the past and their creative responses to living in the [here]-and-now' (2011: 50). Perhaps Hogewey provides a space where the movement between these states is acknowledged and accepted as a part of everyday life. If that is the case, then maybe it also provides an example where varied forms of knowledge, like varied states of being, are accepted and valued. Conceivably, Hogewey provides a place where, to quote Nicholson again, 'different ways of knowing are equally legitimate' (2011:49). Certainly it engages directly with concerns regarding the choice to 'play along' and the validity of the knowledge used to make that decision. As such, it presents an ethos of care that is innovative and potentially inspiring.

The spaces between the public and the private

In Thompson's 2009 book *Performance Affects* the author provides a focus with which to ensure 'the protective and resistant qualities of theatre and performance without minimising or denying their capacity for inducing enjoyment and pleasure' (2009: 2). He does so, at once drawing from Russian-American anarchist Emma Goldman (1869–1940) and the theatre academic Jill Dolan, both of whose ideas regarding the relationship between the creative act and its ability to move those experiencing it are useful to our understanding of applied theatre with, for and by older adults. Reading Goldman, Thompson suggests, 'participation in the joyful is part of the dream of a 'beautiful' future, in the sense that it becomes an inspirational force. Far from being a diversion, it acts to make visible a better world' (2009: 2).

Applied theatre with older adults does not fit always within the conceived intentions attached to the form. Sometimes the objective for producing applied theatre in this area is educational or to encourage development but more often, the remit is about creating a sense of sociality among members of this heterogeneous group. It is about being with others in a particular moment in space and time. Thus the effect of the practice (what happens as a result of the creative intervention) might shadow in comparison to its affect, the emotion that occurs as a result of the moment of interaction and creation. Thompson and Dolan's arguments regarding the importance of observing affect are vital to any analysis of this form particularly where sociality and communality are at the forefront of the practice.

In the section that follows, performance affects, 'the sensory responses to both social and artistic processes' (Thompson, 2009: 8) are considered. Festivals, networks and theatre companies are examined in order to explore aspects of practice 'that practitioners and participants might relish, such as joy, fun, pleasure or beauty, but rarely appear in the articulated intentions, funding applications or evaluation reports that surround the field' (Thompson, 2009: 115).

Festivals and networks

In 2009, a study by Age Concern and Help the Aged found that 60 per cent of older people in the UK agreed age discrimination exists in the daily lives of older people; 53 per cent of adults agreed that once you reach very old age, people tend to treat you as a child; 68 per cent of older people agreed that politicians see older people as a low priority; and 76 per cent of older people believed the country fails to make good use of the skills and talents of older people. Perhaps in response to some of these attitudes, arts practitioners across the globe have developed dedicated arts festivals that explore the needs and issues of older adults. Established in Ireland in 1996, the longest running of these festivals is Bealtaine (meaning May in Gaelic). The festival takes place annually in venues across Ireland. With a mission to celebrate creativity as we age, festival organizers state, 'May belongs to the Bealtaine festival' (Age and Opportunity, 2016).

Each year an estimated 120,000 people take part in the festival, making it one of the largest in Ireland. Supported by Age and Opportunity (a national Irish organization for older adults) and part-funded by the Arts Council of Ireland, the festival organizers' intention appears to be to showcase the talents and creativity of both first-time and professional older artists. With a programme that includes dance, film and theatre, festival organizers suggest Bealtaine offers opportunities 'for people to make new and challenging work' (Age and Opportunity, 2016). A closer examination of the programme in 2014 supports this assertion with work crossing disciplines and ranging in form from collaborations with the CoisCéim dance company, to a dawn chorus, to a collaboration between artist James O'Aodha and an over-fifties bicycle gang. Throughout, and in a similar way to comparable festivals in Northern Ireland (Here and Now), Scotland (Luminate) and Wales (Gwanwyn), United States (Virginia, Creative Ageing Festival), Canada (London Ontario, Creative Ageing Festival) and Australia (Every Age Festival, Celebrate Creative Ageing Festival), the focus of Bealtaine is its participants and audience.

Using both quantitative and qualitative methods, O'Shea and Nì Lèime (from the Irish Centre for Social Gerontology at the National University of Ireland, Galway) have concluded a study on the benefits for health and well-being for the festival's participants. Assessing the impact of the Bealtaine arts programme in 2011 on participants' quality of life, well-being and social interaction, the researchers found that the festival facilitated self-expression among older adults while also impacting positively on their personal development and quality of life. Indeed, in the evaluation questionnaire used, over 87 per cent of older adults involved agreed with the statement 'participation in Bealtaine had increased their level of involvement in their community' (Nì Lèime and O'Shea, 2012: 866). This is echoed in anecdotal responses taken from questionnaires with comments ranging from, 'I'm out and about more and meeting people – I'm also becoming more aware of people and their needs' to 'I'm aware of what's going on in the community' (Nì Lèime and O'Shea, 2012: 866).

While there is no exclusion policy in force, the target population for the festival is individuals of sixty-five and over. Focusing on a theme, each year Age and Opportunity invite groups such as arts centres, libraries, Active Retirement groups, care settings and community groups to run a Bealtaine event 'that celebrates the creativity of older adults and, importantly creativity with, for and by older adults' (Age and Opportunity, 2016). In an effort to celebrate creativity as we age, the organizers of the festival argue Bealtine, 'offers the novice an opportunity to discover a talent until then unseen or a chance for a long-dormant skill to find a new outlet' (Age and Opportunity, 2016). The suggestion then is that the festival actively encourages the communication of traditions between generations and provides an opportunity for older adults to engage with their community. What follows explores that suggestion, while questioning if, rather than producing specific festivals for older adults, a more inclusive policy could be adopted by all festivals, one which would provide the opportunities mentioned above for communication and engagement.

Social psychologists have long since acknowledged the complex relationship between ageing and our understanding of self. Indeed in one study, Thompson et al. note that scarcely any of their respondents thought themselves old, forcing the researchers to note the 'apparent contradiction – a kind of disconnection between how they looked, how they were, how they felt, and what they thought' (1990: 113). Regardless of our perceptions of self, we do not age in a vacuum.

As Mangan notes, 'Biological ageing is one thing; social aging is another – whether we understand this as patterns of intergenerational relationships, as a sequence of ages and age statuses, or as age – based normative expectations' (2011: 5). Social, physical and psychological ageing are all explored in Chapter 1, the discussion alluding to the understanding that concepts of ageing or of being elderly are not easily defined. Whether conceived through our interactions with others or our understanding of self or through the presence of infirmity or degeneration, understanding ageing occurs as a result of a complex system of beliefs, assumptions and power relations. As Woodward notes, 'although knowledge of old age can come to us from our infirmities (our bodies can speak to us of old age) [...] old age is in great part constructed by any given society' (1991: 66). The obvious conclusion then is that any ability to consider ageing positively depends on and is influenced by that construction.

Elsewhere, of course, arts festivals for specific audiences do occur. In Ireland, other months are claimed by the Dublin Gay Theatre Festival, the Feminist Film Festival and the Galway and Cork Arts festivals. Part of the role of these festivals is to celebrate the very thing that makes them specific. Bealtaine and similar festivals focus not on specific markers, political affiliation, sexuality, identity, but on a period of the human life cycle. The development of these festivals is, of course, positive in terms of the recognition of older adults, their creativity and valuable position within society. It could also be argued, however, that they have the potential to limit the scope of that position through the suggestion that exclusive experiences are needed to understand something that is, by definition, a natural part of life, experienced by the majority. It may not be helpful to use the term 'ghettoize', but equally, it is important to note, ageing does not change taste, nor should it produce silos where culture is experienced. The art that one enjoys at fifty is likely to remain the art one enjoys at eighty. Rather than producing separate festivals, perhaps we should work to ensure all festivals are accessible to all members of society. Surely, an inclusive society responds creatively and artistically to all of its members, developing arts practice and in turn arts festivals that consider the young, the old and the in-between in equal measure.

Despite this argument, encouraging participation and engagement through festivals such as Bealtaine, Here and Now, Luminate and Gwanwyn can help to address the needs of older adults removed from cultural and social activity. Of course such festivals provide visibility and provide a political platform where issues relevant to the lives of older adults can be acknowledged and debated. Festivals such as those mentioned can provide an opportunity for a large number of older adults to come together, creating a critical mass with political potential. How this critical mass is used is important, the argument being that properly harnessed, festivals might offer a strategic stepping stone for advocates to encourage imbedded policy relating to arts practice with older adults and inclusivity in general. As well as providing a social, communal and creative outlet, festivals might provide a political force through which ageism and social exclusion are tackled. They might provide an approach that contributes holistically to arts practice with older adults, one that recognizes the needs of individuals while also addressing issues affecting older adults more generally.

Festivals provide one opportunity for work to be brought together and shared; another similar opportunity can be found in the development of networks. Accessed by practitioners, companies, institutions and researchers, networks provide a platform where people involved in arts practice with, for and by older adults can share information about their work and access opportunities to develop their practice. One such network is the Age of Creativity.

On its website the network suggests it provides a national UK platform for those who believe 'creativity can support older people to enjoy better health, wellbeing, and quality of life' (Age of Creativity, n.d.). It does so by providing information about opportunities for older adults to engage in arts practice. For example, on 27 March 2016, the home page of the website advertised work diverse in form and location. The opportunities varied from a playwriting workshop in Oxfordshire supported by AgeUK and the company Living the Drama, a dance workshop for individuals with a recent diagnosis of dementia and their companions with Britain's National Contemporary Dance Company in London and a music/singing workshop supported by Live Music Now (LMN) and Ryedale Carers in Ryedale, North Yorkshire. With the support of AgeUK and the Baring foundation, Age of Creativity aims to create a space where work can be made more accessible to those in the wider ageing sector as well as health care professionals and those involved in policy making (Age of Creativity, n.d.). It does so as a means to inspire further engagement with community practice and the development of new arts projects for older adults.

International examples of a similar network dedicated to arts and ageing include the National Centre for Creative Aging, Washington USA. Their mission, like Age of Creativity's, is to 'support professional development across disciplines and occupations in creative aging that produce an innovative and robust workforce of artists, educators and advocates' as well as supporting community service organizations 'to provide accessible, high quality arts programs that meet the needs of an aging population' (National Centre for Creative Ageing, n.d.). Theirs is also a political agenda with a mission to promote 'research and public policy that enables the development of evidence-based best practices and model programs in the field of creative aging' (National Centre for Creative Ageing, n.d.).

Another international example can be found in the Australian Centre for Arts and Health, which, although not age specific, organizes the annual Celebrate Creative Ageing conference. Held for the first time in Sydney in 2015 the conference has the remit to explore 'the importance of older people engaging in the arts and creative activities to foster good health and wellbeing as they age' (Arts and Health Australia, 2015).

In mainland Europe, the European Theatre Convention (ETC) is a network of public theatres founded in 1988 whose aim is to foster cultural diversity and intercultural dialogue while acting as a platform for professional development and exchange and advocating for the public theatre sector in Europe. In 2012, a report commissioned and published by the European Union entitled the Ageing Report stated: 'An ageing population raises challenges for our societies and economies [...]. The seriousness of the challenge depends on how our economies and societies respond and adapt to these changing demographic conditions' (European Theatre Convention, n.d.). Responding to that report, the ETC developed The Art of Ageing project in an effort to initiate debates between diverse groups all working in this area. Artists, scientists, political and economical stakeholders, as well as audiences, were challenged to come together to discuss changing demographics and the challenges that change presents. Addressing young and old generations alike, their intention was to 'raise awareness for the political, social, biological and economic challenges of our ageing societies and encourage all generations to take an active part in the life of society' (European Theatre Convention, n.d.). The project began in 2013 with national state and city theatres from four countries (Germany, Croatia, Romania and Slovakia) commissioning four playwrights to produce new plays and concluded in 2016 with the performance of each play by a multicultural, multigenerational ensemble.

Theatre companies

Festivals and networks connect people, thereby fostering engagement. This occurs at national and international levels. At a local level, similar activities occur and are of significance to the older adults situated in that place. In the UK, exploring the potential for performance to enrich the lives of older adults has long since been the remit of a number of smaller theatre companies, including Collective Encounters, Liverpool and Spare Tyre, Deptford. More recently, companies such as Frontier Theatre Company, London and Good News from the Future, Cardiff, have been set up to provide opportunities for old actors and theatre makers to continue to be creative as they age.

While these companies focus on providing work for older adults that explores themes pertinent to an older generation, other companies focus on work that brings groups together. The Arcola Theatre in London, Mind the Gap at the Salisbury Playhouse and Shine On at the Belgrade Theatre, Coventry, all create work with their company while engaging in inter-generational performance. Bringing older and younger generations together to share experiences is also part of the mission of London Bubble Theatre Company that works to bridge a gap between arts practice in a theatre and arts practice in residential care homes. With the help of the Baring Foundation's Creative Homes Programme, London Bubble works to connect sheltered homes employing a model which links teenagers and older people as researchers of living history.

This is not an exhaustive list any means; in the UK alone other companies similarly dedicated to producing work with, for and by older adults include Entelechy, the Performance Ensemble, Big Telly, Spare Tyre, Kaleidoscope, Magic Me, Heyday at the West Yorkshire Playhouse and the Elders at the Royal Exchange. This list highlights the amount of work happening in one country alone. If we assume that these examples reflect only a fraction of practice occurring in Britain we begin to imagine the amount of similar work happening globally.

At a local level, one can observe the proliferation of practice in this area over the past decade. As was commented upon earlier, Manchester is the first British city to be awarded the status of WHO Age-friendly City. The award was given in 2010, following a decade of work in this area including such innovation as the establishment of the Older Age Working Party and Better Government for Older People programme, the Positive Images of Ageing awareness campaign and the launch of the Manchester Ageing Strategy launched. Since gaining the status of Age-friendly City, work has continued with the launch of the Manchester Ageing Hub and the publication document profiling individuals who play a leading age-friendly role in the communities within the city. Manchester has several large-scale arts venues; these include the Whitworth Gallery, Manchester Museum, Manchester City Museum, the Contact Theatre, Home (formally the Library Theatre and the Cornerhouse) and the Royal Exchange Theatre. Each of these venues provides accessible activities for older adults, albeit at different levels of engagement and most have a remit to become dementia friendly. While the previous chapter discussed some work situated within the auspices of the Whitworth Gallery and Manchester Museum, this chapter will explore the work facilitated by the Royal Exchange theatre through their Elders Company.

In 2014, the Royal Exchange developed a pilot scheme for a company of older members entitled the Elders Company. With a membership of thirty-five individuals, the company of older adults (aged sixty and over) developed out of an inter-generational project between the Young Company at the Royal Exchange and what was to become the Elders Company. The initial ambition of the scheme was to 'involve people aged 60+ to develop performance skills and make boundary-pushing theatre while also challenging stereotypes of ageing' (Barry, 2015a: 1). To achieve this, the company recruited members from Greater Manchester and developed a programme of weekly ensemble building and skills development workshops led by theatre director Andy Barry. The company used existing links with community partnerships and local housing associations to develop recruitment opportunities, which led to eighty-seven individuals taking part in initial taster sessions. Following these, fifty-three individuals applied for twenty places. The final group selected consisted of ten men and women aged between sixty and eighty-eight, with varying experience of theatre and performance.

For the project to include as many members as possible, a rotational system was developed. This means after a ten-week period, participants have a rest period, which allows other members to take part. According to Barry, 'This encourages sense of trust and ensemble built to cascade out to new members joining meaning the company does not have to start from scratch each time to build a completely new group' (Barry, 2015a: 2). Not starting from scratch is important to the creative progression of the company and is something organizers have worked to negated through taster sessions. These sessions allow potential members to engage with the practice prior to joining, thus maintaining retention levels for those who do choose to join. Once engaged in the programme, participants attend ten weekly workshops led by Barry and other visiting directors and artists working or affiliated with the theatre. Exploring three main themes, Storytelling, The Body in Space and The Voice and Text, these workshops develop in such a way as to encourage participants 'to work physically together to make discoveries about their own bodies and voices while also learning more about the rigorous processes an actor uses as part of their training' (Barry, 2015a: 2).

The company's work with visiting practitioners and artists is facilitated through their position within the walls of the Royal Exchange (both metaphorically and materially). Collaborations with theatre practitioners working or visiting the theatre and with the other companies based in the theatre allow members of the Elders to gain insight into specific areas of practice from established practitioners working in the field. Barry notes that this has helped them to 'feel valued as a community company within our organization and also to develop a range of different skills' (Barry, 2015a: 3).

These skills are visible in the diverse work produced by Elders. From the physical theatre, devising and ensemble work that facilitated the creation of the 2014 *The Goose Girl at the Spring* to their engagement with public installation in the 2015 *We're in the Lounge* (housed in the foyer of the theatre), the range of practice developed by the Elders shows an interest in the company to learn about and engage with different performances strategies.

Thematically, *The Goose Girl at the Spring* explored representations of older adults, especially those presented to children. It was shared with the New Vic Theatre's intergenerational company, Ages and Stages, allowing these themes to be explored and discussed by both companies together in a workshop setting. *We're in the Lounge* encouraged company members to use their homes as inspiration to develop an intimate performance that explored the stories and experiences of the Elders. This production highlights one of the main aims of the company, 'to broaden participants' knowledge and involvement in different types of theatre-making that doesn't necessarily focus on traditional text based performances' (Barry, 2015a: 3).

Much like *The Goose Girl at the Spring*, *Flicker and the Flying Books* (2015) was developed by the Elders to encourage better inter-generational understanding. In collaboration with members of the Royal Exchange's Young Company, the group worked with director Barry to create a play suitable for children aged three to eight that became part of the Manchester Children's Book Festival. The piece was developed through ensemble devising and was performed in the Royal Exchange, the Central Library, Manchester, and the New Vic Theatre, Stoke where it was seen by 204 children and adults. In 2016, the children's play was successfully remounted as part of the Great Big Noise Festival (a festival of work for children and families) at the Royal Exchange where it had two performances and reached a further 119 audience members.

As well as work within the company, members of the Elders have taken part in other intergenerational work attached to the Royal Exchange. Also in 2015, several members of the company took part in Blast Theory's *Too Much Information*, a digital storytelling project. The company produced a digital map for individuals to navigate while listening to older adults and young people discuss life experiences. Most recently, the company has produced two productions within the walls of the theatre, the first *This Is Me*, within the foyer space of the great hall, and a second, *Keeping up with the Elders,* in the theatre's studio space.

In the devising process for *This Is Me*, members of the company took part in creative writing workshops with playwright Zodwa Nyonito creating text from personal experience. The result was a relaxed, joyful performance of music and personal testimony. Revealing delicate and often poignant stories from their own lives, the piece challenged stereotypes of ageing and older adults. Rather than portraying a group isolated, marginalized or invisible, *This Is Me* allowed the company's members to present this lives as they are:

active, engaged, lived in the moment, without reference or fixation to the past or the process of ageing.

The most recent performance by the company, entitled *Keeping Up with the Elders*, was produced as part of a large initiative by the Royal Exchange to engage with its audience in a conversation regarding their experience of theatre. Entitled *You, the Audience*, the project consisted of an eighteen-month conversation between the Royal Exchange and its audience undertaken to gain an understanding of the relationship between theatre and audience member. The project culminated in several public-facing activities, one being a sound instillation and exhibition which included extracts from many of the interviews with audience members. As part of their event the Elders presented their thoughts on the subject in *Keeping up with the Elders*, which unfolded as a manifesto of sorts, outlining the creative intentions and aspirations of the performers and of the company as a whole. Using mask and physical theatre and engaging with audience members directly through one-to-one interaction, members of the Elders developed a piece of performance that allowed them to describe what theatre means to them.

The examples outlined above highlight the use of personal material in the work of the Elders. This autoethnographic interest, however, is not accompanied by a proclivity to subject matter pertaining to ageing. Indeed, members of the group have, at times, expressed a desire not to make work explicitly about ageing. Instead, there is an interest in exploring different performance skills and experiencing different ways of theatre making. As Barry continues, 'This [has] led us to focus on making work whose form or content might surprise an audience, and thus challenge stereotypes of ageing in this way, rather than necessarily making work that thematically explores ageing' (Barry, 2015a: 5). This intention is clear in the intergenerational work undertaken by the company and in their work with younger audiences. In these examples, the work produced by the Elders has made older adults more visible to specific groups without explicitly pointing to a need for that to be the case. It has allowed for a natural intermingling of generations, which is somewhat unnaturally absent in contemporary Western society.

Here the Young Company members from the Royal Exchange express their change in attitude towards older adults as a result of engaged in intergenerational work: '[At the start of the project I thought] ... that Elder performers may develop work slower. This was positively challenged'; 'I learnt that I have common interests with people from other generations' (Barry, 2015b: 3).

While thematically the company does not always address directly issues that affect the lives of older adults in British society, indirectly, there remains a shadow of it in their practice. It is there unapologetically and arrives through what Barry describes above as an exploration of form and performance practice. The Elders may wish to consider their position in society through their practice but they do not wish to look backwards, to reminisce. Their work (particularly in the performance *This Is Me*) reaffirms and celebrates the role of older adults in British society. Members of the company are members precisely because they wish to recognize and develop their creative, social and cultural capacity in the present. As one 71-year-old male member expressed,

> It made me have a different view of what theatre can be – in the moment, real, intimate, live. My past, present and future existed all at the same time. It's important on so many levels, emotional, physical, intellectual. It's expressing myself, sharing with others, moving outside my comfort zone – it makes me realise I am still alive. (Barry, 2015b: 3)

The success of the company to date is outlined by Barry as occurring in two different strands. Firstly, the flexible approach to membership allows for growth while maintaining the interest of existing members and supporting their creative progress. Secondly, the company fosters a sense of belonging nurtured through the open access to the theatre and its communal spaces and also through a democratic ethos where members express opinions about the running of the company and the themes their work addresses. This ethos is important to members. As one individual expressed, 'Meeting and working with new people is not a problem, but meeting people honestly, trusting them and myself;

experiencing the support and humanity of other people was special about this group' (Barry, 2015b: 5). This sense of belonging, of having a say, is reinforced through the introduction of sessions facilitated by visiting or associate artists and their work with other groups attached to the theatre.

Attending an Elders company workshop one is struck by the creativity of the members of the company and the ease with which they rise to challenges and embraced tasks set out in the course of the workshop. Also evident is a level of mastery, an understanding of theatre practice and an ability to articulate and analyse that practice. These are not novices, nor are they experienced performers. They are participants with a healthy curiosity and a sense of confidence in their ability to understand and be critical of performance. This creative curiosity and confidence to engage is also evident in the company's performances strategies which have been known to include direct engagement with the audience in non-traditional performance spaces. When visiting the Elders one also becomes aware of their involvement within the organization that is the Royal Exchange. They attend other participatory workshops in the theatre, assist in visitor events or work as ushers. They also engage with and have access to the theatre as a social space, regularly meeting in the green room at various times not just before or after workshops. This opening up of communal spaces within the workings of the theatre means members of the Elders often mix with staff from the theatre, members of the professional company and other participation groups including the Young Company members. Indeed, they are encouraged to feel part of the day-to-day running of the theatre and the creativity that regularly take place within its walls.

The continuity theory of ageing, Atchley (1989) explains, is evolutionary in that it suggests ideas and skills, which individuals use to adapt and act in relation to their environment, continue to develop and persist over time. If we consider this in relation to the Elders, then opportunities afforded to its membership could be argued to provide opportunities for such adaption. The continuity theory of ageing suggests that an individual has the potential to develop and adapt rather than remain personally unchanged. For many members of the company, membership in the Elders is their first foray into performance. Through this foray, however, social connections are forged, new skills learnt and opportunities to develop confidence offered. Like activity theory (Havinghurst, 1963; Lemon et al., 1972; Victor et al., 1986), which argues the maintenance of meaningful social roles and activities can encourage well-being in older adults, continuity theory is about producing paradigms of old age which embrace ageing as a natural part of life when one can continue to find personal fulfilment in social and creative activity.

The future of the Elders is set with intentions to engage hard-to-reach older adults. The company is working to develop an Elder Champions scheme where members of the group will be trained in recruitment and outreach. The goal is that these champions will work in venues outside the Royal Exchange, in care homes and community centres, in a bid to engage older adults unfamiliar with the Royal Exchange and its work. In her book *Utopia in Performance*, Dolan describes utopian performances as those which allow shared 'experiences of meaning making and imagination that can describe or capture fleeting intimations of a better world' (2005: 2). Perhaps the work of the Elder Champions might provide 'strategies of artistic and critical production [... that] enable the proliferation of utopian performatives, without commodifying them and emptying them of their necessarily spiritual, idiosyncratic is-ness' (169). The aim for the Elders is that it opens its membership to 'groups who are currently under-represented in the company for example people from certain postcodes, ethnic minorities or who are over eighty' (Barry, 2015a: 5). Along with this, the company is currently in a bid to secure funding for a three-year programme of practice which will include professional productions and a symposium that will allow the learning of the Elders to be disseminated and discussed with others interested in similar practice.

Festivals, networks and theatre companies come under the title of 'the space between' because their work is neither public nor private;

sometimes it is one or the other, sometimes both. The work included in 'the space between' is work that specifically offers opportunities for sociality through the communal engagement with creative practice. They do not have a focus that is solely political. Indeed, they may not have an agenda that is focused on development or education, although these outcomes may be a by-produce of the practice. Their main purpose is about continuity, about providing opportunities for individuals to continue their social and cultural lives as they age through engagement in arts practice with others.

Conclusion

As the perspectives on practices included here show, applied theatre with older people does not occur in one way, or one place or, indeed, with one group of people. Practice in this area occurs in ways that are diverse, in every sense of the word. The continuum along which these examples exist considers levels of relationality, sociality, affect, creativity and ability and any attempt to quantify or qualify practice in this area needs to consider these factors.

As both the first and second chapters have shown, contemporary society faces an unprecedented change in demographics. But these changes need not be negative. What has been included here and what follows throughout the second section of the book highlights the need for understanding in relation to ageing and the capacity of older adults. If embraced this capacity could encourage a better relationship in general with ageing, one that might develop with future generations. Ageism occurs and its impact is insidious. There are, however, opportunities for us to do things better, for us to consider ageing not as an inevitable, intolerable aspect of life but as an important aspect in a journey through life. If ageing is viewed as something that occurs across a life span, something that is ongoing from birth to death, then the possibility to remove the stigma attached to ageing might present itself, along with the benefits a longer life has to offer.

The examples of applied theatre discussed in this chapter are grouped together and positioned at different points along the continuum in order to highlight the diversity of practice that occurs in this area. Applied theatre with, for or by older adults is not one thing. It takes into account different needs and abilities, as well as different intentions. Each example (or groups of examples) aligns particular areas of practice with specific theoretical considerations; yet throughout a common theme emerges, that being the universal inherent sociality that this practice engenders.

Moving along the continuum from work that is produced publically as a means to provide visibility in relation to ageing, to work that occurs in private with a remit of care, including work that occurs in the spaces between the two, allows a survey of the field from which further discussions regarding the future of applied theatre practice with, for and by older adults might develop. Applied theatre offers an avenue through which to understand ageing, individually and as a community, better. As these perspectives on practice have shown, theatre can empower, include and engage; it can provide a catalyst for comfort and care and a force with which to negate marginalization and social exclusion. In Part Two, further examples of innovative practice are shared and their benefits explored. It is important not to consider this practice in isolation, as an intervention that can only tackle isolation or the symptoms associated with a particular illness attached to the process of ageing. Instead, as you read, consider these examples as opportunities for ageing to be reconsidered and engage with more positively. Consider what the experience of ageing might be like if the work included was commonplace in the lives of older adults.

Part Two

Complicite, Le Jeu and the Clown: Playful Engagement and Dementia

Michael Balfour, Julie Dunn, Wendy Moyle and Marie Cooke

We are not clowns there to entertain or to make a show for our participants. We are actually there to interact. We are there to be responsive ... to any clues from them. We will initiate things in order to invite some response – and if they respond and lead us somewhere else, then we will follow. It's about inviting participation.[1]

Introduction

This chapter draws on insights from a multidisciplinary study entitled *Playful Engagement*, which was funded by an Australian Research Council Linkage Grant. The study involved Nursing and Applied Theatre academics from Griffith University; staff and residents of five Brisbane-based Wesley Mission Residential Aged Care facilities; and two relational clowns[2] – Anna Yen and Clarke Crystal. The research was focused on identifying the potential of relational clowning to achieve improvements in the quality of life (QoL) for people living with dementia.

Over the past two decades, arts-based practices have been increasingly applied in response to the challenges of rising rates of dementia. Music has traditionally been a strong area of practice in this area (Cooke et al., 2010; Raglio et al., 2010; Svansdottir and Snaedal, 2006), as well as art therapy and art activities (Beard,

2011), dance and movement (Guzmán-García et al., 2013; Ravelin et al., 2013), storytelling (Basting, 2006) and reminiscence theatre (Schweitzer, 2006). The growth of these arts-based approaches derives from recognition that, in the absence of a cure for dementia, there is a need to develop approaches that address its key impacts of social isolation, depressed mood and QoL. Moyle et al. (2011) emphasize the importance of meaningful relationships between people with dementia and others including their families and staff. They note the significance of these relationships for reducing depression and feelings of loneliness and social isolation, while also suggesting that the symptoms of dementia, such as apathy, paranoia, anger and difficulties with recognition, can have a negative influence on the person's relationship with their family, staff and others.

With these considerations in mind, the *Playful Engagement* team applied a relational clowning approach specifically designed to be responsive to the moods of people living with dementia and to improve staff attitudes towards this population. The relational clown is subtle and underplayed, and draws from a legacy of European clowning that has at its heart a philosophy of spontaneity, connection and respectful playfulness. The engagement between a relational clown and a participant is conceived of as a non-threatening encounter, designed to break the institutional tedium, and enable a different kind of relationship to exist. Relational clowns utilize improvisation, stories, reminiscence, humour, songs and music with an emphasis on individual engagement (Dunn et al., 2013; Hendriks, 2012; Warren and Spitzer, 2011). Previous studies focused on relational clowns (or elder clowns as they are sometimes referred to in the literature), have indicated a positive efficacy in psychosocial functioning of participants, and a decrease in feelings of anxiety and isolation (Low et al., 2014; Warren and Spitzer, 2011).

The relational clowns who worked within the *Playful Engagement* project were Clark Crystal and Anna Yen who make up a team called The Lamingtons. The very tall Clark becomes 'Tiny Lamington', with Anna being portrayed as his identical twin sister who engages with residents as 'Dumpling Lamington'. They dress in character costumes from the 1950s and each wears a red nose. Their story is that they live together out of town with their mischievous dachshund dog Peg, catching the bus to the care centres to visit the residents once a week. The siblings carry suitcases with them, with these cases containing games, wigs, old magazines, wool for knitting, musical instruments, sheet music, lengths of material and toys that squeak. They are always lost, tangled, confused, hopeless and in need of help. They do not prepare set pieces or conceptualize their work as entertainment, but instead, playfully create spontaneous interactions by working in the moment.

In this chapter, we report on the approach employed by the applied theatre artists, outlining in particular how key concepts developed by internationally regarded clown and theatre practitioners such as Jacques Lecoq, Phillipe Gaulier and Monika Pagneux, informed and enhanced the efficacy of their work. These concepts include play, complicite, Le Jeu, status and validation and listening.

To foreground this discussion, we provide a brief overview of the methods used within the *Playful Engagement* research programme, highlighting in particular the forms of qualitative data that we specifically draw upon within this chapter. Next we provide a brief review of literature focused on clowning work in health care, with a particular focus on some of the common practices and philosophies that have developed in work with ageing populations. Following this review, we examine the five clowning concepts listed above, drawing on data to illuminate each one in turn. The chapter concludes by offering discussion about the work of relational clowns in dementia settings, specifically noting how such work might be extended and developed.

Methods

The study adopted a mixed methods approach, with data collection processes built on the skills of the multidisciplinary team that included academics from both nursing and applied theatre. Measures from the nursing field included QoL and health surveys of staff and families, while qualitative data collected by the applied theatre team included video recordings; interviews with participants, family members and staff; practitioner journals completed by the applied theatre practitioners; social biographies; ongoing communication and feedback from staff and family; and a range of demographic and medical baseline data. Baseline data was collected prior to the commencement of the visits and was compared to end-point data. Social biographies for individual participants were collected during this phase in order to support the development of individualized interactions. Analysis of both the qualitative and quantitative data supported the development of a layered understanding of the approach and its impact.

The practical work of the two relational clowns was conducted in five Brisbane residential aged-care locations, with one of these locations being the site for the pilot study, while the main work occurred in the four remaining sites. The visits occurred across a six-week period and involved a total of sixty-four residents – forty-nine women and fifteen men. The residents' ages ranged from sixty-eight to eighty-nine with the majority of participants being over seventy years of age. The duration of each visit varied from individual to individual and from visit to visit, but the average length of visit time across the programme was fifteen minutes per individual.

Within this chapter, a series of vignettes is offered. These vignettes are based on a range of data sources including the videos recorded during the visits, post-session reflective conversations, collaborative analysis of the video recordings (Dunn, 2010) and interviews with the applied theatre artists themselves.

Clowning around in health care

Clown work in health care settings was established almost three decades ago (Barkmann et al., 2013; Oppenheim et al., 1997) and is known by a range of terms including clown doctors, elder clowns and hospital clowns (Warren and Spitzer, 2011). Common characteristic of all clowns in health care contexts is the need for the clown activities to be carefully attuned to the clinical and personal needs of the elderly or ill participants (Kontos et al., 2015).

Much of the published literature focuses on clown work with children, although there has been a growing application of clowning to other areas such as psychiatric hospitals, refugee camps and conflict zones, as well as political and spiritual clowning in churches (Peacock, 2009). Early examples of clown work were the Big Apple Circus Clown Care Unit (Christensen, 1999) and Patch Adams (Korr and Williams, 2015). Since these early practices, clowning has grown significantly across international contexts, with documented practice in the UK, Europe, the United States, South America, Africa, Israel, Australia and Asia Pacific (Kontos et al., 2015). There are now numerous clown organizations that train, recruit and facilitate programmes in hospitals. Some clown training has been developed in higher education and care home contexts with clown practices being translated into improving the quality of communication and interpersonal relations of medical students and staff (Kerman, 1992; Nogueira-Martins et al., 2014).

The first documented initiative of clowns in aged care facilities was the work of the Clown Ministries in the United States (Kerman, 1992), with a focus on the clown as a social healer. Since then a number of secular programmes have been developed (Killick, 2003; Kontos et al., 2015; Warren and Spitzer, 2011). While clowns in hospital often have painted faces, relational clowns in aged care are more understated, with their costumes and characters being inspired by life in the 1940s and 1950s. Relational clowns often work in pairs (although not always), and when this is the case, adopt characters that are related in some way. These relationships, such as siblings, are significant as they provide opportunities for tensions and rivalries to be introduced. Playful tensions such as spats over domestic duties, or issues relating to family finances, are useful as they can serve to support and at times drive the creation of humour and subsequently connection (Dunn et al., 2013; Kontos et al., 2015).

Philosophy of the clown

In order to be effective when working as a team, relational clowns need to have a shared philosophy and, ideally, a shared vocabulary of practice. In the case of Clark Crystal and Anna Yen, this shared understanding was made possible through similar training backgrounds, with both having been inspired by the work of Lecoq, while both were trained by Gaulier. Anna also worked extensively with Monika Pagneaux. This shared background and philosophy was important in developing a common play vocabulary, while also generating a similar understanding of the role and function of clowning. Of particular importance in their work are the concepts of complicite (togetherness), Le Jeu (playfulness), status, validation and listening – concepts that have proved useful in translating the art of the clown into relationship work for people living with dementia. These concepts are now discussed in turn, beginning with the overarching notion of play as the core component of clowning. In each section, vignettes of practice, created in response to the data set are used to support the discussion and exemplify each concept.

Play

Etchells (1999: 53) defines play as 'a state in which meaning is in flux, in which possibility thrives, in which versions multiply, in which confines of what is real are blurred, buckled, broken'. When considered within an interaction between a relational clown and an individual living with dementia, one can see that a relational clown must work not only to create fictional worlds and multiple versions of reality (as clowns do) but also to simultaneously accept the multi-fictions and shifting realities that might be at play for the individual living with dementia. The multi-layered meanings that are generated in such interactions create complex and yet exciting possibilities. For example, rather than trying to correct an individuals' reality – a situation many want to try in the case of dementia, the approach works with the realities that exist for the individual in the moment, while simultaneously generating new realities that may or may not be rooted in one or more versions of reality. What is particular to the relational clown then is that the relationships they create are defined by possibility rather than a fixed version of reality, and where meaning exists in continual flux. For the clown in particular, there is an acceptance that what is real may be unstable – with these shifting versions of reality opening up opportunities for playfulness.

The following vignette, built from a range of data sources including observations recorded at the time, provides descriptions based on video recordings of the visit and post-visit dialogues between the research team and the two applied theatre artists. The purpose of this vignette is to provide insights into this multi-layered notion of reality experienced by artists, resident and staff members. It is focused on a playful encounter that occurred during a visit by the Lamingtons to a resident we have chosen to call Margaret. This visit is the third in a series of six, and as such, Tiny and Dumpling are able to draw on information gained during previous sessions. In particular, they have chosen to build on their discovery that Margaret was once a competitive water skier.

Vignette 1: A Week 3 visit with Margaret

The Lamingtons are in the crowded lounge room. There are about thirty residents sitting, mostly slumped, in comfy chairs. The television is on. Nobody is watching. The residents do not interact. Tiny and Dumpling are crouching beside Margaret. They speak softly and talk to each other about water skiing. Tiny pretends to stand on a water-ski board, while Dumpling seeks advice from Margaret about whether or not he is doing it right. Tiny keeps getting it wrong and falls off the board. Margaret stands up and says: 'I should be on there' and so the Lamingtons invite her up. Supported by accompanying sound effects and mimed movements made by Dumpling, Margaret stands and pretends to water-ski with the relational clowns on either side. Her spouse watches on and tells us that they used to water ski together years ago and that this was something that she had enjoyed immensely. She had stood on the shoulders of her water skiing partner and was a very talented water skier. During the play Margaret's face is bright and she laughs along with the Lamingtons. She appears lost in the play as the three of them 'ski' through the corridors and around the room – with Tiny providing commentary and sound effects to accompany. The other residents watch and smile and laugh along. A few clap the performance. Some of the staff get involved too, with one in particular adding to the play by calling out, 'Ah! I am getting wet from the spray'.

This vignette reveals the multi-layered sense of reality inherent within this interaction. Clearly, it is difficult to determine if, for Margaret, the experiences actually feel 'real' or not, but it seems to provide her with an experience that links her with an enjoyable aspect of her past. Her call 'I should be up there' is a clear indication that Margaret is playfully engaged in the action, while her willingness to 'pretend' to ski is evidence of her desire to play. The staff member's playful

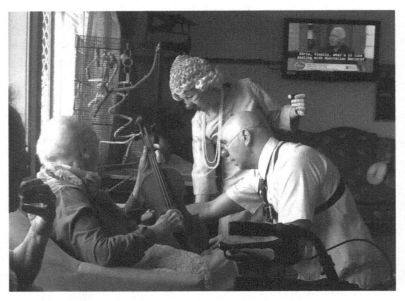

Figure 3.1 Clarke Crystal and Anna Yen. Photographer: Michael Balfour, 2013

offering which suggests that she is 'getting wet from the spray' adds an additional layer, reinforcing Etchells's notion (highlighted above) that 'the confines of what is real are blurred, buckled, broken' within play (53).

Complicite

A second concept critical to the success of the two relational clowns within the *Playful Engagement* work is that of complicite. Lecoq describes complicite in the following way:

> Complicite doesn't just take the form of performers working well together, it is a term used to describe when performers seem to inhabit a world with one another, a form of un-spoken unity where performers are completely receptive to one another and what the situation they are in requires. They don't need to fight for the power onstage, who is in major and who is in minor, instead it is exchanged in a smooth transition from one to the other, opening up the performers' rhythmic agility. (Lecoq, 2000)

The vignette demonstrates the importance of the two artists having a shared sense of purpose and the ability to carefully read and respond to each other's offers, with their shared training and philosophy being crucial in supporting spontaneous decisions about when to lead, when to follow, when to stay silent, when to speak, when to dial up the activity and when to dial back. With each offer and response creating new opportunities and potential new directions, achieving complicite can be difficult and may be one reason why much of the clowning work conducted in dementia settings involves just one artist or makes use of set pieces, rehearsed in advance.

A key tenet of complicite, and indeed of all improvisation work, is that each member of the relational clowning team needs to avoid blocking an offer from another performer, even if they are unsure of its direction or value. In discussing this aspect, Gaulier argues (2007) that it's important to go with the flow of the play. This is especially important in the dementia context where the relational clowns engage in a constant process of adjustment as they attempt to find the most appropriate form and tone of play for each individual. Complicite is therefore a key concept for helping the artists generate a shared understanding of the temperature of the room – a sense of how each individual resident is responding to the play, their sense of wellness in the moment including pain they might be experiencing, or indeed the impact which medications offered earlier in the day have impacted on them.

Le Jeu

Vignette 2: A Week 3 visit with Barbara

Barbara is largely confined to bed. She only utters guttural sounds. The sounds are constant as if she is trying to talk. Barbara's vocals reflect different rhythms. Sometimes they are high tempo, at other times they are like murmurs quiet and lower toned. She is alert and makes eye contact with Dumpling during the visit. Tiny and Dumpling sit with her. They chat a little between themselves. They prop up Barbara's doll and also introduce her to their doll, Cookie. Tiny and Dumpling improvise the introduction of a song 'Three blind mice', Barbara appears to catch the rhythm a little with her sounds. The tempo of the song briefly seems to create a reaction in Barbara. A little later in the visit Tiny and Dumpling introduce another song 'Happy Birthday', Barbara again seems to connect her sounds to the rhythm of the song and to take pleasure from the song and connection with the visitors. She is looking at Dumpling a lot. When Dumpling asks her if she minds singing it again, saying how lovely it is to hear her sing, she turns her head and smiles at Dumpling and says 'yeeees'. After the third repetition of 'Happy Birthday' and on the last verse Barbara sings 'happy birthday to you' clearly using words. Dumpling and Tiny smile and share a moment. At the end of the song Barbara reverts back to sounds, singing to her doll, but it seems like there is greater meaning in the sounds and her engagement with the doll.

Figure 3.2 Clarke Crystal and Anna Yen. Photographer: Michael Balfour, 2013

A concept closely allied to complicite is Le Jeu. Lecoq defined Le Jeu as 'an improvisation for spectators using rhythm, tempo, space, form' (Lecoq, 2000: 29). In performance training it relates to the ability to react, and the performers' attuned readiness to respond to the moment that is happening on stage. Lecoq discussed how the body exists in relation to everything else that is in the space, including objects, other performers, time, music and environment. Responsivity to the space is key to being able to exist in the moment, and in relation to everything else, so that all elements may be part of the play. A secondary meaning of Le Jeu is the pleasure of the performer, and the joy in *being* in the playful present.

The emphasis on pleasure as a key characteristic of the relationship between the clowns and the participant with dementia is important because it accentuates an attuned form of listening and responding. Here the pleasure is not about the simple pleasure of performing a character, but the pleasure in the engagement, in the invitation to play and in the inhabited space of the moment. The pleasure is a form of social grammar that can construct an atmosphere of openness and non-judgemental attitudes that are crucial in order for people with dementia to feel accepted and to improve their feelings of positive self-esteem. The reciprocal pleasure in being present is an important validating cue.

For the artists then, what is critical is their ability to construct a micro-fictive space, with this space being one where there is a close proximity between attunement to the moment and the pleasure of that moment. In such spaces, life and possibility can be celebrated and represented in a process based on joy and playing. For this reason, the Lamington's core philosophy, whether performing to spectators or interacting with an individual in a dementia setting, is the conscious adoption of Le Jeu as a state of being. This approach plays against the dominating social scripts in a residential home – duty, diagnosis, medication, formalized activities and institutional routines. The spontaneous nature of the play, the reactiveness of the performers to what is present in the room and the underlying joy of being and interacting – of taking pleasure in the moment and the relationship, are important and significant aspects of the work with people with dementia.

Le Jeu can be seen in Margaret's vignette above, offering Margaret, who had severe stage dementia, was usually very sedentary and did not recognize her husband who came to visit regularly, the chance to reconnect with embodied memories, bending her legs and moving from side to side (with support). The video data evidenced Margaret's high levels of engagement and pleasure in the activity, and a determination to reconnect with a sport she had loved. Much of the activity was non-verbal, with the relational clowns scaffolding the play through noise and movement. In this instance, Le Jeu was a synthesis of playing and the pleasure in playing. Gaulier (2007: 193) discusses Le Jeu in this way:

> When I talk about the game, I am talking about an immense desire for life, the same desire which makes us breathe. The game of hide and seek: hiding behind a door, or under a mask or disguise. Enjoy disappearing. When the joy of the game wavers, the character in the play appears heavy, true, too true to be honest: theatre dies. Theatre equals the pleasure of the game plus play. When the play is beautiful, the game of hide and seek unfolds, simply and freely.

There is an *art*ful simplicity to Le Jeu, born from considerable professional training and experience, and honed to a point where the performer can play instinctively, integrating multiple intelligences including body, space, affective attunement, being in the moment and being present and reactive. In relation to the Lamington's work, this meant there was a highly developed theatrical and play-based intelligence at work, with the artists being able to respond minutely as well as operatically depending on the needs of the moment. What anchors the play from becoming inappropriate, for example, a performer's ego getting in the way, is the skill in limiting and adapting the play to connect with the space, the room and the person. The clown is in a sense continually reviewing Le Jeu to seek a connection. There were plenty of examples from the research where relationships did not connect, where the clowns attempted to find attunement but where this didn't quite work, or where they tried a number of strategies to create a playful encounter but with no clear results. Equally there were moments where the play was created, but all too soon, lost. The clowns' pursuit of the qualities of Le Jeu was therefore a constant process of failing, trying and failing again in order to do better with the next resident or at the next visit. Like tuning an old wireless radio, sometimes a sense of Le Jeu was disrupted by white noise, while at other times it was clear and present, with crystal clear reception full of joy and pleasure being obvious within the interactions.

Status

Status is a fundamental element in improvisation and performance training. Clowns by definition have very low status, with a key aspect of this low status being their vulnerability. The clown is in trouble all the time, doing things wrong, muddling words up, forgetting what objects to use. Rather than hide these mistakes however, a clown shares these failures and allows others to witness their vulnerability.

Interestingly, in a dementia care setting, it is most often the people living with dementia who have the lowest status, with the operationalizing of care leading to hierarchies of power that ironically place the resident on the margins. During our observations of the *Playful Engagement* practice, we saw wonderful professional and care staff who chose to interpret their job in humanistic ways, and not get caught in an administrative approach to caring that was dominated by duty and tasks. Nevertheless, the sheer scale of management involved in large institutions often means that personhood is an aspiration interpreted in multiple ways, with the status of each of the participants being limited by an overall governing network of authority. Within such networks, people living with dementia inevitably end up with ever-diminishing agency. Enter the clowns, who, as part of the process of playing, position themselves as being lower than a resident, as being someone who needs help. Their pleas for assistance from residents are an unusual occurrence in the everyday routine of aged-care institutions, but by seeking advice about a range of challenges, from personal problems, to sorting out their knitting mess, clowns gift to people living with dementia a much needed lift in status.

In Vignette 3, an example is offered to demonstrate how Tiny and Dumpling played with status.

Vignette 3: A Week 3 visit with Ingrid
    Ingrid has chronic pain and is telling a staff member about this as we arrive. However, her mood noticeably lifts when Tiny and Dumpling step up for a visit. Dumpling begins by asking Ingrid for help. 'We are looking for a wife for my brother', she suggests. Ingrid replies, 'We like each other'

and winks, suggesting that Ingrid may not be all that keen on pursuing this challenge. Dumpling tries a new tack, retrieving knitting from her oversized handbag.

She immediately gets tangled up in the knitting, soon ensnaring Tiny in the mess who appeals to Ingrid for help. Ingrid immediately offers advice while looking across at another resident, and saying with a smile, 'I've been doing it for ages'. The other resident is sitting close by and giggles at what is occurring. Ingrid is really enjoying the play – she can cope with it and she seems to be enjoying the help she is giving. Ingrid instructs Dumpling: 'You don't have to turn around', 'Don't make it so hard!' She is laughing. Tiny finally gets clear and with this task complete, Ingrid offers some extra words of advice to Dumpling about her knitting: 'Here we are ... now what you have to do is not pull so hard.'

The other resident is totally enthralled and interested. Dumpling says to her, 'Ingrid isn't so silly, she wouldn't tangle the wool'. Ingrid has gone from someone who began the visit telling us about chronic pain to someone who is giggling and playing.

There is a pause in the play. Ingrid says, 'My father had a farm' then goes on to suggest to Dumpling, 'Now sit down here'. Dumpling obeys, but the memory is lost. Ingrid has forgotten what it was that she wanted to share ... or even that she wanted to share. Tiny moves the play on.

The link between status giving and agency is clearly evidenced in this vignette, with one of the skills of relational clowns being the ability to reverse status. To be effective, they need to understand how to make an offer that gives agency to the resident, providing them with opportunities to take control of the play, to intervene, shape it and change according to their own whim. In this example, the tangle of wool created by Tiny and Dumpling serve to lower their status, providing Ingrid with the opportunity to become an advisor and problem solver, someone able to suggest and direct (sometimes quite strongly) what should happen to resolve the tangle situation. Similarly, within the first vignette, Tiny's exaggerated falls and failed attempts to water ski, clearly served to encourage Margaret to show him how it should be done.

For both these women, the opportunity to take control of the situation, to come to the aid of others, to offer their experience, wisdom and input is a reprieve from their usual sense of powerlessness. In addition, in both cases, the play seems to trigger something more as well. For Margaret, it appears to be an embodied memory of achievement, of being 'able' and 'successful', while for Ingrid, once the tangle is resolved, memory of a different kind seems to be triggered as she suddenly offers the comment, 'My father had a farm'. In each case, the moment is fleeting and the memories soon dissolve, but the satisfaction of taking control, of being momentarily in charge, seem to have given both Ingrid and Margaret the confidence to voice something they want to share.

Rhythm and listening

The improvisational work of relational clowns in dementia settings is unpredictable and difficult to manualize. For this reason, in addition to the four concepts outlined above, a relational clown also needs to be able to listen and in turn, understand how to manage the rhythm and tempo of a visit. These skills are needed to recognize not only what the nature of the social engagement is but also what it *could be*, to listen and be attuned to the most subtle foreshadowing in a gesture, sound or word. This form of embodied listening creates a relationship that strongly validates the individual, with the artists needing to take time to listen, to pause, sometimes to be silent and wait. Lecoq's training philosophy was always to begin with silence and start an improvisation from a 'state of innocent curiosity' (Lecoq, 2000: 28).

Lipsitz (2015: 11), writing about improvisation and music, discusses how so much can be lost in social life through not listening. He notes:

> Hearing just happens, but listening entails attention and interpretation. Listening is an act of deliberation and discernment, a capacity that gets cultivated through experience. Music is an interactive practice. It is a dialogue, not a monologue ... Improvisation plays a crucial role in creating the capacity for an augmented sense of listening because at its core, improvisation is an act that opens

doors. It creates new understandings of previousness and futurity in order to explore hidden possibilities.

The importance of listening is clearly evident in each of the three vignettes above, with Crystal and Yen continually shifting between listening and action. Rather than rushing in, both would regularly pause and allow space for the next action or words to come from the participant, with these pauses being one beat or many. For example, the third vignette reveals that when engaging with Ingrid, both artists listened carefully to her response about finding a partner for Tiny, taking a beat then before taking the action in a new direction towards the tangled knitting. By contrast, in the first vignette, they immediately responded to Margaret when she exclaimed, 'I should be up there', seizing her enthusiastic reinforcement of their ideas to extend her involvement.

However, while Vignettes 1 and 3 describe visits that were overtly playful and highly interactive, where listening occurred amid a lively and active engagement, Vignette 2 offers a contrasting version of relational clowning. Here silence was the dominant mode, with Crystal's work being slow, patient and deeply responsive. This ability to respond to the individual rhythms of each visit is a manifest adaption of Lecoq and Gaulier's training, with each artist being willing to take a risk by accepting a silence before finding something new to work with. The silence is therefore a form of respectful, attentive waiting. It shapes and provides a grammar for an engagement.

Lecoq discussed silence as a key way to enable the rhythm of an improvisation to emerge, and was clear to distinguish between rhythm and tempo:

> Tempo is geometrical, rhythm is organic. Tempo can be defined, while rhythm is difficult to grasp. Rhythm is the result of an actor's response to another live performer. It may be found in waiting, but also in action. (Lecoq, 2000: 29)

The distinction between these concepts is important when trying to understand the nature of the improvised relationship in Playful

Engagement. Crystal and Yen engaged in a number of different tempos, pacing the interactions in response to the participant's abilities and interests. Invariably, the engagements started off slowly and carefully to establish the mood and possibilities of the interaction. When an engagement 'worked' – where there seemed to be high responsivity and reflexivity – it could take on a natural rhythm and flow in which the tempo sped up, slowed down, as the suggestions and counter suggestions were accepted and played with. All the time Crystal and Yen would carefully be positioning the participant as the leader, playwright or conductor of the engagement, letting them set the pace, and find a rhythm that everyone could work to. When engagement did not work, where there was an evident misfiring, it was sometimes because there was a mismatch in the rhythm. This might occur when, after an engaging visit with someone else and a brief walk along the corridor, there wasn't enough time or deliberation allowed, with the artists failing to re-set their energy back to neutral. In these cases, the energy of one rhythmic engagement got carried into the next one, leading to either too much energy or too little.

As mentioned in the 'Methods' section, visit lengths varied, being roughly 15–20 minutes each. In most cases, there was only a very short gap between visits, with Crystal and Yen visiting up to eight individuals in a session. The time between visits was quite inconsistent too, with residents sometimes being difficult to locate, while at other times they were seated side by side. These factors impacted on the engagement, influencing in particular the rhythm of the work.

New directions

As we observed and studied the improvisations in *Playful Engagement*, it was fascinating to draw out the ways in which Crystal and Yen's common performer training influenced and created the rich possibilities in their practice. These were not just any performers or any kinds of clowns. The specific qualities embodied in their practice were a legacy of the philosophies passed on to them by Lecoq, Gaulier and Pagneaux. These include the need for: a strong understanding of the multiple realities created and accepted within play; complicite between performers (sharing of play worlds with one another) and between performers and participants (co-creators that are given the opportunity to lead the sharing of play activities); Le Jeu, in which the performer finds the pleasure in this interaction, in being in the play; the use of status in enabling participants to own the play, to lead the improvisation and to be given an active role in creativity; and the importance of rhythm and listening. These combined elements came into play in dynamic and variable ways but were constant features of the engagement.

While the practice element of the research concluded in 2014, Wesley Mission Brisbane have continued their involvement, wanting to explore how to extend and develop the insights gained, with additional funding being attained to begin to develop a process of training professional care home staff in understanding and enacting some of the relational approaches used within the *Playful Engagement* programme. In taking this direction, Wesley Mission Brisbane's goal is not to train their staff to become relational clowns (such as the creation of Laughter Bosses as in other programmes), but rather, to distil some of the philosophies used by relational clowns so they might be applied by staff as they interact in more everyday and in the moment ways with people living with dementia. In particular, Wesley Mission Brisbane are interested in training that offers staff different perspectives and skills of communicating with residents with dementia.

Relational clowning in a dementia setting is a constant search for connection and relatedness achieved through the five concepts discussed here. Together they provided opportunities for residents and artists to engage in ways that privilege temporary and ephemeral moments of pleasure, play, silence and indulgence, recognizing that every encounter requires renegotiation and adaptation as situations, moods, and conditions change. These are characteristics of engagement well suited to anyone who seeks a version of aged care that is relational.

Acknowledgement

The authors would like to acknowledge Clark Crystal and Anna Yen's work on the project, and the extensive support of Wesley Mission Brisbane staff, residents and families from the five residential care homes.

The Care Home as a Creative Space

Jayne Lloyd and Helen Nicholson

Imagine a residential care home for the oldest-old, and most people will picture residents slumped in chairs facing a blaring television in an overheated, airless room with the faint smell of cooked food wafting through it. Despite the efforts of many dedicated and often overworked care staff, for many of the oldest and most vulnerable people in society this is at least part of their daily experience. It is also an image of end-of-life care that is perhaps most widely feared, and which family and friends frequently find distressing. The 'feel' of a care home is often a major factor in any decisions about where elderly relatives are placed, and its atmosphere is usually the first thing that visitors observe. Officially, however, the well-being and quality of life of residents is only recognized when individuals can be measured; this means that the more communal, affective and sensory qualities of a residential care setting are often overlooked. This chapter attends to this oversight by considering ways in which artists and residents living with advanced dementia can work together to foster a sense of home and reimagine a care home as a creative space.

Considering a residential care setting as a 'home' draws attention to the ways in which homemaking is sensed and experienced in everyday life. In their study of the cultural geographies of home (*Home*), Alison Blunt and Robyn Dowling point out that a home is both a physical place and a set of feelings. These feelings of attachment and belonging may be related to home as a material environment, but home might also refer to other geographical locations or temporalities, leading Blunt and Dowling to describe home as a 'spatial imaginary that travels across space' (2006: 22). Home does not just happen, they suggest, it is made and, however complex and contradictory the emotions it inspires, homemaking is always a creative and relational process:

> Home is a process of creating and understanding forms of dwelling and belonging. This process has both material and imaginative elements. Thus people create home through social and emotional relationships. Home is materially created – new structures are formed, objects used and placed. (2006: 23)

In terms of residential care for older adults, the suggestion that home is connected both to the materiality of everyday routines and objects and to different spatial and temporal imaginaries poses some complex issues for carers who often find themselves negotiating very different social relationships with home within one residential setting. It also offers creative opportunities for artists, whose work necessarily involves encounters between material and imaginative elements, and who are thus well placed to encourage creative engagements with different imaginaries of home and to foster new social relationships in the material present of a residential setting. Thus understood, homemaking is not only an important marker of individual identity: it also suggests that home is created and recreated reciprocally and relationally, with social relationships that change over time.

One of the principles that informs this chapter is that creative approaches to care pay attention to the interconnectedness of everyone involved in the home, whether they are professional carers, residents, friends, family or other visitors. This approach marks a transition from person-centred care that dominated approaches to dementia towards the end of the twentieth century, and moves debates and practice towards relationship-centred care, which also takes account of the multiplicity of spatial and temporal attachments, and recognizes that both human and non-human relationships contribute to feelings of home. Person-centred care and relationship-centred care derive from different philosophical traditions and theories of selfhood, leading to rationales for creative practice with people with dementia that are differently nuanced. Person-centred care was a radical innovation introduced by social psychologist Tom Kitwood in the 1980s to take account of individual life histories within caring environments. Based on Christian beliefs and liberal humanist principles, Kitwood's person-centred care for people with dementia aimed to preserve the 'essence of personhood' by maintaining models of care based on a faith in a common humanity, on 'what it is to be human' (2007: 230, 231). At the time this was a welcome departure from the medicalization of dementia care, and it led to various creative practices that aimed to 'recover' the person who was 'lost', particularly through reminiscence activities. More recently, however, the normative vocabulary associated with liberal humanism is no longer regarded as culturally appropriate in contemporary society, not least because it individualizes difference and ignores the ways in which cultural, social and environmental factors shape identity. In response to anti-essentialist theories of selfhood and the post-humanist decentring of human agency, questions of relationality are beginning to re-shape dementia care. One of the challenges to person-centred care is political; Ruth Bartlett and Deborah O'Connor argue that it is inherently unequal because 'personhood' is bestowed on the person living with dementia by their carers, thereby failing to understand that all social relationships are reciprocal and mutually affecting (2010: 22).

For artists attending to the sensory, creative and imaginative qualities of residential care, an understanding of relationship-centred care marks an important extension of thought. It further challenges humanist ideals of person-centred care by opening the way for post-humanist understandings of social relationships in residential homes. It also takes account of the ways in which the material environment and non-human world have agentic capacities that affect everyone who lives, works or visits the home. In this chapter, we shall take this as a starting point for analysing two examples of practice undertaken by Jayne Lloyd in one care home between 2013 and 2015. As a fine artist working in a care setting, Jayne's work offers insights into how care homes can become creative spaces by observing the different spatial and temporal imaginaries that bring feelings of attachment to home in its broadest sense, and by building ongoing relationships in the material present. In both examples that follow, her practice as an artist and her everyday life was influenced and shaped by her work with residents. Methodologically, this practice-based research offers an opportunity to explore how the reciprocity of mutually caring relationships can encourage dialogue between the past, present and future.

Walking with Mary: Creating sensory spaces

Between September 2013 and April 2014, Jayne made weekly visits to a care home to observe artists from Age Exchange Theatre Trust work with residents. Each week she entered the care home through the double doors, signed in at reception and made her way up to the second floor. Invariably, by the time she had reached the top of the stairs the heat had hit her. It felt oppressive as she rallied against the feelings of lethargy that it triggered. Still wearing her coat, she would hurry to the dining room where the sessions took place, put down her bag and remove several layers of clothing. Connie always sat by the door wearing a woollen skirt, tights, fluffy slippers, blouse and cardigan. She was the first resident she would greet each week. Every week without fail their conversation would go something like this:

> Connie: It's cold isn't it?
> Jayne: I'm quite warm.
> Connie: Where's your cardigan, are you not cold?
> Jayne: No, I think it's warm in here.
> Connie: It's cold. Are you not cold?
> Jayne: No, I mustn't feel the cold.

Connie would hug herself as she spoke, rubbing her upper arms as if trying to warm up. In most care homes she has worked, Jayne has observed differences between residents' experience of the temperature of the home and her own. While she is sweltering in a T-shirt, the majority of residents arrive at sessions in cardigans or jumpers, and requests for windows and doors to be closed to 'keep out the draft' are not uncommon. The care home residents' experience of the heat was influenced by their physiology; poor circulation, the loss of adipose tissue and becoming less physically active can make the ability to control bodily temperature more difficult. Significantly, for an artist attending to the sensory, creative and imaginative qualities of residential care, the physiology of the residents influenced how they experienced the care environment creating a difference between theirs and Jayne's experience.

This exchange between Jayne and Connie illustrates how the material environment of home not only contributes to residents' physical comfort: it also shows how one location can be experienced in different ways by people who share the same space. Conversations with Connie about the experience of temperature not only illustrate the dual meanings of atmosphere as the physical climate and as a felt experience, they also problematize any suggestion that there is a common or universal experience of a care home; if the temperature could be experienced in such radically different ways, it was important to consider what else could. The temporal rhythms of care homes are experienced in multiple ways, for example, and the experience of living with dementia often means that it becomes increasingly difficult to keep track of time. For this particular project, however, this insight prompted Jayne's interest in how the embodied experience of place is multiply inscribed with meaning, and this inspired her creative work with a resident called Mary.

Mary had often spoken about walking her dog on Streatham Common, a large open space and nature reserve in London. The project Jayne facilitated with her explored how conversations about her walks on the Common might become framed creatively and artistically: what could Jayne understand about Mary's remembered and imagined walks by walking on Streatham Common herself? How could she use arts activities and artefacts collected from the Common to represent the experience of walking that Mary missed in the care home? In an attempt to understand Mary's dog walks, Jayne walked on Streatham Common every week during the ten-week project.

The use of walking as a methodological practice to research the dialogue between experiences of being in a residential care setting and walking outdoors is informed by anthropologist Tim Ingold's ideas about how knowledge of an environment can be developed through walking in it. In his book *Being Alive: Essays on Movement, Knowledge and Description*, Ingold advocates an approach to anthropological research that acknowledges thinking as an embodied and mobile experience. He argues that there is an 'assumption in studies of human cognition that thinking and knowing are the achievements of a stationary mind, encased within a body in motion' (2011: 17). He identifies two implications for how the research is undertaken. First, the journey to and from the site is often not considered part of the research, and this encourages the site to be seen as an isolated place unconnected to its surroundings or other places the researcher or inhabitants of the site have previously visited. Second, Ingold argues that little attention has been paid to how the body makes contact with the ground of the environment within which the research takes place. He contends that the world is experienced in motion and through the whole body, and suggests that research methods should reflect this, with researchers putting their own embodied experience at the centre of their approach to studying the world around them. Ingold challenges the idea that people do not think through their feet, arguing that knowledge of an environment can be gained by feeling the surface or contours of the ground, particularly when walking barefoot. He suggests that there is a need to understand what he terms 'pedestrian touch' with the rhythm and weight of the body behind it because 'it is surely through our feet, in contact with the ground [...], that we are most fundamentally and continually "in touch" with our surroundings' (2011: 45). The steps taken while walking, he suggests, are 'continually and fluently responsive to an ongoing perceptual monitoring of the ground ahead' (2011: 47), and one step, therefore, is never quite the same as the next.

In the account that follows, Jayne writes in the first person to capture the embodied qualities of her experience of walking on the Common and her creative work with Mary in the care home. It explores how and why Mary's and Jayne's experiences of the same care home might significantly differ from each other, and questions how these subjective experiences of the immediate environment in which the project took place affect creative workshops that attempt to trigger experiences of places outside their immediate environment. This account of practice identifies points where their experiences met and discusses how different sensory triggers, arts materials and artefacts facilitate a relationship to place and enable experiences to be shared and reimagined in artistic form.

Walking and creative practice

The weather was still warming up and there was a chill in the air when the walks began. Walking on the Common and visiting the care home each week heightened my awareness of the difference between the scale and materiality of the two places. I could walk a significant distance on the Common without covering the same ground, but in the care home residents who walked trod the same corridors over and over again. The gradients of the ground they walked on were much gentler and the smooth, matt, non-slip flooring was less textured than the grass, pebbles and mud I trekked through in the Common. In the care home there was little sign of the scenery, weather, seasons or even the time of day changing. Furthermore, I did not see the majority of the residents walking around, and many of them remained in the same seat throughout my visit.

At first I was convinced that Mary must be aware of her surroundings in the same way I was. I thought she must be fed up with her sedentary existence in an institutionalized domestic environment. How could she not miss the long walks on the Common that she talked about? As the project progressed, however, I began to question how far our experience of the care home was comparable. The care home residents I met appeared to live much more stationary lives in a much hotter environment than I did, but some of their comments suggested that they did not all experience it as such. Unlike Connie, Mary did not complain about the cold but she did appear oblivious to the intense heat I experienced. Her hands felt cool and she wore a cardigan throughout our workshop sessions. A further difference between our experiences of the care home became apparent each week as I supported her to stand and we walked slowly arm-in-arm down the corridor from the lounge to the dining room. It was the same distance I had walked to get to the lounge but with Mary it took far more time to cover the same ground. The corridor seemed much longer when we walked it together than when I walked it alone. About half way down the corridor Mary often commented on how tired her legs were, suggesting that she experienced this as a significant distance to walk. It struck me that this was now a long walk for Mary who had once regularly taken much longer walks with her dog on the Common.

Mary did not remember my name and, as I explained the purpose of my visit each week, she listened as if hearing this information for the first time. She often repeated herself, asking the same questions with no apparent awareness that she had just asked them. Despite this, I felt there was a growing familiarity between us. As the project went on she greeted me with increasing warmth. There were also occasional indications that she remembered something about the theme of our sessions. When I greeted her at the beginning of the sixth session, one of the first things she shared with me was that her legs were tired, and this was followed by her explanation that 'it must be all the dog walking'. When Mary talked about her dog walks, she sometimes spoke about them as something she used to do, implying an awareness that they no longer took place. Other times they were described in the present tense or situated in the recent or continuous past, but on this day they were described very much as something she still did. Rather than missing the walks, I noted that she referenced them to rationalize her experience of old age in the care home. They provided a reason for her feeling tired and were used to justify why she spent so much time sitting down.

During our first session, I showed Mary a photograph of some trees on Streatham Common, and she responded by telling me that there were lots of trees there. This prompted me to collect leaves from as many different trees on the Common as I could find. During that visit to the Common it was a breezy but sunny day with blue skies. The leaves swayed gently in the breeze. They looked almost translucent and their colours appeared vibrant in the strong sun. I plucked a leaf from each type of tree and placed them in a canvas bag. The following day Mary and I picked them out of the bag one by one and laid them out on a dining table. In the still air of the care home the leaves did not move unless we moved them. I noticed that the dining room light made their colours look disappointingly dull against the dark brown wood of the table.

I described to Mary how I had collected the leaves from Streatham Common. Her body language suggested she was listening, but there was no indication that she made a connection between the leaves and the trees she passed on her dog walks. Only when prompted by my questions did she talk about those walks. Mary picked the leaves up and looked at them. She appeared to enjoy handling them, talking about their shape and colour and choosing which ones she preferred. The leaves, however, isolated from their surroundings and closely examined in the care home environment, did not seem to retain for her a connection to Streatham Common. Perhaps very similar leaves could have been collected from any number of places. The photograph of the trees that I had shown Mary two weeks earlier depicted the whole tree in relation to other trees and the surrounding Common. The image provided a context that appeared to enable Mary to relate it to her memory of the Common in a way that the leaves did not. During our second session, I showed Mary a film that captured an approximation of my view while walking on the Common. The film showed the visual context that the photograph had and provided additional audio information. Furthermore, it represented the Common from the viewpoint of a body in motion, which is much closer to the perspective of a dog walker than a still image. It was the films, with their context and motion, which prompted Mary to talk most about her dog walks and to identify places in them that she recognized.

My sessions with Mary continued into June. In mid-June a heat wave came. The heat outside for once matched, if not surpassed, the temperature inside the care home. When I arrived for our ninth session, Mary and several other residents were sitting on the patio adjacent to the dining room. Mary was wearing a short-sleeved blouse without a cardigan and had a sun hat on. She was slightly reclined in her chair, eyes closed and face tilted to the sun. In contrast to my previous visits to the care home, that day the whole environment indicated it was hot. The sky looked blue with only a few white wispy clouds. The sun was blindingly bright. It lit everything with its strong rays that showed off the vibrant greens and yellows of the plants, bleached the sandy coloured paving stones and cast crisp, dark shadows across them. There was a relaxed 'holiday' atmosphere that matched the weather, care staff kept the residents' cold drinks topped up and when someone spoke about going to the south coast it prompted a fellow resident to sing 'I do like to be beside the seaside.'

One of the first things Mary said when I greeted her that day was to tell me that the heat was 'a bit much for her'. I too felt the intensity of the heat. It appeared that outdoors our experience of the temperature was much more comparable than it was indoors. I wondered if this was because in the care home there is no indication of the temperature other than how it is felt by each individual. The temperature in that sense could be compared to the leaves I had removed from the trees and presented without their context. Mary and I moved inside for the session but sat near the open patio doors so we could still see out and feel the sun. Mary fanned herself as we sat together. She continued to comment on the hot weather throughout the session and her observations about the weather were incorporated into our discussions about walking on Streatham Common. This was in stark contrast to previous weeks where the care home and Mary had appeared unaffected by the weather outside, and in those sessions I had had to work much harder to create a context and atmosphere for our imagined walks.

Mary's walk: Reciprocity and creativity

One aspect of Jayne's work is that her work as an artist in care settings is situated in conversation with both the residents and other artists. Artist Richard Long has had a strong influence on her thinking, and the concept and aesthetic of 'Walking with Mary', the installation she made as a consequence of working with Mary, was influenced by Long's piece *A Line the Length of a Straight Walk from the Bottom to the Top of Silbury Hill* (1970). In this work, Long transferred a walk he took in the countryside into the indoor space of the gallery.

Long made *A Line the Length of a Straight Walk from the Bottom to the Top of Silbury Hill* by walking from the base to the summit of Silbury Hill in Wiltshire in a straight line. To transfer the walk into a gallery space, Long walked in a line that was the same length as the one he had walked up the hill. When he walked it in the gallery, however, he could not walk the distance in a straight line because the dimensions of the space were too small. Instead he chose to walk in a spiral, drawing the line with his feet. When he had walked up the hill the weight of his body pressing through his shoes left an imprint of the sole of the shoe on the earth. When he recreated the walk in the gallery, he dipped his walking boots into mud that he had collected from the hill and made footprints with them on the floor. The floor, unlike the ground outside on the hill, did not allow his footprints to penetrate its surface. Instead the mud sat on top of the hard, non-porous surface designed to be cleaned and to leave no trace of the feet that walk over it. These two significant differences between Long's walk up the hill and his recreation of the walk in the gallery highlight how the representation of the experience needed to be adjusted to accommodate the differences in scale and materiality between the outdoor and indoor spaces.

Although the gallery space is a very different type of space from the care home, it is on a comparable scale to many of the rooms in which the sessions took place and is an indoor environment that shares some similarities with their physical qualities, for example, the non-porous flooring and artificial lighting. The curled up line of muddy footprints set on the gallery floor provides a strong visual metaphor for the issues of scale and materiality Jayne contended with when she tried to represent outdoor walking inside the care home. Understanding how Long transferred his walks into the gallery space serves to highlight some of the challenges of scale and materiality Jayne faced in her projects. It also highlights the very different aesthetic of the indoor walk to the outdoor one. As an artwork, however, the line walked indoors is just as visually interesting as the one outdoors, if not more so because it is framed by the indoor environment: the containment of the line and the protrusion of the prints lend it a stronger visual impact than the line dispersed in the vast outdoors. As such, bringing the walk indoors does not always detract from the experience, and its metaphorical qualities may serve to amplify it. This suggests that artworks made in care settings need not be poor representations of secondary experience but can provide significant aesthetic involvement for residents as well as creative engagement in the making process.

In her book *Home Truths*, Sarah Pink discusses the ways in which homes are pluri-sensory contexts, and observes that people often use metaphor to express their sensory experiences of home. Drawing on the work of Judith Okely, she argues that although it is impossible to share the same sensory experiences as others because the senses are always mediated, it is possible to find points of connection: 'Through being there, we cannot claim to have exactly the same sensory experiences as others, but we can "creatively construct correspondences between" experiences' (Okely, 1994: 47 quoted in Pink, 2004: 34). Furthermore, Pink suggests, the creative understanding of metaphor can encourage empathetic responses to home environments that are not one's own. Applied to residential care settings, Pink's analysis has two interrelated consequences. First, it suggests that residents are supported in creating feelings of home when their everyday sensory experiences find symbolic expression and when the sensory qualities of their imagined past are represented in metaphor. Second, visiting artists might gain a deeper understanding of the experience of living in a care home if they take time to engage creatively with residents in constructing new metaphors in response to their sensory experiences – both from the past and in the present. This reciprocity is central to relationship-centred care, where it is understood that social relations are created in dialogue and through shared sensory engagement in the present.

Artists are in a unique position to extend this reciprocity to metaphors that engage in an imagined past as well as the materiality of everyday life. Furthermore, Jayne's work as an artist was enriched and inspired by knowing Mary, and Mary's act of generosity in engaging with Jayne recognizes how newly created relationships can have a positive influence on others.

A taste of life: Creating social space

The idea that a residential care setting is a social space is central to many different models of care, but relationship-centred care particularly emphasizes the care home as a community, in which everyone is regarded as an active member, whether they are carers, visitors or residents. In practice, however, the many different tasks that carers need to undertake to ensure the welfare of residents can take precedence over community-building activities that create feelings of belonging. Gerontologist Michael Nolan explicitly refers to the senses in his framework for relationship-centred care, stressing the need for carers, staff and older people to be affectively involved in creating a caring community. In his 'Six Senses Framework', Nolan suggests that caring environments are enriched when everyone experiences feelings of security, belonging, purpose, significance, achievement and a sense of continuity by making links between the past, present and future (Nolan et al., 2008: 80, 81). This suggestion that people living with dementia might actively contribute to creating a social space involves a shift in focus, inviting artists who work in residential care settings to move from individualized practices with residents to creative activities that involve people from across the home's community.

In response to the idea that people living in residential care might enjoy relationships with their carers and fellow residents that are reciprocal and mutually beneficial, Jayne developed a project with John, a Jamaican man living in the same South London care home as Mary. She had observed John's contribution to reminiscence arts workshops run by Age Exchange practitioners, where he often talked passionately about the meals he enjoyed cooking and eating. He could give detailed instructions of how to cook numerous Caribbean dishes, communicating memories related to food with a clarity that was rarely evident when he discussed other topics. Strongly associating food with socializing, he often talked about eating 'good food in good company'. Sometimes when he had been talking about food he would close his eyes and a smile would spread across his face, as if imagining that he was eating a Caribbean feast with friends and family. One of his favourite dishes was ackee and salt fish, which he once described as 'a taste of life', a phrase that eloquently captured how much food meant to him and the integral role it played in his identity and happiness. Attuned to the ways in which John expressed his emotional connection with food, Jayne worked alongside him over a period of ten weeks in which she learned to cook his favourite recipes, often with the assistance of care staff, and designed a cookery book in response.

This project illustrates how attention to the relational qualities of care enabled one care home resident to gain a sense of purpose and achievement by taking the opportunity to teach his favourite recipes to others. The sessions provided John with a space to discuss and taste food that he had grown up with and that was an integral part of his Jamaican heritage. As one of only a few Caribbean residents in a home staffed mainly by carers who identified as Caribbean, John was able to create a social space in which other residents and care staff shared his enthusiasm for Caribbean food. Sharing of Caribbean recipes in the context of this care home was particularly pertinent because most of the food that was served there was what could be described as traditional 'English' meals, despite being prepared by a Jamaican cook. Furthermore, it strengthened feelings of the reciprocity between John, other care home residents and staff, and as workshop facilitator, Jayne, describes here in the first person, the effect the project had beyond the care home on her everyday life.

Learning to cook ackee

Ackee is the national fruit of Jamaica. After it is picked from the tree the poisonous seeds and outer skin need to be carefully removed. It is the soft, slightly greasy, pale yellow flesh of the ackee that is eaten. It is difficult to find something to compare the taste of ackee to but it is close in texture to avocado. Probably because parts of the fruit are inedible, in England you can only buy the flesh of the ackee in tins. It is available in many shops in Herne Hill and in Brixton Market. There are many restaurants around Herne Hill that serve good versions of the popular Caribbean dish ackee and salt fish. I live near Brixton where John used to shop. I often wander round Brixton Market, but at the time I knew very little about the Jamaican produce that was sold there. I quickly realized that John could teach me, and this became the focus of our creative sessions that took place over ten weeks in the summer of 2014.

Each week I brought in food items or photographs of food I had bought in Brixton Market. John and Gloria, a member of care staff who had grown up in the Caribbean and joined the sessions, would explain what they were and give me a recipe I could cook with them. Following their direction I would source additional ingredients and cook the dishes at home. I would return the following week with photographic documentation of the cooking process and samples for them to taste. They would give me their verdict and tips on how I could improve the dish. For example, John's tip for improving my attempt at ackee and salt fish was to 'add black pepper and more tomatoes and serve yam and banana plantain on the side'. Often an ingredient I had brought would lead to discussions of another dish and ingredients that I would go away and source to bring in the following week.

The sessions were initially set up with John's interests in mind. On hearing our discussions and seeing the food, however, several Caribbean care staff and one of the cleaners joined us and shared their stories, recipes and cooking tips. As the weeks progressed and care staff continued to engage with our sessions, I realized that this was an important (and perhaps rare) opportunity for them to share something about their cultural identities at work, extending their habitual roles as professional carers and enabling John to relate to his carers beyond the cared for/carer relationship. A notable example of this was a very passionate discussion between John and Gloria about how many tomatoes to put in the ackee and salt fish. Gloria only wanted to add one tomato to allow the taste of the ackee to come through, but John wanted to add four or five to infuse the dish with the sweetness of the tomatoes. In the end they compromised and we agreed to include three tomatoes. The discussion was significant because for a moment they appeared to forget their roles as care staff and resident, becoming in that moment just two people with a love and knowledge of cooking debating on equal terms how they liked to make a familiar dish. Furthermore, in that instance, John played an active role in the selection and preparation of food. This was in contrast to his usual position in the care home as someone who was cooked for and cared for.

John's knowledge of Jamaican food was further recognized when two other residents from the care home joined us for the final five sessions of the project. As far as I know, they were both unfamiliar with Caribbean food. One of the residents was Mary, with whom I had shared stories of walking on Streatham Common. Mary enjoyed trying the food, often asking for a second or third portion, and she appeared to want to learn about it. Before each session I placed food items and ackee tins (Figure 4.1) on the table, and Mary often looked

Figure 4.1 Ackee. Photographer: Jayne Lloyd, 2015

at the labels on the tins, reading the word 'ackee' out loud then asking me if it was a type of nut or a type of rice. In turn, I would ask John to describe ackee to Mary, and he usually accepted my prompt. The enjoyment Mary appeared to get from her new interest emphasized two things to me. First, that it was important that the knowledge of a person's past interests did not limit the experiences they were offered in the present. In many ways, Mary seemed more engaged in tasting and asking questions about the Jamaican food, which, as far as I know, was a new experience for her, then she had been in drawing on her past experiences to talk about walking her dog. Second, I have encountered many care home residents who have told me something about their diverse and rich life experiences. As this project suggests, if they were supported to share their knowledge and interests with each other they could potentially offer one another access to new experiences and opportunities to learn and teach, to be experts.

The idea of people with dementia learning from each other could easily be dismissed because most people with dementia have difficulty retaining new information. However, I would argue that providing people living with dementia with opportunities to learn is still possible and important, particularly when it is associated with sensory experiences. Although Mary often asked the same questions about the food, there was evidence of her learning in the steady increase I observed in the confidence and coherence with which she asked the questions. There was also one particular comment she made that led me to believe she might have retained some memory of the sessions. In one of the later sessions she contributed to a discussion about Jamaican food by telling the group that she used to have Jamaican friends who cooked for her and how much she enjoyed this. It is possible that this was a memory from her earlier life, but she had never mentioned it before. I wondered, therefore, if this was her way of remembering previous sessions by integrating into her own life story something from them that she had remembered but was not able to place.

Everyone involved in the group spent time exploring the food we shared and in turn spent time with each other. One of the most important outcomes of the project was that the food enabled social interactions that I had not observed in the day-to-day life of the care home. Not only did this involve care staff and residents, it was also notable in the interactions between the residents. I had never seen John and Mary talking to each other before and in the initial sessions they did not engage in conversation without significant prompting. During the eighth session, however, I overheard Mary asking John what Jamaica was like, suggesting her interest in the Jamaican food had prompted her to start a conversation with John. The other resident who joined the session was Pearl, who had had a rich social life with a lot of friends and family and a strong involvement in her local church and community. When I sat with her each week and she smiled at me, her smile lit up her whole face indicating she still enjoyed being in company. Now in the advanced stages of dementia, Pearl struggled to find words and form sentences; therefore, socializing had become a challenge for her. In the sessions some of her difficulties seemed to ease, and she often became animated and contributed to the conversations by smiling, laughing, nodding or saying 'oh yes'. Occasionally she said odd words that indicated she understood the content of the conversation, for example, 'oh yes cooking'. However, what appeared to be important about her being in the group was that she was able to socialize without the pressure of having to formulate coherent sentences or necessarily follow everything that was said.

By cooking and eating John's favourite dishes, the project temporarily shifted the roles of care staff and residents and the relationships between them. During our last session together, John and I cooked ackee and salt fish accompanied by roasted breadfruit and fried plantain for the other staff and residents on his floor of the care home. After the session I cleared up and told John I had put the leftovers in the fridge in a container with his name on so he could eat them later. He looked at me and asked 'but where will you be?' These words stuck with me, not least because they made me question what happens after visiting arts practitioners leave the care home. What, if any, lasting changes do temporary creative projects make? After the project finished I did not visit the care home again for over a year. I did not know if John still remembered the project, if any discussions or making of Caribbean food still took place in the home – or even if the residents I worked with were still alive. What I did know was the lasting impact John has had on my life. Now, over a year after the project ended, I continue to make the recipes he taught me for friends and family and to shop in Brixton Market with a little more knowledge of the produce on sale. Ackee and salt fish is now a firm favourite of mine and has become a regular meal in our house.

Creative spaces of care

As an artist, Jayne's response to the project in the care home was to create a cookbook, *A Taste of Life*. The cookbook aimed to share what she had learnt in the care home with a wider audience and contains the recipes she learnt, including tips from the residents and care staff. The images in the cookbook are reproductions of hand-pulled screen prints she made, influenced by pop artist Andy Warhol's prints of everyday household products. The inspiration for this came while preparing for one of the sessions. Sitting with nine different brands of tinned ackee in front of her, the numerous variations of the same type of tinned food reminded her of Andy Warhol's *Campbell's Soup Cans* (1962), a series of screen prints of the thirty-two varieties of Campbell's soup. The majority of viewers of Warhol's *Campbell's Soup Cans* will immediately recognize the product and bring their own autobiographical stories and associations to their reading of the work. However, unlike the soup cans, she anticipated that the prints of the ackee tins (Figure 4.1) and other Caribbean foods would be unfamiliar to the majority of people who read the cookbook. She was interested in the moment she anticipated this would create for some readers when the images hovered between portraying foods they did not recognize and foods about which they were gaining some knowledge. Importantly, this knowledge was primarily provided by a care home resident living with dementia and demonstrates that people, even the oldest old living in residential care, still have much to offer others.

In August 2015, over a year after the end of the project, Jayne returned to the care home to take John and Gloria a cookbook. When she greeted John he looked at her blankly, showing no indication that he recognized her. However, when she told him that he had taught her to cook ackee and saltfish his face lit up and he said 'that was a good day'. She gave him a cookbook and he began to look through it. He was not able to read the text, but he really engaged with the images, commenting on the different foods they portrayed. Turning to a page with an image of three plantains on it, he described each one, 'ripe plantain, yellow plantain, green plantain', followed by 'ummm' indicating that he enjoyed eating them. They conversed for nearly half an hour and Gloria joined in the conversation, reminding John of the week Jayne had brought the carrier bag with all the ackee in and picking out the colours of the Jamaican flag on the cover of the cookbook. It was notable how the connection between them that had developed through discussions of food that John and Gloria loved to cook could still facilitate lively and engaging conversations one year on.

In their study of home, Blunt and Dowling point out that feelings of attachment to home are often predicated on an ideal of intimate relationships and close family ties (2006: 110–112), and domestic objects and routines of living become inscribed with meaning, memorably invoked by Kathleen Stewart as the 'ordinary affects' of everyday life. Blunt and Dowling describe homemaking as 'creative and imaginative as well as materially grounded' (2006: 254), imbued with memories and carrying the tastes, interests and expectations of its inhabitants. By contrast, the communality of residential care homes can feel sterile and impersonal, lacking the intimacy that is associated with positive feelings of home. Redefining a residential care home as a creative space involves an openness to difference, a willingness to encourage generous and reciprocal relationships, and attention to the non-human qualities of atmosphere and environment.

Artists curate the sensory qualities associated with home in the residential care home by temporarily introducing and animating objects with material and sensory properties that are not usually present in that rather astringent environment. The creative space that artists curate in care homes is a complex and aestheticized dialogue between the sensory qualities of the care home environment and the many and diverse associations its residents have with home. As visitors to the care home without the personal care responsibilities of care staff, they have the time to learn what makes a home for its residents. They bring to the care home an understanding of aesthetics and metaphor, and experience of engaging with the materiality and sensory properties of objects and environments. This artistic knowledge makes them sensitive to the sensory and material properties of the care home and supports them to respond creatively to the space and those who live and work there. Often their interventions do not exactly replicate the activity or place that the resident associated with home; instead, everyday sensory experiences find symbolic expression and the sensory qualities of the individuals' imagined pasts are represented in metaphor. The sensory qualities of a home the arts practitioners are trying to evoke will always exist in dialogue with those of the resident's current (care) home. This does not necessarily detract from the experience but often frames it and can heighten it. Metaphorical and symbolic representations of home coupled with material and sensory engagement can create a focal point around which to build relationships between those who live and work in the care home. These relationships have the potential to create the strongest sense of being at home.

A Gentle Inquiry into Dark Matter in Arts-based Research

Clive Parkinson

Introduction

We are bombarded with the possibilities of miracles from the cradle to the grave – of life eternal on one hand – and cosmic riddles of the universe on the other. Medicine, it seems, can offer an endless range of interventions to extend our lives, and when it ultimately fails, religion offers us eternal salvation from our bodily woes. In the heart of Europe, deep underground, the Large Hadron Collider offers us teasing glimpses of the hypotheses of our brightest scientific minds made real, typified most poignantly by the 'God Particle'. We are told that we are on the brink of new revolutionary discoveries. And while the great whirling apparatus of science smashes sub-atomic particles together at 13TeV (Anonymous, 2015: 2) in the hope of explaining the mysteries of dark matter and quantum gravity, a thousand miles away confused wars rage in the name of religion and greed. The poet Philip Larkin usefully reminds us of the fussing and sometimes impotent presence of science and religion in his poem *Days* (1964: 3). We will see that artists explore and expose the essence of what it is to be human, which in its turn presents us with unique artist-led research that we are perhaps not yet sophisticated enough to value in its own right because of our blinkered worship of science. This chapter will explore what is considered evidence, value and impact, and what social psychologist Professor Tom Kitwood describes as 'the subjective reality of lived experience' (1997: 4).

Through an exploration of work of playwrights and filmmakers, artists and poets, one can investigate the instrumental potential of the arts, alongside their intrinsic cultural value. From Florian Zeller's visceral portrayal of dementia in his play *The Father* (Zeller, 2015: 5) to Peter Schaffer's questioning of the blunt tools of psychiatry in *Equus* (Schaffer, 1973: 6) and Sarah Kane's exploration of her own psyche in *4:48 Psychosis* (2000: 7), artists offer us time and space to question both subjective reality and the dominance of medical science. While evidence of the impact of arts on health and well-being is growing, this chapter will suggest that our understanding of cultural value might best not be understood through the lens of medicine but its own language.

Day-to-day extremis

There is a little theatre that buffers this experience of life, from the induced rapid suction into the flat-pack world of our birth, to the sometimes rather protracted, technophilic end days, drawn out, intubated and devoid of ritual and meaning. The intervening years may be peppered with the high camp of all that religion offers through its various ceremonies and barbarisms, but by and large, the theatre of the every day is that of the television, the internet and all the unmediated fears that they propagate. If we travel across the life-course from fictional newborn Baby A to the very real Patient Z, we may get a picture of how positive innovations in technology have something of a flip side and, by proxy, begin to understand how the arts might offer some sophisticated and wholly humanistic counter blasts to our burgeoning technocracy.

Case studies: Baby A and Patient Z

Baby A: The first anxieties

The neonatal incubator has undoubtedly played a profound part in saving the lives of countless infants born too early into the world, or else delivered into it with life-threatening disease. It may be surprising to know that these gently purring greenhouses of the neonates produce an array of noises that have the potential to damage hearing permanently and influence physiological damage. These impacts include 'apnea; bradycardia; and abrupt fluctuations in heart rate, respiratory rate, blood pressure, and oxygen saturation' (Philbin and Klass, 2000: 8).

To understand the disturbing nature of sounds on a neonatal intensive care unit, we can look into data from the American Academy of Paediatrics, Committee on Environmental Health, who in the research report, 'Noise: A Hazard for the Foetus and New Born' (Committee on Environmental Health, 1997: 9), paint a disturbing picture of sound equivalents from the interior of incubators. If 45 decibels (dB) is the acceptable level of ambient sound in the neonatal ward and the sound of a vacuum cleaner is 70 dB, the bubbling sound of air tubes provides the equivalent sound within an incubator. Taken further the simple tapping of fingers on the plastic lid of the incubator equates to the 80 dB of heavy traffic or a phone ringing. At its most extreme the closing of the plastic porthole is the same as a power mower at 100 dB, and simply dropping the head of the infant onto the mattress is the equivalent of a painful and distressing 120 dB car stereo playing you very worst kind of music.

Patient Z: The final indignities

In May 2015, an independent Parliamentary and Health Service Ombudsman published its report, *Dying without Dignity*, which is an investigation into complaints about end of life care in the UK. The report cites the case of one patient who at the age of seventy-four was admitted to hospital for investigations after experiencing prolonged abdominal pain. Patient Z spent five days in hospital before he died. During this time, he suffered 'ongoing abdominal pain, nausea and vomiting, build-up of fluid on his lungs, breathlessness, chest pain and excessive sweating' (Parliamentary and Health Service Ombudsman, 2015: 10). When admitted, Patient Z had a CT scan that revealed abdominal cancer that had spread to his liver. Because the cancer was inoperable, palliative care was decided to be in the best interest of the patient and to relieve his symptoms and distress, subcutaneous medication was prescribed. Patient Z's drip accidentally came out and three junior doctors made fourteen failed attempts to reinsert it into his vein. Following these attempts the next step was to contact the on-call anaesthetist but he or she failed to respond until the next day, at which point Patient Z was close to death. It took the anaesthetist another forty minutes to insert the drip. Patient Z died shortly afterwards.

The report concludes it was clear that all involved in his treatment knew that Patient Z was close to death and that a drip was not appropriate. Alternative means to provide medication should have been secured and by not doing so medical practitioners failed to provide treatment to alleviate his stress, discomfort and fear. To quote from the report, 'the junior doctors and anaesthetist should have acted on the advice of the palliative care nurse and provided him with the necessary medication subcutaneously to make him more comfortable' (Parliamentary and Health Service Ombudsman, 2015: 10). It was revealed in the report that hospital staff had tried to administer pain relief orally despite Patient Z not being able to swallow and that his pain levels had been recorded as not being managed effectively. It is without question that Patient Z suffered unnecessarily at the end of his life and that witnessing this caused his family anguish 'on top of their inevitable distress at his diagnosis' (Parliamentary and Health Service Ombudsman, 2015: 11).

Research from A to Z: A gentle instrumentalism

Behaviour change and good design on a neonatal unit could swiftly address the impact of noise – and as a counter-blast to this – adding positive sounds could have an impact on physiological outcomes. Through her interrogation of existing data around the impact of music on neonates, research nurse Dr Kimberley Allen suggests that premature infants with respiratory distress, during endotracheal intubation, ventilation and when receiving regular endotracheal suctioning, saw improvements when exposed to music, with statistically significant higher oxygen saturation during the thirty-minute recovery period (Allen, 2014: 2).

Premature and inconsolable intubated infants, who were exposed to music during a naturally occurring episode of crying or agitation, and observed for a further ten minutes following the music exposure, 'had statistically significantly improved oxygen saturation, heart rate, and returned to a drowsy or alert state after the music intervention. The introduction of music to intubated, premature infants who are agitated may improve the clinical status of the infant' (Allen, 2014: 13).

Significantly, Allen points to a survey of neonatal nurses in Finland, which showed a majority of nurses believed music could increase the feeling of security, improve sleep, decrease stress and reduce pain in premature infants. This belief was supported in a further study, in which parents similarly thought music decreased stress, improve sleep and decrease crying in their child in paediatric intensive care.

With the potential of full lives stretching ahead of them, it is easy to justify rich collaborative research in neonatal intensive care; the plight of the older individual at the end of their life perhaps demands a different kind of thinking. Writing in *The British Medical Journal*, general practitioner and former president of the Royal College of General Practitioners Dr Iona Heath provides us with some difficult food for thought around this conversation on ageing, illness and mortality. Heath suggests that as governments strive to reduce mortality, they are ultimately fighting a losing battle, as 'the mortality rate for the population will always be 100%', and if 'we continue to fight all causes of mortality, particularly in extreme old age, we have no hope of success, and we will consume an ever increasing proportion of healthcare resources for ever diminishing returns' (2010: 4).

Heath suggests that despite all the evidence, preventative medicines like statins are prescribed to people over seventy, which successfully reduce deaths from cardiovascular disease, only to increase mortality rates through cancer and dementia. She cites a US study of care in people dying of advanced cancer or with dementia in acute hospitals, which found that 'for 24% of both groups cardiopulmonary resuscitation was attempted and that 55% of those with dementia died with feeding tubes in place' (Heath, 2010: 15). Her explicit question being: is this '[w]hat we want for ourselves or those we love – or indeed for anyone?' (Heath, 2010: 16).

Fear of our own mortality and the commodification of well-being is reflected in the way that, 'more and more of life's inevitable processes and difficulties – birth, sexuality, ageing, unhappiness, tiredness and loneliness – are being medicalised' as Dr Richard Smith (one-time editor of *The British Medical Journal* argues) (2010: 17). For him, 'medicine alone cannot address these problems [...] common values and attitudes towards the management of death, whilst well known about in scientific circles, have yet to be acted upon because of lack of imagination' (2010: 17).

While the modern version of the Hippocratic oath urges clinicians to avoid the 'twin traps of over treatment and therapeutic nihilism' (Lasagne, 1964: 18), it also stresses that 'there is art to medicine as well as science, and that warmth, sympathy, and understanding may outweigh the surgeon's knife or the chemist's drug' (Lasagne, 1964: 19). Smith's implicit message is that the arts might just be the vehicle to address these points.

Artists and arts therapists have established diverse roles within multidisciplinary teams in end of life services, primarily within hospices and palliative care. While it's generally accepted that the arts enable and aid difficult communication through metaphor, signs and symbols, the use of the arts to create the conditions for innovation in the workplace to enable cultural change is perhaps a newer idea.

Research undertaken by Dr Joan Yalden et al. explores the possibility that arts-informed approaches can transform end-of-life care, through 'visible, shared meanings' (Yalden et al., 2013: 20). The development of a strategic and evidence-informed tool known as the 'palliative care chest of drawers' (PCCOD) is useful to explore when attempting to understand how we can humanize the heavily managed processes of our dying. A portable five-drawer cabinet, designed through a workshop process with multidisciplinary team, contains personalized artefacts and material to support physical, psychological, social and spiritual care – material are a mix of the metaphorical and the practical, including personal mementos alongside care plans and advanced directives.

In terms of research, this gently instrumental aesthetic tool has been created using the 'experimental knowledge' of all those involved. In its design, the innovation goes beyond physical care and embodies the subjective reality of lived experience, echoing the nurses and patients in Finland, who instinctively believed that music played a real part in reducing the stress of premature and seriously ill infants.

Cultural value beyond technocratic measurement

In March 2015, shortly before *Dying without Dignity* published its indictment of the unintentional small acts of day-to-day abuse meted out to Patient Z, an altogether different story of a 78-year-old woman's dying days became a social media sensation. When the Dutch volunteer organization Stichting Ambulance Wens, the Netherlands (Anonymous, 2015: 21), took three terminally ill people to see the Late Rembrandt Exhibition at the Rijksmuseum in Amsterdam (featuring work that the artist produced during the final phase of his life), the gallery threw open its doors to the individuals who, in their very last weeks of life, expressed an interest in seeing the work.

Perhaps this moving image and the actions of those involved represent what Iona Heath describes as 'authentic health care for the old and frail, which has much more to do with helping to preserve their dignity, treating them with affection, and supporting their continued involvement in social activities, rather than the pursuit of ever-more elusive cures' (Heath, 2006: 22), and an embodiment of Kitwood's subjective reality of lived experience (Figure 5.1).

Figure 5.1 Stichting Ambulance. Photographer: Wens Nederland, 2015

Surgeon and writer Dr Atul Gawande (2010: 23) consistently suggests that while the goal of medicine and surgery is to prolong life it runs the risk of sacrificing quality of life by pursuing every available intervention, however traumatic, for the possibility of extra time. It appears that twenty-first-century patients have bought into the consumer myth of invincibility wholesale, an indicator perhaps of selfish consumerism at its most blinkered.

The arts might enable deeper and more engaged conversations around a new philosophy of how we live our lives and, explicitly, end our days; a difficult conversation perhaps, but one that the arts are uniquely placed to address. This, however, will require a significant cultural shift.

Fifteenth-century priests offered advice on the protocols and procedures of a good Christian death through an instructional Latin text on how to die well. Any contemporary *Ars moriendi*, or art of dying (Duclow, 2003: 24), might not focus on how you might avoid the five temptations in your final moments – of lack of faith, despair, impatience, spiritual pride and avarice – but instead offer more humanistic guidance to those nurses, doctors and technicians, who inevitably surround the dying individual. What might a contemporary *Ars moriendi* look like – designed to look past what the poet Philip Larkin described as 'that vast moth-eaten musical brocade, created to pretend we never die' (1964: 25), particularly in the light of a secular and arguably science-obsessed society?

In the case of medicine, this is often cast in the language of battle lines and of a war on disease that is mediated by the complicit relationship between the pharmaceutical giants and profits-driven research, but in truth, any notion of creativity and culture in acute care seems irrelevant if measured against the scientific instruments and well-funded field of medical research. Perhaps we are trying to understand the value of the arts in the wrong language and context. While constantly aspiring to some gold standard of measurement, we may be ignoring the golden methods of understanding our own potency and reach.

Randomized controlled trials (RCTs) are widely held up as the gold standard in testing clinical efficacy; how useful would an RCT be in a cultural context, or is the arts and health agenda more about vision, values and believing that things can be different? Dr Nancy Cartwright speaking at the London School of Economics usefully suggests that, 'There is no gold standard; no universally best method. Gold methods however, are whatever methods will provide the information you need, reliably, from what you can do, and from what you can know on the occasion' (Cartwright, 2007: 26). This raises a concern though: Aren't we too fixated on understanding the impact of the arts on countering ill health, when the arts surely have most value across the life course?

A wealth of studies illustrates the short-term benefits of arts engagement, but little consideration has been given to the ways in which our health may be affected through engaging in the arts over a longer period. In a bid to redress the balance, Arts for Health set up a six-month research programme, in which Dr Rebecca Gordon-Nesbitt asked a simple question, 'Is there a relationship between engaging in the arts and long-term health benefits, and, if so, can we find evidence of it?' (Gordon-Nesbitt, 2015: 27).

This research isn't confined to symptoms of ill health but looks across the broader social and physiological factors underlying health conditions and the ways in which arts engagement might mitigate these relationships. This research has revealed fifteen highly relevant, key longitudinal Nordic research projects that interrogate population scale data from the past thirty years, and that taken together demonstrate a positive association between engagement in high-quality arts activities and life expectancy, disease resistance and mental acuity.

In considering the effect upon physical and mental health of engaging in arts activities in non-clinical settings including galleries and museums, theatres, cinemas and concert halls, the research reveals arts engagement to have many second-order benefits in a variety of diseases and health concerns including dementia (Wang et al., 2002: 28), coronary heart disease (Sundquist et al., 2004: 29), obesity (Cuypers et al., 2012: 32; Kouvonen et al., 2012: 31; Lajunen et al., 2009: 30) and cancers (Bygren et al., 1996: 33 and 2009: 34).

However, this narrative is not about 'interventions', in the medical sense, instead it is about opportunities for voluntary participation and the positive effects this participation might have on physical and mental health. The aggregated research explores who has access to the arts and critically, how the arts impact on health through a mix of cognition, psycho-neuroimmunology and epigenetics, as we will see.

Studies repeatedly demonstrate that the production of our stress hormone, cortisol, has wide-reaching effects on the brain. Some of the core structures that regulate emotions and mood (hypothalamus, pituitary and adrenal glands – the HPA axis) become suppressed and less effective when the body or mind is under stress. This impairs our defence against depression. In contrast, the production of dopamine is positively associated with 'flow' that 'psychological state of high but subjectively effortless attention, low self-awareness, sense of control and enjoyment that can occur during the performance of tasks that are challenging, but matched in difficulty to the skill level of the person' (Gordon-Nesbitt, 2015: 35), a state which is frequently induced by creativity and is central to being absorbed by the arts.

Towards the end of the twentieth century, it was posited that, rather than being autonomous, self-regulating entities, the nervous, immune and endocrine systems function in a reciprocal way in response to environmental and psychological stimuli. In a study of the impact of psychosocial and behavioural factors upon cancer, it was found that distress negatively influenced mechanisms central to carcinogenesis, including the ability of cells to repair damaged DNA. The significance of studies of this kind is that, in making a connection between stress, distress and chronic morbidity via psychoimmuno-neurological pathways, they pave the way for an exploration of arts engagement as a factor, which might reduce the negative side of this equation.

Perhaps one of the most revelatory hypotheses in this field is around epigenetics and an exploration of the role environmental factors play in determining which genes are switched on or off in the body at any given time, potentially inducing physiological changes that result in disease or protection from disease. Short-term exposure to a range of external factors can cause long-term changes and, as Swedish researcher Lars Olov Bygren (2009: 36) suggests, exposure to enriched environments can have a positive epigenetic effect. This suggests great potential for arts engagement in mitigating a range of acute morbidities. Cultural participation may yet prove to moderate the epigenetic transfer of disease susceptibility through the generations.

From a cultural perspective, population-level research of this kind potentially reduces pressure on arts organizations to constantly justify their value to the public purse. Added to this, the fact that the quality of arts projects is taken to be paramount in manifesting health effects may ultimately serve to focus attention away from quantitative measurements of cultural value. That notion of quality, however, is subjective and loaded with bias and is something I will return to.

Ambiguity and uncertainty

While this is the ammunition we might crave to evidence our value in terms of medical science, my opening gambit was a suggestion that the arts and health field might be better off liberating its understanding of impact and value from the language and evaluation of medicine. Samuel Beckett's *Not I* is a short, one-act play in which an illuminated mouth delivers a high-octane monologue of the fractured memories of a fragile and seemingly very real woman. It was first performed in 1973 and undoubtedly would have been utterly incomprehensible to my mindset as a young working-class boy – but would it? Perhaps my family simply had a deficit of aspiration and was complicit in the divisive order, which dictates that contemporary art is the soul preserve of the educated elite, while the working classes could consume popular culture, predominantly through the television.

The artist Joseph Bueys (Adriani et al., 1979: 37) declared we are all artists, but I'm not sure that this is right. We are all born with the potential to be creative, but increasingly the arts are marginalized in school curricula through target-driven educational systems. As artists, as passive or active participants, or as free thinkers, we all inhabit a cultural spectrum of some sorts. It might be intentionally medicinal or unintentionally impact our long-term health and quality of life, or it may simply have the power to shift our ways of thinking, and seeing the world and our shared place in it.

Seemingly a polar opposite to Beckett's *Not I*, the British playwright Sarah Kane (1971–1999) charted her lived experience of clinical depression in the play *4:48 Psychosis*, which premiered following her suicide at the turn of the twenty-first century. Complex, harrowing and deeply affecting, her work reminds us of the often blunt tools of psychiatry that reduce, distil and pathologize the nuances in all our mental difference. As an artist and as a human being affected by the extremes of mental ill health, Kane eloquently offers us a stinging critique of psychiatry and the technocratic fantasy that reinforces the dominance of a discipline which reduces the human psyche into neurons and synapses, dendrites and plaques.

Often disregarding the personal narrative that leads to a mental health crisis, in *4:48 Psychosis*, Kane reminds of the subjective reality of lived experience in the face of diagnosis and treatment. This critique of psychiatry is not new to literature or theatre, and perhaps the fictional child-psychiatrist Dr Dysart (played by Richard Burton in the film of Peter Schaffer's *Equus*) best illustrates the god-like role imbued on clinicians. Attempting to 'cure' the pathological religious and sexual fascination with horses: that his young patient has, Dysart begins to question his own part in reducing child patients into compliant and unimaginative adults. Dysart dreams of worship and passion: the very characteristics that he is charged with suppressing in his patients, and yet which he craves himself. The fundamental questions of why we are and who we are have no place in the psychiatrists consulting room, he suggests, at least, not in the re-moulding of passive and good little citizens, or in the excising of existential pain. To the chagrin of many clinicians in the field, Dysart closed his final defeatist monologue with the legend that passion 'can be destroyed by a doctor, it cannot be created' (Schaffer, 1973: 40).

This is stinging, and while I am not arguing that an arts and health agenda should divorce itself entirely from understanding its potency through the language of medicine, perhaps we might better share our understanding of cultural value with some of the conviction of a theoretical physicist.

The Large Hadron Collider took about a decade to construct; it cost around $4.75 billion and its total operational budget runs to about $1 billion per year. Forbes estimate the total cost of finding the Higgs boson (God particle) at about $13.25 billion (Knapp, 2012: 41). Money is also invested in hypothetical explorations into Dark Matter and Dark

Energy; matter with properties that are inferred from gravitational effects on visible matter, and which can't be seen with telescopes, but which account for most of the matter in the universe. Theoretical physicists like Professor Stephen Hawking have to learn to live with ambiguity and uncertainty in their mission to describe the universe using mathematics and, critically, their imaginations.

While the arts will never generate the research funding that CERN brings in, aren't we interested in some of those fundamental and difficult questions – questions that aren't easy counted out and measured by the crude efforts of trialists? In Larkin's poem 'Days', the poet addresses the realization that humans and time have an unequal relationship and while religion and science aim to understand the why and how of the universe, it is perhaps artists who are best placed to help us understand what it is to be human, to have finite life, to seek meaning of our fragility and to impose order on the chaos of our existence.

French writer Florian Zeller's play *The Father* (Zeller, 2015: 42) perhaps helps us span that blurred and often disputed space between the instrumental and intrinsic, and in doing so, provides a useful motif in understanding narrative, value and the barriers that prevent a wider range of people experiencing the arts. Ostensibly, the play tells the story of one man's experience of dementia and that of his daughter who runs the gamut of emotions in making decisions about his care. The play depicts a common human story, but one explored through unexpected theatrical devices that elevate it beyond nanny-state instrumentalism. Critically, as Susannah Clapp in the *Guardian* notes, 'Zeller's play is not a study or a discussion of Alzheimer's. It is more profoundly theatrical. It plunges the audience into the experience of dementia. It throws the switches in your brain' (2015: 43).

Interestingly, in his introduction to the play, Zeller describes it not as a piece of work about dementia, but an attempt 'to understand, through theatre, the situation of an old man who has lost his bearings and arrived at that moment where his kingdom dissolves' (2015: 44). In holding up 'a mirror to its audience', the playwright helps us recognize and understand ourselves more deeply. I would argue that he does this more effectively than any well-intentioned NHS information leaflet, and perhaps gets closer to Kitwood's notion of the subjective reality of lived experience than any other art form. By becoming lost in the protagonists fractured, subjective reality, we are temporarily immersed in a shared reality – a shared grief – that in very real terms, may prepare us for the fragilities of old age and our inevitable mortality.

The play offers no certainty or explanation, and moreover, it contradicts its own narrative and yet is imbued with deep human warmth, which Holly Williams in the *Independent* usefully describes as 'one of those plays that makes your brain hum with the unique potential of theatre' and 'perfect [in] unity of form and content' (2015: 45). But who is the audience to this play? Karena Johnson writing in the *Guardian* reminds us of what we know all too well, that 'working-class people and culture are an endangered group in our subsidised theatres, invisible in our auditoria and rarely seen on our stages' (2015: 46). The expanding arts and health evidence base, as explicitly stated by Gordon-Nesbitt, illustrates two significant obstacles to attributing causality between arts engagement and health. She asserts the assumption that people with poor health tend to take a diminished part in cultural activities, thereby skewing research results; similarly, scrutiny of non-participation in surveys has revealed low socio-economic status and disease to be the two main reasons for non-response.

If, through consciously chosen leisure activity, engagement in the arts is generally shown to have a positive impact upon the body's physiology, in turn improving health and quality of life, then it is equally clear that those who have fewer resources will continue to see culture and arts as being the sole preserve of those with perceived wealth, education and resources. Contentiously, and from a cultural perspective, population-level research of the kind described by Gordon-Nesbitt potentially exempts arts organizations from continually having to justify their value to the public purse. Added to this, the fact that the quality of arts projects is taken to be paramount in manifesting health effects may ultimately serve to focus attention away from quantitative measurements of cultural value.

Is there room for ambiguity and uncertainty in medicine and health care? Unquestionably the answer must be no, but like our theoretical physicists, artists thrive in the liminal space between human knowledge and imagination. From addressing behaviour change in neonatal units and end-of-life care to bringing people up close and personal with artistic revelation, cultural engagement and participation offers a more ambiguous and nuanced conversation about what it is to be human. Scientific theories and hypotheses are not proven to be true or correct but rather supported by tests and experimentation.

The researcher Lars Olov Bygren suggests that the arts are a 'perishable commodity' (2009: 47), something that if we don't value and practice may just negatively affect our lives. Conversely, our deeper engagement may indeed contribute to richer, fuller, longer lives. This is an important hypothesis and, as I've suggested, is grounded in serious research. I would like to add to this and propose that it is not simply a discussion about the arts as some instrumental 'high-quality' cultural tool meted out to the poor and uneducated and dispensed by a nanny-state. It suggests something far deeper. Arguably, in an increasingly secular society, the challenging and difficult, the darker and sometimes avant-garde work of artists that taxes us and makes us uncomfortable – in all its ambiguity and uncertainty – feeds a gaping need for something to nurture our very essence. More than ameliorating against disease, this may enable deeper understanding of the subjective realities and diverse lived experiences of others.

From Islands to Networks: Using Improvisation to Build Relationships among Individuals and Systems

Anne Davis Basting

This chapter is the story of a theatre research project, the Islands of Milwaukee (IoM), which I co-facilitated from 2012 to 2014. My goal here is to share the journey of IoM as a case study and, in so doing, point out several unique challenges and opportunities of engaging in applied theatre research, particularly when working collaboratively with older adults and the agencies that partner to support them.

A few points before we begin

Through twenty years of working in the arts and community engagement, I have made a choice to use language that is accessible to all those that my research might engage and interest. This choice gets very interesting when the bulk of one's work is with people with cognitive challenges. Still, I remain committed to this approach. If there are terms that various fields use (fields of gerontology, applied theatre research or community-based participatory research), I will include those in parentheticals when it feels important. I do this not to annoy the reader, but with the hope that we all might expand our vocabulary without making anyone feel like they don't understand the basic flow of the story. The language that I use to describe a project has become an artistic product of the project itself –

carefully honed over the course of multiple years of collaborating with stakeholders.

I am telling a story about a project that involved hundreds of people. Every one of them shared their own expertise in the project. My expertise/role was as the principal investigator, as a facilitator of project stakeholders in countless meetings, as a teacher of students who participated in the project and as an artist who wrote the script for the performance and who served as co-lead artist of the overarching effort along with Maureen Towey of Sojourn Theatre.

The story begins with another project

To understand the evolution of IoM, I take you back to an approach I have been using since 1998, when I was working in a locked unit of a nursing home in the United States. I was trying out creative dramatic techniques, adapted from work with children, with people with Alzheimer's and dementia in a rather chaotic day room, with rather heavily medicated residents. I found that by shifting away from the expectation of memory, and inviting residents to improvise a new story from their imaginations, that the residents communicated more, appeared to enjoy themselves (what researchers might call improved affect), and formed relationships with each other, developing a sense of group identity and belonging. I called that approach TimeSlips in order to capture the free flow of the stories that did not necessarily follow traditional plot structures (beginning, middle and end). Instead, the stories follow whatever direction the tellers take and can include sounds, gestures and multiple plots in non-linear time.

Over the years TimeSlips' improvisational storytelling has become ritualized into a series of steps that are easy for anyone to learn. It begins with a welcoming of the storytellers, an introduction of a prompt (usually an image or question), and proceeds with a facilitator asking open-ended questions and echoing responses as they co-create a collage-like poem or story. The process ends with thanking the participants for their efforts. The ritual of TimeSlips is built on the core philosophy of improvisation that goes back to theatre artist and educator Viola Spolin – one says 'yes' to whatever input is given to you, and says 'and ...' by building on that input in a positive way. As the field of dementia care evolved (with Thomas Kitwood's important life's work) to become 'person-centered' (Kitwood, 1997), improvisational storytelling has proven to be a simple way to feel what it means to be person-centred without getting lost in the conceptual definitions of it (Kitwood has seventeen elements of person-centred care). Because of its simple, ritualized structure, it is also relatively easy to identify TimeSlips in concrete steps and train people to use it. This makes TimeSlips an easily researchable method.

Studies have supported the early observations of the outcomes of the method: improved affect; increased quality and quantity of engagement between staff and residents (Fritsch et al., 2009); improved attitudes towards older adults and people with dementia by student volunteers (George et al., 2011; George et al., 2012); reduction in behaviours that are often called challenging or are seen as signs of distress in the person with dementia (George and Houser, 2014; Phillips et al., 2010). One study suggests that with a large enough sample size, TimeSlips storytelling as a weekly activity has the potential to reduce the use of anti-psychotic medications that are commonly used to sedate people with dementia who have distressed behaviours that can be challenging to care partners at home or in care settings (Houser et al., 2014). TimeSlips' improvisational approach is an effective way for staff, families and volunteers to engage and invite people with dementia to express themselves.

In the framework of applied theatre, TimeSlips' power is in participation – inviting and fostering expression from people whose views are commonly overlooked by mainstream culture. However, in TimeSlips, there is also a clear benefit for the care partners. The approach helps care staff and volunteers who learn to facilitate the improvisational storytelling to see their work as meaningful and as having an impact. The shift towards engaging through imagination helps care partners more deeply understand the people whose stories (and identity) they had difficulty accessing because of memory loss. Training the staff, families and student volunteers to facilitate the improvisational storytelling method can sustain and deepen the impact of the approach over time. In shaping TimeSlips, we avoid looking at the storytelling method as oppositional – as freeing the expression of people with dementia from their care partners. Instead, we frame it as a tool to transform the care relationship itself. Publicly sharing the stories that emerge from the story workshops, as we did through multiple play productions for example, in turn educated audiences about the expressive strengths of people with dementia and the promise that improvisation holds for transforming care relationships.

In 2009, I began working on a large-scale application of TimeSlips' improvisational storytelling approach in collaboration with Luther Manor Retirement Community, Sojourn Theatre, and students and colleagues in the Theatre Department of the University of Wisconsin Milwaukee. We used Homer's *Odyssey* as a prompt for a two-year project that we called the Penelope Project. The impulse for the project began as a way to create professional quality art that emerged out of long and deep improvisation and collaboration inside of a care community. In the end, the Penelope Project became an experiment in infusing improvisation into a care system itself – beyond just single groups of elders and their care partners/facilitators. In the Penelope Project, students, staff and artists all facilitated improvisational workshops in all four areas of care: independent living, assisted living, skilled nursing and the adult day centre. We wrapped extensive evaluation around The Penelope Project, including pre- and post-attitude surveys for staff and students, surveys of audience members, focus group meetings throughout the two-year process, interviews with key players (residents and staff) and ethnographic field notes. All artistic products, from visual art to poems and the culminating play, were also considered data. The research on this project is chronicled in the 2016 book *Playing Penelope*. I include a few highlights here to provide background for the IoM project.

The Penelope Project set up a stakeholder group – leaders in each of the four areas of care (independent, assisted, skilled and adult day), representatives from Sojourn Theatre (director Maureen Towey) and lead faculty from the University of Wisconsin Milwaukee (myself and colleague Robin Mello). We set up monthly conference calls and a series of in-person meetings to collectively shape and enact the project over the course of the two years. Through the notes to these meetings, we realized that improvisation and collaboration was happening not just in the creative workshops on Penelope (visual art, dance, poetry, storytelling, etc.), but also in the meetings themselves.

When the designer from Sojourn Theatre asked the group if they could weave something as long as the route the play would take through the care community (nearly a mile long), a staff member quickly responded:, 'Yes. I don't know how, but we'll figure it out.' Perhaps most importantly, in the final focus group that met one month after the play last appeared at Luther Manor, the staff took it upon themselves to invite more stakeholders. I had asked only that the 'stakeholders' come to the focus group. But when I arrived to the meeting, in addition to the familiar faces of staff representatives from each area, there were family members, volunteers, residents, the head of pastoral care, the head of volunteers, the lead administrators of each care area and the CEO. The system itself had changed to become more inclusive, more person-centred, by inviting residents to be part of conversations about their care, and by acknowledging volunteers and family members as part of the care community.

In the United States, long-term care settings are heavily regulated and face significant fines if inspectors discover violations. Violations can range from not properly dating items in a refrigerator to not distributing medications on time. Skilled nursing settings are designed to reduce risk for vulnerable residents. This can make innovation and experimentation with new ways to improve care very difficult. As the Penelope team evaluated the considerable data from the project, it became clear to us that the improvisational roots of the TimeSlips approach were having an impact on multiple levels.

As with the previously noted published studies on TimeSlips, we knew the improvisational workshops in the Penelope Project were increasing the participation of people with dementia and improving their relationships with staff and volunteers. The workshops were reducing anxiety and anxious behaviours. But the longevity and the breadth of the project (engaging the entire care community) had additional positive effects. Analysis of interviews, field notes and meeting notes showed that the collaborative partnership was able to build community beyond the groups in the individual creative workshops that took place over the course of more than a year. We also created a sense of belonging and shared identity in Luther Manor as a whole. People with dementia were enfolded into the community as equal participants. And most interesting to me – the system itself began to collaborate and improvise. In the final focus group, I asked the simple question, 'What did you learn?' One staff member responded: 'I learned that Assisted Living is right over there through that window. And that we could collaborate with them on programming.' Another responded: 'I learned to trust and take risks – that it's okay if we don't know how to do something. We can figure it out together.'

In my field notes, I also captured a moment that the focus group didn't call out. In one of the rehearsal sessions for the play, the director was guiding the cast (made up of professional actors, students, staff and residents) through a scene in which one of the main characters gets scared while visiting the nursing home and tries to climb out a window. Improvising, the actor took off the screen and started to climb out a first-floor window in the lobby outside their Faith and Education centre. Within minutes, a staff member came and told us that someone reported to the CEO that we had just gone out the window. 'Was it true?' she asked us. Yes. It was. As the writer of the script, I was already starting to troubleshoot how to change the scene when she said, 'the CEO wants to know if it is instrumental to the plot of the play that you go out the window'. I said, yes, it was. She said then it was okay. Art-making – meaning-making – had become enough of a reason to say 'yes, and', in a facility designed to reduce risk to residents.

Collaboration with systems and individuals

In her book *Social Works*, Shannon Jackson profiles multiple arts and performance projects that take a unique approach to working in systems. It is relatively common for applied theatre research to focus on amplifying the voices of the under-represented (poor, minority) and, in so doing, to set those voices in resistance to the systems that have under-served them. For example, in their introduction to *Applied Theatre Research: Radical Departures*, O'Connor and Anderson describe their mission as 'positioning applied theater research as part of liberatory and critical research tradition' (2015: 6) that does not aim for neutrality, but to show a clear bias towards bringing out the voices of the marginalized. Jackson invites us to take a different view. Instead of framing the performance projects as oppositional, she looks at them as inter-dependent – as working with the systems: 'While the activist orientation of some social practice displays the importance of an anti-institutional stance in political art, I am equally interested in art forms that help us to imagine sustainable social institutions' (2015: 14).

As we assessed the results of the Penelope Project, this was our most significant discovery – that the improvisation inside the creative workshops with residents, staff, volunteers, artists and families had been absorbed into the care system itself and begun to change how they worked together, how decisions were made, and who they invited to the table. The Penelope Project had also successfully built a sense of belonging and community among people separated by fear and stigma – those residents with cognitive and physical disabilities and staff, residents, students and artists without them. People were drawn into a common, meaningful, long-range project. Hungry to see if this approach could be repeated and expanded, Sojourn Theatre's Maureen Towey (director of *Finding Penelope*, the culminating play of the Penelope Project) and I began outlining a new project that would reach outside the walls of a care community to people living alone at home.

We followed a path of phases similar to those of the Penelope Project, and that generally follow the course of community-based participatory research models:

1. partnership development (arriving at shared goals and language)
2. preliminary research (studying partnering systems)
3. creative data generation (creative workshops)
4. reflection and shaping a plan for next steps
5. rehearsal/refining
6. culminating event
7. reflection
8. dissemination and evolution of project energy

In the earliest phase of IoM in 2012, Towey and I temporarily called the project 'Shipwrecked', after two artistic images that inspired it – the story of Robinson Crusoe and the possible staging of Shakespeare's *The Tempest* in a suburban cul-de-sac. This latter image was meant to capture the experience of people who work their whole lives and successfully achieve their dreams only to find themselves ageing and isolated in suburban homes with no public transportation and no social network. The first phase of development of the project was to assemble potential stakeholders and share and refine ideas and solidify partnerships. It was clear from early meetings that the term 'Shipwrecked' had too many negative connotations for elders. They would not want to engage with a project that negatively captured their situation. In a meeting with the Executive Director of the Milwaukee County Department on Aging, the head of the Home Delivered Meal services for the county, the Executive Director of Interfaith Older Adult Programs (a non-profit providing transportation, companionship and programming and volunteer opportunities to elders in Milwaukee) and several older adults serving as County Commissioners on Aging, they suggested that we call the project The Islands of Milwaukee. And so we did.

The question with which Towey and I began the project was, 'Can we create a sustainable system to bring creative engagement to isolated older adults?' – with the assumption that creative engagement would improve quality of life and the quality of relationships with care partners. The language of isolation also evolved relatively quickly as stakeholders expressed concern that older adults, even if they are living alone and chronically lonely (using volunteer services for companionship), do not identify with being isolated. As a collaborative group of stakeholders, we shaped the language and mission of the project around three core questions:

1. How do we create a more connected Milwaukee that values and includes older voices in civic life and public decision-making?
2. How can we bring meaningful engagement to older adults living alone or under-connected to community?
3. How can we deepen the capacity of existing systems to create a sustainable mechanism to invite and nurture engagement with older adults living alone or under-connected to community?

As a practice, this crucial, early stage of cross-sector collaboration establishes goals and a shared language for a project. It can be challenging to secure funding to support this early stage, as many funders require a clear vision of what the end products will be. But separating the project into Planning and Implementation stages can make it difficult for the project to build momentum. Stage-based funding streams can create gaps during which the stakeholders change and the process must start anew. When we completed the partnership development phase of IoM, we articulated our three goals and identified several existing care systems (ways to reach older adults living alone) that would become our core partners, including Home Delivered Meals (free meals delivered to low-income elders who otherwise cannot access them) run through Goodwill Services in Southeastern Wisconsin; Stowell Associates, which provides managed homecare; and Interfaith Older Adult Programs' telephone reassurance and companion care services. I applied for Institutional Review Board human subjects approval for the study, creating a universal consent form for all participants to allow us to use their creative work, images and words as part of a larger project to bring creative engagement to older adults living alone or under-connected to community. There was no risk to their involvement, and it was indeed possible that participants enjoy themselves as a benefit. Staff, volunteers, students, elders and collaborating artists all signed consent forms, which also included permission for us to interview them for their feedback about the project as a whole.

As part of the preliminary research phase, I worked with graduate student assistants, undergraduates enrolled in my 'Performing Community' class, and members of Sojourn Theatre to learn how each service/programme is delivered, and where creative engagement might be fit into the system. We applied site-specific art techniques to systems by aiming to understand how engagement already happens as a result of these service/programme interventions, how we might deliver opportunities to be creative, how we might gather their creative input, build on it, and return it to them so they could begin to see their work as part of a larger whole. We arranged and conducted several ride-alongs with Home Delivered Meals drivers, following them on their routes and to the doors of clients as they exchanged pleasantries and dropped off the meal. We also trained the undergraduates as official volunteers for Interfaith, and they began their own companion visits with an older adult.

In the first two stakeholder meetings, we found that partners had difficulty explaining the project to their staff, volunteers and elder participants. They stumbled with language as they described the project as arts and crafts to the elders and were met by icy silence. As a result, we shifted the language from inviting elders to participate in an arts project, to the simplest and least threatening invitation we could think of. Rather than invite people to engage in art-making, we would appeal to their curiosity: 'I have a Question of the Day – would you like to hear it?' Together the Sojourn team, the graduate assistants and I generated a list of Questions of the Day (QoD) that we vetted with the stakeholders. The QoDs ranged considerably. Some were practical questions. Some invited people to see their homes and lives differently – to imagine their spaces with a fresh lens. Others asked them to consider their strengths. Many questions were 'one-offs' – just a single question. Others appeared in sequence, developing from week to week.

An example of the outcome of QoDs can be explored through the story of June's interaction with the project. Two students made home visits with June.[1] June's daughter lived with her, but was gone all day at work, leaving June alone. The students asked her the question, 'What do you treasure in your home and why?' June's response was 'my oven', which came as a surprise to the students. When they asked why, June told of being known in her family for baking and the joy of sharing treats with her children and grandchildren. She hadn't baked in years. The students asked if her oven still worked – and it did. They asked if they could bring ingredients and bake with her. So the following week, they gathered ingredients for June's favourite recipe (almond cookies with banana frosting) and baked together. In their field notes, they told of feeling giddy as they shared stories while the smell of cookies filled the house. Together they made a plan for how to share the cookies. They would put three cookies into a plastic bag and fasten it with a card. On each card they would print the recipe on one side, and on the other print 'This recipe comes from June's oven, which is her treasure. What do you treasure?' The students distributed the cookies to the Home Delivered Meals drivers as a thank you for their work, or for them to share with their clients – their choice. In their field notes, students described the session as 'more casual' with more laughter and smiling, particularly in response to the cookies baking and designing the tag for the bags of cookies.

At semester's end, the students designed their own culminating celebration with the elders they worked with as their final course project. They created a table display in the campus's Student Union that said 'Question for a Cookie'. They invited passers-by to answer a QoD – the same questions they had asked their elder participants – and gave them cookies from June's recipe in exchange. After several hours of gathering answers, they printed them up and gave them back to the elders in a small treasure box.

We tested the QoDs through ride-alongs with Home Delivered Meals drivers, at workshops with volunteers and at meetings with core stakeholders. We worked with each system to identify how best to introduce the concept to volunteers and staff, and how best to gather the input from their creative exchanges. Questions went out through four-colour-printed cards hand-delivered by Home Delivered Meals drivers and shared at Meal Sites place settings, through the project's Facebook page and website, through our Google Voice answering system and through emails sent to volunteers and coordinators.[2]

Responses to the QoDs came back to us through our Google voice line, hand-written cards gathered by Meal Drivers and Meal Site Coordinators, and our website and Facebook page. Project assistants organized responses into our shared file system (Dropbox, Google Docs, etc.). Anyone leaving a name and number was called back and asked if they would like an artistic house call as a way to deepen the engagement. After we gathered responses, we shared them back with respondents to let them know they had been both received and built upon. We did this through hand-delivered posters (that went to Home Delivered Meals and Meal Sites), a weekly segment on public radio, our website and publications in newsletters and papers about the project (Figure 6.1).

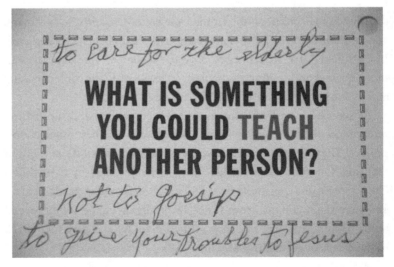

Figure 6.1 A Question of the Day and response. Photographer: Anne Basting, 2014

In total, we received 2,500 hand-written responses to our QoDs. By far the majority of our responses came from hand-written cards at both the Meal Sites and the Home Delivered Meals systems. In total, we estimate that we received 500 additional responses from the website, Facebook, and Google Voice. The most popular questions were:

1. What is something you treasure in your home, and why?
2. Is there an intersection you wish you could cross but feel it is too dangerous?
3. What is the most beautiful sound in your home?
4. What is the most beautiful sound in the world?

It was helpful to work in a series of questions that built over several weeks. Examination of field notes showed that we garnered more responses and interest and enthusiasm from the 'envoys' (those who helped us deliver the QoDs). It also suggested that it was more successful to create a series with the questions that started with the past and moved to the present and future and/or more poetic interpretations. Envoys reported that elders were more likely to answer a question about the past, and then become intrigued with the series of questions. Designing the series in this way enabled us to meet people where they were most comfortable engaging, and then encourage them to move beyond that point towards the symbolic. Take, for example, the series:

1. What is a well-worn path in your home?
2. What is a well-worn path outside your home?
3. What blocks your path?

In home visits, QoDs were designed as the first step to engagement. Many participants responded to multiple questions. If they left their name and phone number (by phone or hand-written card), we called and talked with them, thanking them for their participation and inquiring whether they might like an artistic house call. The vast majority of respondents did not leave their number, but among those who did, we had a 90 per cent response rate to this inquiry, and we engaged with: Fran, Jim, Antoinette, Tony, June, Angie, Ernest and Taylor. Angie created paintings and wrote poems. Bill told stories and sang. Ernest told stories by phone. Taylor told stories. June baked. Antoinette, Jim and Fran danced, and Tony shared stories and guided the project as an advisor (as did Fran). These artistic house calls were not designed to be sustained but to guide the person to a meaningful experience by making it (1) related to the person's identity, (2) a rigorous art-making experience that built skill and (3) connected to the larger world. We did this by learning about what was important to each person, making art together and building on that interaction by sharing the art with others for the larger purpose of creating a dynamic discussion about creating a more connected community as we age.

To keep stakeholders and friends (those who expressed interest) of the IoM up to date on our many endeavours as the project evolved, we created an electronic newsletter that went out monthly, starting in January 2014; an Islands of Milwaukee Facebook page; a Twitter account; and a website. The final iteration of the website prepared the project for growth and shared the exhibit and performances as models for other cities and partnerships.

On ride-alongs with Home Delivered Meal drivers, we noticed that many meals were delivered to apartments or homes that were across the street from food services. But the multi-laned streets were nearly impassable to pedestrians. Social isolation among older adults can be a result of our built environment – and the loss of confidence or comfort in walking and crossing the street.

To address this aspect of Islands, we collaborated with Southshore Connecting Caring Communities (SSCCC) on their pedestrian safety initiative over 2013–2014 and, through a street performance, amplified their efforts to create a city that sees and stops for pedestrians. Together we identified three problematic intersections in three different municipalities. We selected intersections for their perceived dangerousness to pedestrians and for their proximity to senior apartment buildings – the residents of which would grow into collaborative partners for the events. We reached out to a dozen senior apartment buildings and conducted interactive workshops (entitled 'How to Stop Traffic') to engage elder residents, particularly those with disabilities. We invited civic officials at the city, county and state levels to cross with us, and invited press to cover it. I worked with the University of Wisconsin Milwaukee theatre students and Sojourn Theatre artists to create the street performances, which took place on 1 and 2 May 2014. The experience led to real policy changes at two of the three intersections. A Crossings Guide provides details on this extensive project and is available for download at www.islandsofmilwaukee.org (Figure 6.2).[3]

Figure 6.2 Islands of Milwaukee listening stations, Milwaukee's City Hall. Photographer: Shannon Scrofano, 2014

Culminating exhibit and performance

We shared the results of our two-year effort in a performance/exhibit at Milwaukee's City Hall on 20 and 21 September 2014 in conjunction with Doors Open Milwaukee, a city-wide open house that is based at City Hall. Theatre's Shannon Scrofano designed a large island on the ground floor of City Hall featuring audio and visual stations inspired by our engagement with elders through our artistic house calls. Each station offered an emotional impression of the elder and was connected (literally) by string leading to a panel on the second or third floor. The panel described how we met each elder and gave details of our encounter. Each panel also displayed the QoD to which the elder responded. Strings suspended near the panel featured hand-written responses to that same QoD by other elders participating in the project. Blank cards and pencils invited audience members to write their own responses and add them to the interactive display.

Opening on 20 and 21 September allowed the exhibition to be strategically aligned with Doors Open Milwaukee, a city-wide open house that draws thousands of visitors to City Hall to get tickets for tours and to tour the building itself. Each day, we staged hourly ten-minute performances to animate the exhibit and invite audience members to engage with it. The performances provided context to the issue of social connectedness for elders, and shared a range of responses to several of the QoDs. The performers were positioned throughout the eight-storey atrium, moving slowly down to the large island itself where their voices and movements merged with audio from several artistic house calls. In one we called 'The Dance of the Driftwood', the three performers adapted a dance that Jim shared with me on an artistic house call in response to the question 'How does water move?' I had met with Jim and his wife Fran several times in the kitchen of their duplex. Fran was caring for Jim at home with the help of home care workers. I knew that Jim loved the outdoors. Because he was beyond language, I asked him a question that could be answered with movement. And in fact, in response to my question, Jim picked up a piece of driftwood from his kitchen table and danced with it for nearly thirty minutes.

The performance in City Hall also featured audio of a story by Ernest. Ernest answered many QoDs. When we asked him if would like an artistic house call, he said he would enjoy talking with someone on the phone to share stories. After months of talking with Sojourn performer James Hart on the phone, the opening day of the performance was the first time the two met in person. The brief performance ended with nearly 300 QoD cards floating down from the top floor of the atrium, and the performers inviting audience members to use them to start a conversation with a stranger.

Exhibit docents foster collaboration

Along with Graduate Assistant Sarah Freimuth, I coordinated a roster of volunteers from the partnership network to be docents at the six interactive question stations within the exhibition. Volunteers took two-hour shifts throughout the two full days of performances. Each station also featured an artfully designed card that profiled the programme through which we met an elder in the project. Docents engaged audience members, explaining the project, addressing the issue of social isolation and ringing a triangle every time someone answered a QoD and added it to the display. The docent system brought the exhibit alive, and enabled staff and volunteers from the various partnering agencies to talk and play with each other in a new collaborative setting.

City Hall setting attracts families

The partnership with Doors Open Milwaukee enabled us to engage with a diverse spectrum of people across race, age and gender. The design of the exhibit enticed the curious to listen to the voices of older adults and wrestle with issues of community connectedness. The City Hall setting also fostered a direct connection with civic officials, and positioned the elders as citizens, rather than recipients of social or medical service.

What did we learn and how?

We received Institutional Review Board human subjects' research approval for this project through UWM and gathered consent from all elders who received artistic house calls, all artists and all staff/volunteers who participated. To assess the benefits and challenges of this initial pilot, we analysed all field notes, minutes from stakeholder meetings, and two anonymous surveys sent to stakeholders, one in the middle of the project and one after the exhibit/performance was complete. A total of nine out of fifteen stakeholders responded to the survey that focused on if/how we accomplished our goals.

Our first goal was to create a sustainable partnership network to bring meaningful engagement to older adults living alone or under-connected to community. In response to the survey, 33 per cent of stakeholders said we were somewhat effective; 33 per cent said we were effective; 22 per cent said we were very effective; and 0 per cent responded with neutral, somewhat ineffective or ineffective. When asked to provide examples, comments focused on creating new partnerships, creating lasting and meaningful relationships with elders, and finding a simple way to engage elders. Stakeholder textual responses included: 'The meetings included a variety of partners all bringing special talents to the project'; 'The questions got people talking'; 'I thought the QoD was genius and really helped start conversations at the dining sites'; and 'Isolated seniors were physically connected to community members in an engaging way'. One response specifically pointed out the network of new relationships that were built through the process:

> A couple of participants have developed a lasting relationship with the artists they worked with – which is significant. Much of the

strategic building of the project created new kinds of relationships between entities that wouldn't previously communicate, or wouldn't have communicated about hopes, desires, imagination, the city, etc. Drivers seem to have gotten a lot out of this before they got tired of the questions.

When asked for suggestions to improve, respondents said we should expand to more meal dispatch sites, improve recording techniques and expand our volunteer base to better transition from QoDs to artistic house calls.

Our second goal was to 'create a public conversation about the importance of staying connected to community as we age'. The survey revealed the following results: 33 per cent of respondents said we were somewhat effective; 33 per cent said we were effective; 22 per cent said we were very effective; 0 per cent responded with neutral, somewhat ineffective, or ineffective. When asked for specific examples, respondents pointed to the Crossings events and the intergenerational audiences at the City Hall exhibit and performance. When asked for suggestions for improvement, respondents pointed to greater media exposure.

Finally, we asked stakeholders how they would like to continue the project. Stakeholders provided a wide range of responses, including: 63 per cent would hold workshops for staff/volunteers in creative engagement; 63 per cent would feature the creative expression of older adults living alone in their various communication systems; 50 per cent would collaborate to hold more Crossings events; 88 per cent would continue to develop QoDs and distribute them to their networks; 88 per cent would continue to like to collaborate with artists in some way. When surveyed for general feedback about the project, respondents said that as the project evolved, they grew more engaged, and that as the partnerships formed, they felt 'a network of organizations that had a wealth of basic assistance, but a dearth of social/emotional assistance' began to talk about arts and imagination – 'Keep it up!'

Beyond survey: What we learned

After analysing field notes from logistics team meetings (graduate students and myself), artistic team meetings (Sojourn members and Basting) and stakeholder meetings (core partners and Basting), we identified several key elements to the success of the project.

Language is crucial

We spent an entire stakeholder meeting coming to agreement on a tagline for the project – one in which staff, families, artists and elders would recognize themselves. We also wrestled with how to refer to targets of the project. 'Social isolation', 'lonely', 'under-served' and 'homebound' are not words elders embraced or recognized for themselves. We arrived at 'older adults living alone or under-connected to community'. We include 'finding a common language' as an outcome in our grant proposals to ensure that we allow time for this crucial process and that it is recognized as a foundational step on which to build a project. Early in the project, we also realized that a barrier to participation was that partnering staff and volunteers were describing the project as 'arts and crafts'. When we encouraged staff and volunteers to shift from leading with language of the arts towards 'Questions of the Day', this barrier eased considerably.

The creative feedback loop is crucial

Elders, volunteers and staff all need to know 'where are these answers going', or they will lose faith in the process and tire of responding. We initially thought that radio would be the best way to create a high-profile, high-value way to share the stories back with respondents, but realized that few participants were listening to the broadcasts. To counteract this, we sent discs of the radio segments to meal sites and meal dispatch sites. We also created 'micro-exhibits' that could go back out through the Home Delivered Meals drivers to the people who responded. These were small booklets that featured highlighted QoDs and a range of the handwritten answers (captured with a graphic design program) we received.

The Meal Site participants did not feel as connected to the feedback loop. Posters with responses we made were not distributed or were posted on bulletin boards removed from the diners. They were 'tired' of the process of answering QoDs, according to staff. Participants need to feel a connection between question, response, the joining of that response to other voices, and the building upon all responses by artists. They need to feel the direct path of answer to community building and meaning-making.

Learn the systems and build into their strengths

We spent nearly a year in meetings, site visits and ride-alongs learning the systems in place to reach older adults living alone and under-connected to community. We held stakeholder meetings to identify goals and language for the project. Only through this process were we able to engage such a broad range of people in the process of creative engagement to accomplish our goals. It also enabled us to create a process that fitted into the strengths and capacities of each group, that encouraged their own creativity, and that would ensure that the process could continue.

Communicate, communicate, communicate

To maintain the momentum of the partnership network between meetings, and to grow the public dialogue about the issues at the root of the project, we created a newsletter that went out each month. We printed and mailed it to those without computers. We updated our Twitter feed, website and Facebook page regularly to engage staff, families and volunteers associated with our network and their partners. We planned rolling press exposure to maintain a presence in the public eye throughout the process and build a sense of anticipation for the final exhibit/performance. It proved important to our goals to re-explain our project multiple times to multiple stakeholders, so that administrators, staff and volunteers could witness the impact their ideas had on the shaping of the project, just as we were creating feedback loops for the participants.

Peer-to-peer training is crucial

Once the Home Delivered Meals drivers came on board, the project blossomed. When a volunteer or staff member understood how the QoD could be used to deepen relationships and invite creative expression, we invited them to share their thoughts with others. As we prepare to expand to more meal dispatch sites, we will deepen the peer training component as well, modelling the engagement in video to share with other drivers.

Artistic house calls should respond to the individual's interests and invite them to grow. Angie wanted to experiment with painting so we arranged for a painter to visit with her. We also invited her to stretch herself and write a poem. Bill shared stories about his farm. We invited him to adapt the lyrics to a hymn to create an original song based on his stories. We learned to always listen to the participants' interests – to always invite people to grow; and, indeed, to listen to when they have had enough. People certainly have the choice to detach from the project. After several visits, one of our house call participants told us he was done. We sent him a thank you packet and left open the invitation to engage us again.

Looking forward

The goals of IoM were set on creating a sustainable system and partnership network to bring creative engagement to elders living alone or under-connected to community. It did not specify ability or disability. This marks a shift in approach to working with elders from disease-specific towards inclusion. Rather than focus centrally on elder participation, IoM focused on the collaboration between elders and their care partners and on the systems that support those care partners. IoM extends the improvisational 'yes, and' approach from TimeSlips, from individuals and small groups towards systems themselves. By doing this, the benefits of such applied theatre practices can become sustainable over time; by doing this, we shift focus from identifying elders by diagnosis, towards accessibility – making sure that creative activities are adaptable to all elders.

While the QoD and the project website were designed to be a tool for volunteers, staff and family, without an ongoing energy source to create content and drive traffic, use of the site has been minimal. We aim to expand the project from two to four Home Delivered Meal dispatch sites, including videos of peer-to-peer training/advocacy, but, as of this writing, have not yet received funding to support this effort. Still, the evolution of the IoM project continues. The partnering organizations from IoM were invited to join the Creative Trust, an alliance of care communities and programmes committed to fostering life-long learning through the arts (www.creativetrustmke.com). This group meets quarterly to brainstorm and shape creative projects that are then carried out in collaboration – most commonly with Peck School of the Arts students and faculty focused on community-engaged practice.

In 2015, I received a grant to support eight Student Artists in Residence (SAIRs) that would be partnered and placed in a Creative Trust site. Two of those SAIRs are currently working in IoM sites to continue the evolution of the project. Each spring, collaborative arts projects that are part of the Creative Trust are featured in the Flourish Festival. Also as of this writing, I am in the beginning phases of a large-scale project that can engage elders through the IoM network and the network of care homes in the Creative Trust and will culminate in an intergenerational, city-wide celebration.

In closing, I return to Shannon Jackson's prescient thoughts – that in the practice of applied theatre, we not only foster expression of the under-represented and vulnerable but also engage and imagine how the systems that are built to support them can be mobilized to make those efforts sustainable. The improvisational roots of the work, that invite and celebrate the creative imaginings of people with memory loss, can be extended into the care systems themselves to bring staff, family, volunteers and elders – regardless of their range of abilities – into community.

Performing and Ageing: A Conversation with Mike Pearson

Sheila McCormick

Mike Pearson is the foremost authority on site-specific performance in the UK. Internationally renowned, he is a theatre maker, scholar and teacher. As Emeritus Professor of Performance Studies at Aberystwyth University and with forty-five years experience in performance, Pearson is a highly influential figure in contemporary British and international theatre. He is co-author with Michael Shanks of *Theatre/Archaeology* (2001) and author of *In Comes I: Performance, Memory and Landscape* (2006), *Site-Specific Performance* (2010), *Mickery Theater: An Imperfect Archaeology* (2011) and *Marking Time: Performance, Archaeology and the City* (2013).

Pearson's work is rooted in Wales with companies such as RAT Theatre, Cardiff Laboratory Theatre and BrithGof (of which he was a founding member). His work also translates internationally with successful collaborations with European companies including Eugenio Barba's Odin Teatret in Denmark. He has devised, directed or performed in over one hundred pieces of performance, at times doing all three. Most recently, his long-time collaboration with artist and designer Mike Brookes has yielded the *The Persians* (2010), *Coriolan/us* (2012) and *Iliad* (2015) for National Theatre Wales.

In 2012, Pearson was awarded a two-year Major Research Fellowship by the Leverhulme Trust for a project entitled 'Marking Time: Performance, Archaeology and the City'. The funding allowed for a series of research activities and public engagements including organized guided tours, demonstrations, workshops and the restaging of performances that trace the origins and development of theatre making in Cardiff, Wales from the 1960s to the present day. The project allowed Pearson to chart and locate procedures of theatre making from his past within wider cultural, social and political contexts with his findings being published and disseminated in a book with the same name.

In relation to *Applied Theatre: Creative Ageing*, these findings also allow for an interesting examination of personal ageing. Several of the research activities attached to that project are discussed in this interview, including the restaging of his two extended solo performances – the mainly physical 'Flesh' and the largely spoken 'Asylum' from *The Lesson of Anatomy* (1974) in 2014;[1] and his on-going work with elders theatre group Good News from the Future.

On 5 July 2014, I was privileged to see Pearson perform *The Lesson of Anatomy* at the Sherman Cymru theatre, Cardiff. The piece, based on the writings of Antonin Artaud, had previously been performed on 5 July 1974 by Pearson with the then newly founded Cardiff Laboratory for Theatrical Research (later Cardiff Laboratory Theatre) in the Sherman Arena during that theatre's opening season. In the forty years that have passed, both experimental theatre and Pearson as a performer have developed and changed. Thus, the restaging offered a unique opportunity to observe the influence of the passage of time on theatre practice.

Knowing little about the event prior to attending, I was unaware that it would mark a seminal moment in my experience of contemporary performance and would offer a poignant reminder of the impacts of ageing on the performer and performance manifestation. On both dates, Pearson performed with many of the same audience members in attendance. Some of these were colleagues and friends of Pearson who had worked with him from his early days and aged alongside him as part of the theatre community of Cardiff and beyond.

Attempting the original choreography but with little by way of a script, Pearson relied on images taken of the original performance by his friend Steve Allison. These images provided a text of sorts through which to chart the performance. Accompanying the 2014 event, the book of images designed by Allison includes stills from both performances, providing an artefact to document the original performance, its restaging forty years later and the adaptive means by which this was achieved. Serving as a beautiful reminder of the temporal shift between the performances, the images also provide a visual document of the life lived by Pearson in the interim. The fresh-faced performer in the earlier images, with shaven head and long lean limbs is juxtaposed throughout by its aged counterpart serving not only to highlight Pearson's remarkable ability to perform but also the strategies and allowances created to enable the two iterations of *The Lesson of Anatomy*.

Lessons of Anatomy

SMcC: *What interests me is the sort of segregatory notions about ageing. You hit an age and suddenly you are older. So having come to see* The Lesson of Anatomy *what seemed very interesting to me was the notion of the passing of time, the memory of it and the experience of it in the present, the physical body that you are in now and the one that existed in your 'youth' and the relationship between the two. If I can just ask you about* The Lesson of Anatomy *performance, the restaged performance and how that came about first?*

MP: I've got to rewind to *In Comes I* – the book and the project – which is about memory, about memories of my childhood in relation to specific places in the Lincolnshire landscape. In performing the work in 2000 with a group of villagers, my relatives and others, I became aware of two things: one was that they were constantly correcting me during the performance, adding information too or even contradicting whatever I said. Although I had learned a very long text (two hours), there was a constant addition to what I was talking about. And the second was that every time I stopped speaking, they started because this was the landscape of their childhood too (sorry I made the jump there, the book focuses upon the specific performance *Bubbling Tom* performed on the streets of Hibaldstow in 2000, and visiting places important for me at the age of six). I became fascinated by this relationship between memory and place and how actual locations can act as a mnemonic – to open up, unlock deep histories: when we stand in the school yard, what kind of histories are revealed from that multigenerational group. And it did seem to me that the work could be regarded as multigenerational, that it could appeal to an audience of very different ages. When then I came to formulate the Marking Time project (which is an attempt to make a complement to *In Comes I* and *Bubbling Tom* but within an urban context – to think about Cardiff once again) I was interested in the way that specific places acted as containers of memory. That had two very practical outcomes: one was the way that visiting places helped to recall events and particular performances there. The spin-off of that was the coach tour that Heike Roms and I organized, taking an audience to these locations to collectively remember certain events from the past. The second was to wonder whether the places themselves could help to recall performance in detail, practically, so rather than being a work of memory being a practical project. Looking at the material I had, it seemed to me that with *The Lesson of Anatomy*, were it possible to stage it in the very place it had been conceived, that would be extremely stimulating, because the material conditions had not altered there that much. What had changed was me, and so that became the ambition. Then to begin to look at the documentary material that exists; it's relatively thin but there is the series of 156 black and white photographs that my friend and colleague Steve Allison took in 1974.

SMcC: *And your words as well ...*

MP: Yes and my words. They came the year after ... or a few months after the event.

SMcC: *So they are reflections.*

MP: Yes, they are more like reflections, but they must've been very close [in time] because the account of the process is quite precise. The act of recovery was to order those photographs: fortunately, we do have the contact sheets, so we can order them. And then to pitch in. Physically I was aware that objects like the table and the suit were extremely important in the process of recollection because the work wasn't choreographed *per se*. In the present, I still had to find the same kind of physical logic to put it together. This wasn't the kind of authentic... somehow working from the film or whatever ... the physical work was marginally easier than the textual work.

SMcC: *Really?*

MP Yes.... With the text, there are only a dozen photographs of what I was doing there. There aren't a great number of recorded actions that would enable you to recall a certain text going with them, so I had to work from clues in notebook. It would be two words or a line from the text – that's how I had to archaeologically put the script together. It was close but I can't pretend that it was exactly what was said in 1974. Certain sections I remember really well. I remember saying that thing; otherwise, I was completely lost. I never worked without the table; we had it from the outset. I was able to work in Aberystwyth; I worked with Nigel Watson my colleague in the over-sixties group and Louise Ritchie – looking at the original work, thinking about it. The difference of course is the degree of abandonment that is no longer possible.

SMcC: *Mentally or physically?*

MP: Physically .... mentally I ... well ...

SMcC: *Because there is a certain bravery ...*

MP: Yes. I'm well aware that in 1974 I was jumping off the table; and in 2014, I was putting my hand on the table, and then jumping off. It's all about elasticity and the joints ....

SMcC: *But also about the certain level of bravery needed physically to do those things? Looking back at the images (referring to the book) I keep thinking about Kristeva and abjection. The body, the smelling, touching, licking, all of that must have taken a certain level of bravery?*

MP: In 1974, it was quite shocking in a way but on the other hand the social and cultural tenor of the times was quite different; we expected to see that kind of thing in theatre in 1974 …

SMcC: *And how about 2014?*

MP: Well now there's a kind of transgression: to see a 64-year-old man doing it, that's the difference. A 64-year-old doing it, without drawing attention to it in any kind of way, that's the added poignancy to the work. It's actually about the decay of the body and the way it's changed.

SMcC: *But you don't mark that at all… in the opening …*

MP: No absolutely, absolutely not …

SMcC: *That's really important, I hadn't seen the book so I didn't know the image of you as a younger man. I had nothing to go on which was of course different for other audience members who had been at the original performance. Can I ask you about that wonderful moment when you took your teeth out.*

MP: (*laughs*) It's trangressive, yeah, sure. In 1974, the transgressive acts were things like shaving my head at a period when all my colleagues had very long hair. Nobody knew I'd done it until the moment of popping my head out.

SMcC: *I'm thinking about the specific moments, the moment of the sound of the match being struck for example, and the sort of intrigued literal navel gazing and moment the character discovers sexual pleasure. I think you describe it in the book feeling an enjoyment, then fear, then rapture, then absolute fear.*

MP: There is a 'turning out' and a 'turning in' that we talked a lot about. David Wiles has done some work about the impact of the black box studio that is quite profound in this context. I can't work out whether in the relationship of space and exposition it's a sort of chicken and egg – the fact is that you're on stage and in full view all the time with nowhere to go. This changes performative techniques substantially (sorry this is a fairly obvious) – because there's no fourth wall, then there's nothing to look into. There was that moment in the late 1960s when performance turned and faced the audience, so in 1974 that would not have been unusual, me looking at the audience all the time, talking as if I'm talking to the audience and so on and so on. But maybe in 2014 that kind of work... in a way that might be quite odd.

SMcC: *In that moment you were exploring your body it's very clear that we are watching you because the houselights are up and we can see each at each other watching a man explore himself, it is sort of a communal voyeurism.*

MP: In 1974, a kind theatrical filter hadn't yet descended. A lot of the people making theatre were not trained actors or where not coming out of a [conventional] way of producing. And they weren't being educated by people in the practices of their favourite groups from when they were students... because there weren't any. The difference in *The Lesson of Anatomy* was that the two young French directors Jean Grémion and Patrick Guinand were coming out of a particular French theatrical tradition. There was a particular expectation – I worked alone quite a lot of the time, days by myself in a room; and them coming at the end of the day and asking to see what I'd done ... I'd start to show it and they would just walk out (*laughs*). It was very hard. There were no fixed methodologies in training for physical theatre ...

SMcC: *So no one was heading to study with Lecoq?*

MP: Absolutely no, and it was all being created by the groups themselves from exercises they were getting from here and there, from work they'd seen; that was a very strong impetus of the time. Great, let's try that, let's try and do that as well, that thing we saw. Can we do that as well? And so technique – it was more of a collection of things that made sense at the time..

SMcC: *Those techniques have changed and developed over the course of your career, so restaging* The Lesson of Anatomy *in 2014, did you recall these techniques? Were you remembering not just the way you did things but the way you found things? You have got the techniques that you have now but in recalling your technique then you're remembering being a sort of novice ...*

MP: Yes and again there is that strange moment in between. What
            happened was in the early/mid-1990s a group of us in BrithGof
            realized, or I realized, I had notebooks and notebooks full
            of exercises but basically these exercises were only doing a
            dozen things. So we set out to develop what we called In All
            Languages which is a physical technique that one that can use
            with colleagues of any experience. It's quite a sophisticated
            thing and we are using in the over-sixties group. You could
            use it with children; you could use it with mature colleagues,
            but doing *The Lesson of Anatomy* I almost had to forget that
            moment. It was like an archaeology of techniques: it was going
            back to a point before that formalization; trying to remember
            what that material was, and what the ways of working were.
            In the rehearsals for the 2014 performance, Nigel Watson was
            working with me one day and the camera was rolling – he
            just started reminiscing and then demonstrating things he
            remembered from 1974. There was still this terrific impulse in
            what he was doing.

SMcC: *Like muscle memory.*

MP: Like that, but we were trying to remember what we saw a
            specific exercise and the moment when we first saw it. I don't
            think I went back to the exercises themselves in developing
            The Lesson of Anatomy (2014), but I was trying to recall the
            attitudes that they engendered exactly.

SMcC: *There's an image just as you say that … an image that I was
            fascinated by in the book. It's where you enter the stage for the
            second time and (even as a younger man) suddenly seem older,
            pathetic even. But I look at the images of you as an older man
            doing the same action and it's different, I don't see the same level
            of pathetic. You're in almost exactly the same position but there's
            something dignified about the second image.*

MP: What you can't do is strip out what has happened physically
            between then and now, what traces there are in the body.
            I don't know whether you remember in the discussion after the
            show – André [Stitt] would just not let it rest. I was quite tired

so I couldn't work out the question that he was asking. I think what his basic question was, was – Why would you want to do that? At the age of twenty-three or twenty-four, why would you want to do that?

SMcC: *Why not?*

MP: I was trying to explain that it was the moment; and that maybe now I had actually caught up with the text.

SMcC: *I can understand that. For a 24-year-old, the physical and mental challenge is understanding what it would be like for Artaud in the last two years of his life. One might think as the 64-year-old man you would find it be easier to play that section, to understand the exhausted, pathetic nature of the text and so there's almost this lovely dichotomy where in the images you see a 24-year-old struggling to understand a man who has sort of lived far beyond those years.*

MP: That was Andre's implication, so maybe in some way I did manage to get under the skin of the text in 2014; and he couldn't imagine how that would ever have been the same when I was twenty-four.

SMcC: *But then I suppose that's the experience, trying something and then living life and then trying to remember, to remember what it was like before trying again. It is interesting as a whole but there is something about the first section ['Flesh'], the exploration of ageing body that is really beautiful. There is a quote in the book in relation to* The Lesson of Anatomy *specifically where you question 'how additional dramatic affects may result from the impact of ageing on the performer'. So it seems in 2014, it's not just about reproducing an event, it's something more which I feel like I saw that in that picture.*

MP: Yes, but how to do that, without making reference to it if you like. That's the point.

SMcC: *So highlighting the age.*

MP: Highlighting the age, exactly. That's the point very definitely with the so-called over-sixties group. But again, the last thing we're ever going to talk about is ageing.

Good News from the Future

SMcC: *Terminology around ageing, I'm uncomfortable, I don't know what terms to use with older adults but at the same time, I'm ageing. We are all ageing. I am forty next year and have felt age more profoundly in the last two years that ever before. What does that word mean to you?*

MP: We're the baby boomers; we never thought we'd get old anyway, so I'm not sure we've got a settled terminology for it. I'm not even sure we are likely to refer to it when we're talking about the work. That's why we decided to call the group Good News from the Future maybe. Most terms are unnecessary. I got my bus pass, I got my state pension but I don't feel like a pensioner. It's very odd. We recently had a social evening, fifteen of us, all of the group and we sat and watched Pina Bausch's *Kontakthof with Ladies and Gentlemen over '65* – what a great way to put it, that's just it, so 'for the ladies and gentlemen over 65' ...

SMcC: *A friend was recently talking about having a baby at forty and being termed 'geriatric' by the medical profession; at forty you're a geriatric mother. And there are other phrases that are equally challenging; that just seem inappropriate in relation to current notions of ageing.*

MP: Yes, it was interesting reading Mick Mangan's book, *Staging Ageing* – a lot of that was about representations of ageing as opposed to 'mature performers'. But there are some striking moments – like Michael Gambon's decision not to continue with stage work because he can't actually remember the text in the way that he once could.

SMcC: *But then there is Peggy Shaw's* Ruff. *After her stroke, she and Lois Weaver worked together to make sure she can still perform despite issues with memory. They developed strategies together. They have worked out ways to facilitate each other's ageing as performers and that interests me, the notion that you can have cooperative relationships with other artists so that you can all continue to create.*

MP: With Good News from the Future, two things become apparent: one is that everybody is entirely happy in their own skin, so nobody is having an identity crisis during the work, so …

SMcC: *So I'm going to feel young and make theatre work to make myself feel young kind of thing?*

MP: No, I can be totally stupid because I don't care. I can go and touch you because I'll touch you and there's no other implication other than I'm touching you. And we can do this ridiculous thing because there's nothing to lose. All of those things becoming an interesting dynamic. What they do is bring back that late 1960s and early 1970s ethos. So here it is, but we're not doing it in parenthesis, as if we are pretending to be hippies again. It simply comes back, but it's got that patina of ageing on it …

SMcC: *These people you worked with before, so professional theatre makers, but isn't there also an applied theatre community element to it.*

MP: It's mixed and that's a great thing about it. With the method that we are working with, whether one is experienced or not isn't relevant; there is a levelling out. What comes back quite strongly is a group ethos … and care. All of those initiatives that we were involved with in the late 1960s/early 1970s, whether artistic or social or whatever, they were all self-help; they weren't institutionally bound, we didn't have to create institutions to operate. I'm curious about what that ethos of self-help can do now because I'm fairly certain in ten years' time nobody is one going to want to look after us, so we might as well start looking after each other.

SMcC: *So caring for each other.*

MP: Yes; and in performance, there's always that element of care. The recovery of that ethos, as well as certain kinds of technique and attitudes from that period are equally socially valuable.

SMcC: *So do you think there is the same level of care as when you were working in the 1970s or community?*

MP: Of community, absolutely, But our companies were bound together in ways that might not be very appropriate these days *(laughs)*. For example, Nigel Watson was in a company called Triple Action and I was in RAT theatre and we held a Triple Action versus RAT workshop – which was just to see who was going to be left standing.

SMcC: *So that feeling like there isn't going to be a certain amount of care in ten years' time and here in Good News from the Future is a practice for care, how do you think that fits with the applied label. Do you think this is something that could be taken as a template and translated elsewhere or do you think that that's a very specific set of circumstances with a specific group of people?*

MP: In the long view, I am always suspicious of terminology. When I graduated, the first year that I worked, I worked in a community theatre group [Transitions]. That's what we called it. In the 1970s, the Welsh Arts Council funded a theatre-in-education company in every county. And so on and so on and so on. There are currently different levels of socially engaged work and there just seems to be a moment where it is a 'thing' but what is really interesting is that is it comes in a moment of complete de-politicization so it doesn't seem to be an agency of political change. We know all agencies of political change fail but you should still try.

SMcC: *The reason I ask is because I shudder a bit with the interest in dementia. There are a lot of people who were elderly or growing older who have different needs, some of which have nothing to do with memory. The other thing is the notion of measurement. Everything has to be measured, evaluated if it's going to continue. And what happens if things don't continue? What happens to those relationships? But Good News from the Future seems sustainable. It does not rely on funding so does not need constant evaluation.*

MP: No absolutely not.

SMcC: *So that's why I see it potentially as a sort of template for other groups. Although it's strength also seems to lie in the fact that it has been built from the ground up.*

MP: Sure, forty years ago if you told me I was espousing a certain methodology then I would've run a mile; but with In All Languages we did work hard to offer an opportunity to be physically engaged and without complex training, and that's its benefit. And it is very transferable.

SMcC: *Can you explain In All Languages more?*

MP: Ornette Coleman [1930–2015] is a jazz man of a certain age; he is one of my heroes, and in the early 1960s he developed this method call harmolodics, a combination of harmony and melody that not many people understand. Pat Metheny, the guitarist, he understands it and they recorded together. It is a kind of principle or set of principles of improvisation that Ornette worked with. He made a double album [*In All Languages*] and the first record is his quartet from the 1960s and the second his electric band, with two guitarists from the late 1980s. They are playing with same principles, from the 1960s to the late 1980s. And that's why I wanted to call it In All Languages. For Good News from the Future, there are these principles from the 1970s that we were still using the 1990s and now; so that was the idea. It's not complex but it is about principles: it's not necessarily about this exercise or that exercise; instead we boiled it down to principles …

SMcC: *What would I see if I were in the room?*

MP: So, there are three solos, three duets, three groups – and each consists of ten words or movements. For one solo, it might be fall, clap, jump … Duo two works with mirroring, copying, modelling …. Once the movements are set then articulations are introduced. Each series has ten articulations; for example, more or less time, size, more or less energy, repetition, do it backwards, do it with a different part of the body. Then there are ten what we call mediations; so again, for example, do it on concrete, do it under water, do it with a sound track. When you put all that together in an improvisation it takes quite a long time but you can develop very sophisticated work. It's a language and what's nice about that is you can speak it with anyone else who can speak it. Now that sounds awfully prescriptive but it's not meant to be. It is to enable even the most trepidatious colleague to begin immediately. Because there's no qualitative judgement on how you're doing it.

SMcC: *Sounds great.*

MP: But of course because one disabled performer Dave Levett couldn't stand [during the development of In All Languages], then we simply did the work mediated – the mediation was to do it lying on the floor.

SMcC: *So there's an equality, if there is one person who can't do a certain move then everyone has to find an alternative.*

MP: Exactly, but then for Good News from the Future it's all there; but there is that quality of care about it and that quality of care is for oneself and for one's colleagues. Nevertheless people are doing the most ridiculous and extraordinary things.

All of those exercises that we were doing in the past: what were the principles? If you're improvising with somebody what are you doing with them? Very often you're actually mirroring what they're doing. Just thinking about what the base is of what you're observing … And physical improvisation … It's about getting down to this nub and then you can go anywhere you like.

SMcC: *Do you ever add intention?*

MP: No because you have to deal with circumstances as they come at you. You can add intention but you can't guarantee anybody will respond to that intention. What we do is provide a basic format for the work: just as a simple principle, that every time you meet somebody, something is going to happen. So that's the simplest kind of format. You could go up to somebody and start doing mirroring and they might think that you're doing something else entirely, so they'll start doing that. You constantly have to work out what is this thing that we're doing together. It's fun to do, and it's also really serious. It needs a level of concentration which again is quite useful: the more you concentrate the more complex it can become. Equally, it can happen in a much more relaxed manner as well.

SMcC: *But do you think it's successful now because you have those relationships?*

MP: We developed it and we tried it. When it comes to working with more mature colleagues, labelling doesn't seem to be very useful.

SMcC: *I love that idea of care though. And you obviously spend a lot of time together, so it's not just about to practice.*

MP: There are two things: one is more careful of oneself; and one is hopefully more careful of others. One hopes being careful about one's self doesn't change or alter the physical attitude – as in 'I'm being careful' – but it also then becomes a kind of meter on engagement with others. With In All Languages, if you suddenly confront somebody and you enter into physical improvisation, then those two levels of care are operating, care for myself and also the person I'm working with. This then creates the quality in the work. It is an unforced thing but when I look at it and watch my colleagues working I can see that it is there. You can see it in Pina Bausch's work *With Ladies and Gentlemen over '65.*

SMcC: *Do you see that with younger people?*

MP: No because they want to be seen. That's the kind of interesting thing in an improvisation, they want to get as close to you as they can in order that you see them doing it.

SMcC: *So how does that relate then to the Marking Time project, to bringing forward forty years of devised theatre? How does that all link together?*

MP: Well that was a whole series of things... as I illustrate in the book, first to do this series of walks where certain histories of performance are recognized as not being divorced from the architecture, the social history the city, and so on. Then to look specifically at work from my history in relation to those locations and consider whether precise moments were recoverable. I've been struck by the notion of the revenant, that moment when you get all of the original circumstances together and the past suddenly comes flying back only in a ghostly way.

SMcC: *That's what it felt like in the audience to certain extent. I almost felt like a visitor, even though I wasn't. As an audience member, I understood the context. Here were a group of people experiencing an event that recalled their experience of a past event and all that was happening in a relationship with the performer who was doing the same thing. I was watching the performance but also the people. I was watching people who were experiencing the past while you were experiencing the past.*

MP: That was the experience of doing *Bubbling Tom* because they were the 'inside insiders'.

SMcC: *Does it feel backwards [book first then practice]?*

MP: It does feel backwards, but then it did give me more time in the second year of the project to think about the practical components, about what these workshops for a mature group, for Good News from the Future, would look like.

SMcC: And *the idea of doing the performance to teenagers.*

MP: Yes, we (Nigel and I) are aiming towards making a performance, and we've got two things in mind. One is to create an improvisational piece using In All Languages, and I think it sustains it well. There are a couple of other things we've got quite fascinated by. One is the book for actors called *The Characters* by Theophrastus. It was written in 319 BC; it's a description of character types in theatre but all of the good characters are lost, so it's just the bad characters.

SMcC: *Genuinely lost? Or lost kind of in the book?*

MP: They are genuinely lost so it's only the bad characters – like the Toady and the Chatterer – he is the kind of bloke who comes down and sits next to you and starts talking about his wife and the weather and how many foreigners there are in Athens, wow fantastic! So we think there is a way that within In All Language improvisations these characters could appear just for a moment; and so, if we could work out an improvisation technique where suddenly all fifteen participants are the same character to the point where it becomes abstract improvisation. That's one thing we will aim at, and that is feasible within the way we've been working. Nigel has then got an idea for a second shorter piece he thinks we could work on – Orpheus – because we did wonder whether metamorphosis might throw up some interesting images for a mature group of mature performers. But that would be more formal, more theatrical work, so I suspect that might take much longer to bring about, particularly if we are only working [once] every fortnight.

SMcC: *So how many of these participants still acts professionally? Has there been a period of the time where they most haven't acted or made theatre?*

MP: Many have worked [professionally] but the group is also composed of hobbyists. There is a tradition in Cardiff of a mature dance company and some colleagues have worked with that, so they have done physical work. There are also a number of old colleagues from Cardiff including funders and administrators as well as artists plus enthusiasts – all making work together.

SMcC: *And do you think as a group you have any political motivation or is it not really about that?*

MP: Well I hope by revealing a certain age group in society, making provocative work, then that is political. Also in recent years in Wales, traditions of alternative theatre practice have all but disappeared. If they could suddenly spring back in the most unexpected manner by this group of 65-year-olds, politically and within cultural policy that might be really challenging.

SMcC: *So as you've gotten older has what you're thematically interested in changed?*

MP: Well again that was what was interesting recalling these Artaud texts. The question by André was why would one want to do that; it is difficult to remember the currency that Artaud had at that time largely because the work was only being translated throughout the 1960s and so people weren't very aware of it … those texts that we used from the last period of his life were obviously theatrical but relatively less well known in Britain. Now kids 'do' Artaud but they have no idea what it's about. My Aberystwyth colleagues wanted me to come and do the show to students in Aberystwyth in order to reintroduce

Artaud who seems to have fallen out of a central currency of theatrical thinking. The big question to me now is, given the chance, would I be looking at Artaud texts ... In recent years, Mike Brookes and I have made *The Persians*, *Coriolanus* and *Iliad* with National Theatre Wales.

SMcC: *So it doesn't have to be thematically driven?*

MP: Not thematically no. As theatre makers we're always as concerned with the mechanics, the challenges, as with the theme.

SMcC: *So the themes haven't changed as you've gotten older?*

MP: *(laughs)* Well, I'm just wondering whether I should do anything after *Iliad* because the very first thing we did in university was the *Odyssey*. Start off with Homer and end with Homer. That's really perfect.

SMcC: *Don't say that (laughs). To finish up, I am wondering about two things. You get asked about archaeology all the time and I'm interested in this notion of archaeology of memory and what you still recall or don't recall. For example, you seem more interested in mechanics over the thematic, where does that come from? You've got all of these experiences as a theatre maker, what do you choose to get rid of and what do you choose to keep and how do you as an archaeologist dig through whatever those memories are because you've got forty years of practice to draw on?*

MP: Yes well you heard it here first. Michael Shanks and I are going to do a new version of *Theatre/Archaeology*, revise the book [of 2001]. I'm not sure whether we're going to call it the *Theatre/Archaeology*. What we are thinking about is what has happened in the fifteen years since it was first published. What has happened in the interim? If I look at Michael's writing now he talks about pragmatics. To remember to work pragmatically again is most useful .... So having these experiences ... you just select in any one moment ... you intuit what may or may not be useful. Plugging some stylistic through-line or whatever is never helpful. It's about looking at circumstance and opportunity.

SMcC: *So do you disregard or is everything stored, ready just to be pulled out when necessary?*

MP: The problem is that when you get to a certain age or when (you know Mike Brooks is not, I mean he's only just 50) you've been working together for seventeen/eighteen years, people try to work out what your strategy is. But we just stand around quite a lot of the time without speaking to each other, filtering all that stuff to address – what the moment really needs.

Community Arts and Creative Well-Being for Dementia

Beth Luxmoore

Dementia and creativity

Dementia is fast becoming one of the most prevalent conditions across the globe. In the UK, 850,000 people are living with dementia. The likelihood of developing dementia increases significantly with age, with one in every fourteen people over the age of sixty-five in the UK affected (Alzheimer's Society, 2014), making dementia one of the most significant challenges facing an ageing population.

Dementia can impact all cognitive abilities including memory, concentration, language, visuospatial skills, inhibitions and orientation, with each individual's experience of the condition as unique as that person. As a condition that affects every aspect of a person's life, the support provided for people living with dementia should not be limited to addressing only medical needs and instead should address all aspects of well-being (Killick and Allan, 1999).

Alternative and complementary approaches to care can provide a wide range of benefits, even beyond the management of psychological and behavioural symptoms, including reduced feelings of isolation, physical exercise and enjoyment. The person-centred care model (Kitwood, 1997) draws the focus away from the person as entirely defined by the disease with all emphasis on deficit and deterioration. Instead, an individual's abilities are considered and opportunities are provided to improve or enhance existing cognitive function.

Over recent decades there has been increased interest and evidence to support the use of the arts as an intervention within health and social care (Clift et al., 2009), and interest in the scope and power of such interventions as a method of supporting people to live well with dementia has grown (Beard, 2011).

Many people living with dementia experience non-cognitive symptoms which can manifest themselves as behavioural and psychological changes. These may include, but are not limited to, agitation, aggression, changes in mood and psychosis (Douglas et al., 2004). Guidelines for the treatment of these symptoms recommend first excluding the possibility of physical illness; secondly using non-pharmacological interventions and only using pharmaceutical interventions as a last resort (NICE, 2012).

In practice, however, non-pharmaceutical interventions are often overlooked, ultimately resulting in the inappropriate prescription of antipsychotic medications. A review, produced by the Department of Health (2009), found that 180,000 people with dementia in the UK are prescribed antipsychotic medication, around 23 per cent of the total population of people living with dementia. It was found that 78 per cent of these prescriptions were inappropriate (Department of Health, 2009).

Antipsychotic medications can have significant, adverse side effects including sedation, falls and movement disorders (Douglas et al., 2004). Studies have also indicated that these medications may contribute to reductions in quality of life (QoL) through limiting physical abilities and increased marginalization (Ballard et al., 2001) and can accelerate the rate of cognitive decline (McShane et al., 1997).

The use of non-pharmaceutical interventions, if successful, has the potential to forestall the use of antipsychotic medications with their adverse side effects. Indeed, multisensory stimulation, leisure pursuits, arts activities and social interactions for people with dementia, properly supported by their loved ones, carers, health professionals, therapists and artists can ensure activities are meaningful, beneficial and enjoyable for the individual with dementia.

Taking part in activities that provide cognitive stimulation has been shown to improve cognitive function with additional positive effects on social interaction, communication and QoL (Woods et al., 2012). Arts-based activities can provide opportunities for creativity, self-expression, communication and physical activity and can offer an alternative approach to meeting people's need to a more traditional medicalized model.

The application of arts as an intervention for people living with dementia is a developing field of interest. Beard's review of art therapies for dementia care (2011) presents a comprehensive summary of the literature and illustrates the use of a range of techniques to achieve specified medical outcomes, such as behaviour modification and symptom reduction. Beard stresses the need for a new focus on personal experience and outcomes related to QoL, and the report highlights the lack of studies based in community settings as opposed to residential care facilities.

It has been suggested that the creative and expressive nature of the arts can provide valuable opportunities for people with dementia to connect; to their creative selves and to others, even when cognitive and physical abilities are diminished. For example, neurologist Oliver Sacks succinctly presented the potential for arts to improve the well-being of all people living with dementia: 'however great the organic damage… there remains the undiminished possibility of reintegration by art, by communion, by touching the human spirit: and this can be preserved in what seems at first a hopeless state of neurological devastation' (1985: 39).

An example of the potential efficacy of arts-based services to improve well-being for people living with dementia is Singing for the Brain. This pioneering service was developed by Alzheimer's Society in 2003 and brings people living with dementia and carers together to sing as a group (Bannan and Montgomery-Smith, 2008). The structured group sessions use music to encourage communication and participation and include opportunities to socialize with peers. Each session follows a specific model that combines aspects of reminiscence, cognitive stimulation and music therapy. The sessions have been reported to improve social inclusion, relationships, memory and well-being (Osman et al., 2016). The success and popularity of this service is illustrated by the replication of the service across the UK, with over 100 services now delivered by Alzheimer's Society. The provision of interventions through group-based services can contribute additional benefits by providing a social network that can help to reduce isolation and provide opportunities for peer support and are a cost-effective approach (Health Innovation Network, 2015).

The Non-Pharmaceutical Intervention project

Based on this developing body of evidence and the success of Singing for the Brain, in 2012 Alzheimer's Society was commissioned by NHS primary health services in Merseyside to pilot a range of activity groups for people with dementia in collaboration with local arts organizations. Through the Non-Pharmaceutical Intervention (NPI) project, six types of creative activity groups for people living with dementia and their families were developed and delivered in twenty-three locations across the Merseyside area (UK) for a period of eighteen months. By commissioning these services as a one-off project, the funders hoped to accrue a basis of evidence for the efficacy of such interventions in managing behavioural and psychological symptoms of dementia in a community setting, ultimately reducing reliance on health services and anti-psychotic medications. It was intended that the evidence gained could then be of use for future funding decisions.

In developing this project, the Singing for the Brain model was replicated and applied to different art forms. The services that were delivered through the project were:

1. Singing for the Brain: a group singing session in which music therapy and reminiscence techniques are used to bring people together in a friendly and stimulating social environment, delivered in collaboration with independent musicians.

2. Music for well-being: an interactive music session in which participants use percussion instruments, body percussion and voice to explore a range of musical styles and activities, delivered in collaboration with independent musicians.
3. Dance and movement: from physical activities to music specifically designed to suit the needs, abilities and preferences of participants, delivered in collaboration with Merseyside Dance Initiative.
4. Reading together: a group reading session in which short stories and poetry are read aloud and discussed by facilitators and participants, developed in collaboration with the Reader Organisation.
5. Visual arts: arts-based sessions exploring a range of media and techniques, culminating in a personal project for display at a semi-annual public exhibition, delivered in collaboration with the Bluecoat, an art centre in Liverpool.
6. Maintaining skills: varied activity session incorporating creativity and cognitive processing intended to encourage people living with dementia to stay involved in everyday activities.

The services were delivered in a range of community settings including libraries, art centres and community rooms. The frequency of the sessions varied between weekly, twice per month and once per month depending on the activity and location. At each session, the activities were led by an artist or instructor through collaboration with local arts organizations and individuals. These facilitators were supported by a member of staff and volunteers from Alzheimer's Society who were trained in dementia support.

Based on the Singing for the Brain model, the sessions were structured to facilitate a friendly and informal atmosphere. Each session lasted two hours and was designed to be dementia friendly, in that venues and activities were accessible and adaptable to meet the various different needs of people with dementia. For example, one hour of each session was set aside for activity and the other hour was allocated to allow time at the beginning of the session for people with dementia to become orientated to the environment and to allow opportunity for socializing, and at the end for refreshments and a relaxed exit from the venue.

The pace of activities always allowed ample time for people to process instructions. An example of this can be found in the music-based activities which were deliberately not accompanied by backing tracks to ensure that people with dementia could dictate the pace that most suited them. Each session was made dementia friendly by ensuring that everything within that session was inclusive in a way that enabled all participants to contribute to the activities in their preferred manner. Using the same routine and structure at each session also helped to provide reassurance to participants through familiarity (Alzheimer's Society, 2012).

It was intended that the session would go beyond being simply dementia friendly to actively facilitate improvements in well-being for people with dementia through cognitive stimulation, self-expression and opportunities for communication. Additionally, the project commissioners had identified the need for evidence to support the future funding of such services based on health-related outcomes. In order to ensure both, monitoring and evaluation of the services and the outcomes for the participants was a key component of the project.

A range of evaluation tools was designed to capture the impact that the sessions had on the QoL for those involved. The methods used were intended to cause minimal intrusion on the sessions and to be accessible to people with dementia. All participants of the sessions were invited to take part in the evaluations. Completion of the evaluations was optional. The following evaluation tools were used:

1. Six monthly questionnaires: intended to track changes in the health, social life and QoL of the participants living with dementia.
2. In-session emotions evaluation: to assess the short-term impacts on how the participants with dementia were feeling before and after the activities.

3. Case study interviews: used to gain a deeper understanding of individuals' experiences of the sessions from the perspective of those living with dementia and those who attended as companions.
4. Staff observations: Alzheimer's Society staff members recorded observations at every session to monitor challenges and successes and any pertinent expressions or events.
5. Attendance rates: recorded for all sessions to analyse patterns across the whole project, within services and for individuals.

The results of these evaluations are summarized later.

The experience of participation

The participants of the sessions came from a variety of socio-economic backgrounds with a wide range of life experiences, although the vast majority had little or no recent experience in the arts activities that they tried. There were various reasons for this lack of experience. For a few, it was simply that they had never had the interest or drive, or that they did not associate these activities with their 'shy' or 'non-creative' personality. Others reported a previous lack of opportunities or a feeling of not belonging when it came to interactions with the arts and institutions, with one participant, for example, stating 'places like this [art centre] don't feel like they are meant for people like us'.

Many participants who had previously enjoyed arts activities in their youth had usually lost touch with these experiences and had not continued these into adulthood. Most participants could recall their experience of music, drama, dance and visual arts during their schooldays, and it was often observed that these childhood experiences had made a lasting effect. Many people reported how they had been told at school that they did not have any natural creative talents, with one participant commenting, for example, that she 'was never allowed in the school choir'. These early experiences had at times resulted in a lifelong belief that creative engagement was not worthwhile. These participants sometimes required some persuasion from the organizers to attend the sessions.

Many people were attracted by the opportunity to spend time in a dementia-friendly environment. The sessions were at regular time and place that could be depended on for a break from the stress that is often experienced on an everyday basis by people living with dementia or caring for others with dementia (Alzheimer's Society, 2014). One carer commented: 'Although [my husband and I] are together it is a very lonely life for me. The feeling of isolation is great at times and I feel I have no life of my own so that is why when the [NPI] project began we decided to give it a try'. Many valued the opportunity to meet people in a similar situation and to find new social opportunities and support from peers.

To reinforce this, welcoming, supportive and non-judgemental environments were fostered at each session, within which all parties had a knowledge and understanding of dementia through prior training. As one carer who attended with her husband observed, 'Tim was reluctant at first but when we arrived we were made so welcome by the staff and volunteers … [they were] so patient and understanding and it really didn't matter to them if Tim said or did something funny.'

Once a group of facilitators and participants had been established, engaging in activity together helped to further foster the environment, as was observed by one facilitator: 'When everyone is equally committed and exposed the activity becomes communal and the group gains new feelings of shared ownership and trust' (Merseyside Dance Initiative, 2014).

The activities were designed to be fun and relaxing with creative expressions observed without judgement. One participant, who had fronto-temporal dementia observed: 'Everyone who was there, in this group, was there to do it for themselves and to be nice to people and to work together.' Creative activities such as music, dance and art provided opportunities for many people to try learn new skills.

This encouraged people to concentrate, experiment and innovate; these new experiences helped to provide new patterns of cognitive stimulation (Fischer, 1980). It was intended that these experiences would help to facilitate improvements in QoL and to manage some of the psychological symptoms of dementia.

The beneficial effects of music for people with dementia have been well documented (Bannan and Montgomery-Smith, 2008) and were often observed by facilitators of the singing and music sessions, with one leader commenting: 'I have seen the ability music and song has to awaken something inside someone, to unlock memories and even help find a voice where communication has been difficult.'

Across all the activities, it was importance for facilitators to enable and guide alternative methods of communication and self-expression. One dance facilitator commented: 'Instead of teaching people, you are pulling something out of them' (MDI, 2014). This required skill and empathy from the facilitator, to be able to gauge and read a person's state of mind and being at the start of a session and respond and work with this appropriately. This approach of emphatic communication has been applied to person-centred dementia care in more traditional services, such as domiciliary care (McEvoy and Plant, 2014), and was important to the facilitation of these sessions.

Facilitators needed to be adaptable, with the ability to respond to and work with participants' creative expressions in a manner that was supportive, dignified and encouraged further creativity. Examples included dance facilitators mirroring and evolving the movements of participants and art facilitators proposing imaginative interpretations of participants' abstract paintings during reflective discussions.

Responding with sensitivity was important and facilitators learnt to modify their reactions to have maximum impact on individuals. It was important to give praise when appropriate, but equally personal boundaries were respected and at times facilitators learnt to internalize their personal reactions to allow participants to express themselves without too much attention (MDI, 2014).

Alongside the development of these skills, it was also important for facilitators to develop relationships with the participants. Facilitators made efforts to remember individual's preferences and to notice what worked creatively for the individuals, over time working with the participants to develop personalized practices, supporting the delivery of a person-centred intervention. Within the reading groups, this included the use of rhythmic poetry and rhyming couplets to stimulate and capture the attention of an individual with dementia who found it difficult to maintain focus when reading prose. Dance facilitators reported planning sessions with particular people in mind (MDI, 2014), for example, always incorporating an activity that used feather boas for a woman who favoured these.

With time, facilitators learnt what was possible and how their actions could help to improve a participants' mood or behaviour through the course of the session, as recounted by music facilitator Rosy Rea-Smith:

> In order to deliver a high quality inclusive experience for each and every participant I have found it vital that I continuously search for ways to engage with each group member no matter how difficult this may be. A participant might be unresponsive in many ways – they may have lost their verbal communication, they may lack concentration or exhibit wandering behaviours, they may be (or appear to be) asleep or simply disinterested, but there is almost always a particular song, instrument, or recording that can light up that person and draw from them some kind of response. They might mouth the words of the song, or suddenly stand up and dance, or begin to whistle along or even just a smile. It is important to me that I recognise every moment like this, no matter how tiny, and note it and revisit it regularly throughout following sessions.

Relationships were also seen to blossom between the individuals with dementia and accompanying carers or family members as they engaged in activities together, as observed by one facilitator who noted, 'the act of creating something together with a loved one is a powerful tool'.

Evaluation outcomes

The evaluations outlined earlier in the chapter provide data which was analysed to assess the effects of the sessions on the health and well-being of participants.

Evidence to assess the impact of the services on health-related outcomes was sparse. Return rates for the six-monthly questionnaires were low throughout the project with only 33 per cent of those attending the sessions completing the data.

Of those that were returned, analysis showed little change in health and social measures for participants. These results were interpreted as a positive outcome, suggesting that the cohort maintained stable conditions while living with a degenerative disease. The number of people reporting hospital admissions increased by only 7 per cent over the course of a year. At the beginning of the project, only 22 per cent of respondents reported making new friends in the past six months, which increased to 44 per cent by the end of the project. However, results such as these cannot be directly attributed to participation in the NPI programme due to sessions being delivered on a weekly frequency at most.

The case studies conducted captured some of the personal experiences of participants. Thematic assessment identified the commonly perceived benefits of participation in the sessions. The most common benefits discussed in the case studies were that participants enjoyed the activities, that they had made new friends at the sessions and that the activities lifted their mood. Over 50 per cent of the case studies reported that the sessions helped people to deal with the symptoms of dementia, for example, through improved concentration.

Staff observations, although subjective, interpreted participants as frequently being fully engaged in the activities of the session and enjoying themselves. Another key theme identified within the staff observations was that the sessions appeared to be empowering for people living with dementia; they were able to make active and valued contributions to the group and were provided with opportunities to express preferences, opinions and decisions.

The in-session evaluations provided useful quantitative data on the short-term impact of the sessions on the mood of participants with dementia. On arrival at the sessions, 79 per cent of emotions recorded were positive. This increased to 94 per cent at the end of the session, indicating that participants were arriving at the sessions in a positive state of mind, and this was either maintained or improved during the session, as described by one participant who has dementia: 'As soon as I come here I feel relaxed because it's so lovely to be with them all. I go home feeling a lot more positive.' The recorded decrease in negative emotions indicates that the sessions contributed to reduced levels of distress.

The attendance rates at the sessions in general increased over the duration of the project. In the first month of the project, 219 contacts were made with service users, over the course of the project this increased to 351 contacts in the final month. It was observed that many of the groups required time to build up in popularity as people became more familiar with the services and more open to trying new experiences. This data was useful in identifying popularity between services.

Attendance rates varied between service types and geographic areas. The Singing for the Brain sessions were universally popular, which was attributed to the service being a long-established and well-known offering from Alzheimer's Society. The Dance and Movement and Reading Together groups struggled to attract full attendance in all areas. However, those who attended these groups valued their experiences at the sessions, suggesting that pre-conceptions of the services may initially discourage participants from trying new activities, as described by one carer who attended sessions with her mother who has dementia: 'I think she also enjoys the dance, the first time, she wasn't sure because she's not a dancer, but once she realised what it was, she enjoyed it.' It was found that low attendance did at times have a negative impact on the sessions. This was particularly relevant in the Dance and Movement groups with low attendance producing an atmosphere which may have encouraged feelings of vulnerability and embarrassment not associated with a larger group experience.

Discussion

This project provided innovative services that were novel to both Alzheimer's Society and the partner arts organizations. The experience of these services was enjoyed by both facilitators and participants and appeared to add a new dimension of experience to the lives of people affected by dementia.

The development and evaluation of arts-based services facilitated a holistic view point of the care needs of people affected by dementia living within the community. An individual's QoL extends beyond the meeting the basic needs of health and security. These sessions enabled experiences that could have positive impacts on the less tangible human needs such as love, social support and sense of purpose.

Evaluation design

The evaluation of the services provided was an important component of this project. This aspect of the work intended to address the service commissioners' need for outcome-based evidence to continue to fund these types of intervention.

As previously presented, the evaluation data collected went some way to show that the services were successful in reducing social isolation and helped to improve the QoL and well-being for people living with dementia through social engagement, confidence building and enriching experiences. However, the data recorded is of limited scope and reliability.

The nature of the activities and services provided posed challenges in making the evaluations meaningful. With participants attending sessions at most for two hours per week, there were many extraneous factors that could have had significant effects on their health, well-being and dementia-related symptoms, such as changes in the living environment, experiences at other services or periods of stress or ill health. Thus, the outcomes focused on more immediate impacts of the activities, over the duration of session and that day, rather than overall QoL assessments, during which time periods the changes experienced by an individual could be more confidently attributed to their involvement in sessions. The impact of the sessions as a boost to mood was described by one participant who has dementia: 'I love it, I just wish there were a bit more because it feels like good therapy, it lifts the spirits.'

This approach provided useful information on the impact of the services on short-term mood; however, it was difficult to relate participation to changes in measures that encompass broader QoL, well-being and health. For example, a participant's need to visit the general practitioner may have reduced during the period of attendance at the services or their perceived levels of well-being may have improved; however, the evaluations were not significantly robust to correlate these changes to participation in the groups.

The services were commissioned in order to improve health and well-being for people with dementia. As such, the outcomes were expected to be evaluated using health-related indicators developed in medicalized settings. This study has illustrated the importance of relating expectations of the service outcomes to the service activities and the experience of the creative process. Early stage discussions should focus on what can be achieved by participation in arts activities and how these outcomes can be measured using an approach that is respectful of the service user, the artistic process and the relationship between facilitator and participant.

Despite the limitations of the evaluation approach used, the implementation of this process has provided a basis of experience that could be valuable for future arts-based health interventions. The person-centred approaches to evaluations, such as the case study interviews and in-session observations, provided the data that was of most meaning to both the individual and the practitioners. Future evaluations could endeavour to include the feedback and opinions of those who are actively engaged in the participation of the sessions in the design of evaluations to ensure a person-centred approach to outcome measures.

Partnership working

The development of these services has highlighted the need for improved partnership working between commissioners, health and social care providers, arts organizations and service users, through all stages of service design, implementation and evaluation.

Although participants were actively involved in developing the programme, there was little service user involvement during the project initiation stage. Due to limited time constraints on project delivery, the funders prescribed a range of activity types that were distributed geographically with the intention that as many people as possible would have a group that was close to where they live. As such, people affected by dementia did not contribute to the decisions of what types of activity were delivered in each area.

Had the project incorporated greater involvement of the people living with dementia in each community in the development of the programme, different activities may have been delivered and different user groups may have been attracted to participate. However, with a predefined range of activities, people were encouraged to try something new, as opposed implementing more of the services that were already familiar to many people, such as Singing for the Brain™.

Once services were established, people affected by dementia were encouraged at all stages to be involved in the development of the services and the activities within the sessions. For example, the three dance groups that were delivered evolved into very different services, with one focusing on chair-based aerobics exercise, another preferring traditional circle dances and one that embraced partner dances such as ballroom.

Developing relationships

The creative activities were often seen as a time and a space for the participants with dementia and their loved ones to enjoy together, during which, existing bonds could be nurtured. Collective participation in the programme allowed family members to reconnect through arts participation, as described by one carer of her experiences with her husband: 'The main thing was it was something we could do together and enjoy together and laugh together. We have always worked, played and laughed together but slowly that is disappearing.'

Preconceptions regarding individuals' capabilities could be challenged and potentially rebuilt, as explained by Pat, who cares for her husband Peter: 'The arts group has proved a fantastic outlet for Peter. By the look on his face and in his eyes when he is engaging in the art group, you can tell that there is something going on. It actually enables us to have a conversation through the painting.'

Family members and friends were welcome to participate, creating an opportunity for a wider circle of loved ones to get involved in the support of the person living with dementia. This could be through family members who are not direct carers attending the sessions or through continuing activities and discussions at home, as was the case for Pat and Peter's family: 'It allows him to engage with our two children and four grandchildren again, because they all sit around the table painting. It gives them something they can do with Peter, a common interest that they can enjoy together.'

The sessions bought people together and created new friendships that were built on the common grounds of the shared experience of living with dementia and also from the experience of learning new skills and enjoying new challenges together, as described by one carer: 'It's so warm, when you go into a group; everyone is smiling, welcoming and positive.'

Improving well-being

For many people, the period after receiving a diagnosis of dementia can be fraught with self-doubt, fear, low moods and feelings of uselessness (Alzheimer's Society, 2012). The experiences offered through this project provided a platform through which people living with dementia could become motivated to re-engage with life. Pink (2011) identifies three elements that encourage motivation – autonomy, mastery and purpose, all of which were encouraged through these sessions.

Autonomy was encouraged through freedom for participants to express and create as they wished, and to make choices to follow the paths that were of greatest interest to them, be that a decision between attending a dance session or a singing group or a decision to work with paints or clay within an art group. As was explained by one participant living with dementia: 'It's the first time that a big place like this has come to me, and I've worked in it and I've felt myself, because the fact that I did my own stuff was different to me ... I've loved it.'

By trying new or long-neglected activities, many participants learnt and developed new skills, providing the confidence boost that comes from mastery of a subject (Pink, 2011). This, along with the structure and regularity of sessions, provided a purpose and reason to engage with the wider world as communicated by Michelle who cares for her husband John, an individual living with dementia: 'He likes to be on the go all the time. He doesn't get lost but he's always up and about, so this is somewhere to go ... The effects of the group lasts, definitely, it's something where he's been somewhere, he's enjoyed it, he's mixed with other people as well ... The music has definitely helped.'

A positive experience of trying something new can have beneficial impacts on an individual's confidence and self-esteem, which can be invaluable at a time when skills and abilities can be diminishing. To have these experiences in a supportive environment can be further validating, as explained by one carer about his wife who has dementia: 'All these successes are in public – for other people to see. She is participating in a joint enterprise with other people, with dementia and without, on equal terms, and they're fun, absolutely marvellous for her sense of well-being, self-confidence and self-esteem.'

For some, participation in the services caused a sense of reinvigoration beyond the sessions, developing a motivation and drive that positively impacted their daily routines and outlook on life. Indeed, a few participants even reported finding that the effects of their dementia could, at times, help them to challenge barriers that may have previously restricted their involvement in creative practices.

Meeting the needs of people living with dementia

The outcomes of this project have illustrated how arts-based activity groups can help to improve the QoL for people living with dementia and their loved ones or carers. Through Maslow's widely accepted Hierarchy of Needs (1943), the benefits of these outcomes can be shown to address the needs of people with dementia beyond the physiological and safety needs catered for by traditional, basic care models, as illustrated in Figure 8.1.

Active groups, such as dance and movement, provide opportunity for physical activity: through the provision of a supportive environment that is both physically and socially accepting of individuals with dementia, to encourage feelings of safety and security. The group format of the activities provides a network of peer support and friendship that generates a sense of belonging and community; through trying new activities and receiving public approval from others, individuals can build their confidence and self-esteem.

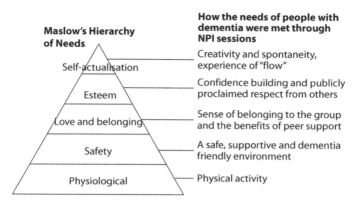

Figure 8.1 How the outcomes of arts activity groups address Maslow's Hierarchy of Needs for people living with dementia (Luxmoore, adapted from Maslow, 1943)

The need to concentrate and fully engage in the activities created opportunities for people living with dementia to experience a state of 'flow' as named by Csikszentmihalyi (1997). When in a state of flow, a person performing an activity is fully immersed, with a feeling of energized focus, motivation and enjoyment in the process of the activity, fulfilling the highest of Maslow's needs: self-actualization.

Within this state a person's focus is drawn away from their thoughts and emotions and is intent only on the activity. This, Csikszentmihalyi suggests, is a result of the brain focusing so keenly on the task at hand it has no spare capacity for distractions. One could argue that at its most productive, each session allowed the space for such a focus and state of flow to occur, the result of which provided subsequent benefits in health and well-being for the engaged participant.

To achieve a service with beneficial outcomes, meeting the needs of the individual with a diagnosis of dementia, requires hard work and dedication from facilitators who must be creative and understanding of the needs of participants in order to implement a fully person-centred and relationship-based approach which can only be developed over time.

For all participants, both people living with dementia and their companions, there were opportunities for people to temporarily shake off their typical roles of 'a person with dementia', a 'patient' or a 'carer', instead adopt new roles including the role of the 'artist', the 'performer' or the 'peer'.

The experience of engaging in creative activities was beneficial for almost all participants. The sessions became a space to engage in therapeutic and enjoyable activities that resulted from their first step of experimenting with a new activity. The importance of person-centred care and the benefits that can come when we look to address the impact of dementia on every facet of the human condition are now well known and accepted (Kitwood, 1997). When we start to understand and accept the true capabilities of people with dementia, we can quickly move on to explore the unique possibilities that can be accessed when the creative mind is unlocked and the potential benefits that can be achieved (Killick and Allen, 1999).

Conclusions

The development and delivery of this project have been a valuable learning process for all stakeholders. Both the commissioning bodies and Alzheimer's Society have gained experience in delivering a new approach to dementia support services; the arts practitioners and organizations have been exposed to working with a client group with different needs and objectives; people affected by dementia have experienced novel creative approaches to tackling some of the challenges of living with dementia.

Through the process, it has been highlighted how important it is that all stakeholders are actively involved in the development and delivery of these new approaches. Evaluations are vital to obtain the evidence that is needed to justify continued funding; however, a medicalized approach to service outcomes will not provide an illustrative and useful view of the services' impact. A person-centred approach is required to service delivery and participants need to be actively involved in the continued development of services.

Evaluation approaches should also be carefully considered. The effectiveness of outcome-based, quantitative or medicalized evaluation methods should be carefully considered in the context of the experiential nature of the interventions and the client base.

The potential for creative activities to improve the QoL for people affected by dementia has been shown through several key messages of the project. From a social perspective, the activity sessions have become tools for facilitating friendship and peer support in new relationships, while existing relationships have been given time and space to develop feelings of togetherness. Engaging in new experiences has provided stimulation and enjoyment suggesting once initial steps are taken, the benefits of enjoyment, stimulation and involvement found in arts participation are quickly reaped, helping to build feelings of confidence and self-esteem.

Looking to creative approaches to meeting the needs of people with dementia has helped to support people to continue to live well in their community, through fostering connections and meeting the needs of individuals through the arts at what can be a challenging time for anyone affected by dementia, as explained by one couple: 'The activities give a structure to our lives, a beacon of brightness in the darkness of this terrible disease. The staff and fellow participants are part of our family – for loving kindness and mutual support.'

Afterword

Applied Theatre: Creative Ageing as a collection explores the complex needs of a diverse group in contemporary Western society. In doing so, it examines the work of contemporary applied theatre in relation to those needs. Including both a survey of the field and specific critical analyses, the book examines innovative national and international applied theatre practice that responds to and facilitates the needs of older adults in an effort to encourage outcomes that include, but are not limited to, well-being and social inclusion. It does so while exploring scholarship that addresses how society engages socially, culturally and politically with the process of ageing.

Applied theatre in its many forms seeks to involve all members of society in a range of performance practices. As a form of social engagement, whatever each practitioner's intended outcome, applied theatre aims to be inclusive. Practitioners in the field make work for, by and with members of a community in an attempt to engage creatively with that community. As applied theatre develops in professionalism and proficiency, its legitimacy also grows and it is this legitimacy that has encouraged its embrace beyond artistic circles with social, cultural and political apparatuses now acknowledging its ability to improve health, well-being and social inclusion.

Applied theatre developed with, for and by older adults is as specialized as any other applied practice and, as such, must remain adaptable to the needs of the community it serves. One specific section of our society is set to rise exponentially over the next twenty years. As the population of older adults grows, its heterogeneous nature and complex medical and social needs also become evident. With this understanding come initiatives to move away from medical models of care and pharmaceutical intervention towards social and cultural alternatives. Dedicated to recurring themes that surround the natural process of ageing, the aim of this book has been to bring together authoritative insights on pioneering practice and scholarship so as to advance understanding of socially engaged creative practice in this area. The contributions included also allow points of commonality which exist to be examined, particularly in relation to the challenges associated to the practice along with the subsequent innovations developed to address and overcome these challenges.

Encouraging conversations into the process of ageing and how we, as a society, might engage with that process better, several recurring themes have emerged throughout *Applied Theatre: Creative Ageing*. These themes include the significance of affect over effect in relation to applied theatre and ageing, the importance of continuing to be creative as one ages and the relevance of sociality in applied theatre with, for and by older adults. The book and its contributors explore these themes relating them to concepts such as: the movement from medical models to person-centred and relational approaches to care; the changing attitudes towards cognitive impairment and the multiple layers of meaning that exist in work with older adults with cognitive impairment; the issues that exist in relation to evaluation and the inability of established evaluation tools to adequately capture the outcomes of applied practice in this area; and the importance of continuing to create and/or develop artistry as one ages. In doing so, the book examines innovative methodologies that support these concepts.

Examples within the book allude to practice that facilitates and supports changing attitudes towards ageing, particularly in relation to cognitive impairment. This reconsideration or adaption of traditional methodologies in applied theatre with older adults which, in the past, privileged reminiscence includes work that embraces cognitive changes and adapts practice to engage creatively with these changes. At particular points in the book, conversations regarding work with individuals with a diagnosis of dementia allowed investigation into what Balfour et al. call 'versions of reality' (this volume, 110). What these conversations explore is the ability of applied theatre to work across spatial and temporal norms and to traverse practice where a firm grasp of time, space, or indeed understanding is needed, to practice which allows individuals with a diagnosis of dementia to express their alternate realities in a way that subsequently encourage creativity.

Much of *Applied Theatre: Creative Ageing* privileges the person-centred and relational approaches to care. With these approaches it is the individual and the relationship between artist and individual that is considered, not age and/or diagnosis. This consideration supports arguments in the first section of the book which highlight the heterogeneous nature of older adults as a community. The shift from the medicalized model is particularly appropriate when applied theatre is adopted in a medical setting and where relatedness, connectivity and sociality are privileged above other outcomes. These three outcomes are repeated using different adjectives throughout the publication and, as such, underline the importance of affect in the experience of applied theatre with, for and by older adults, something also articulated throughout the book.

The concept that practice can be developed in such a way as to have a life beyond the artist/facilitator's intervention and that it can become imbedded in whatever setting it is development, adopted by individuals working in these setting is argued by several contributors. Similarly, the notion that co-dependence in artistic engagement can lead to independence in terms of creative capacity is also alluded to and examined in both sections. Here practices were considered that introduce an ethos of creativity that continues after a project ends – an ethos that is subsequently adopted by individuals (often not artists) working in that area. The concept that the adoption of an artistic ethos allows life beyond a project also ties to discussions regarding interdisciplinarity and the benefits that occur through collaborative practice between artist, caregiver, family member and older adult.

Many of the examples cited within the pages here embrace the importance of artistry and of continuing to be creative as one ages. Examples where individuals continue to create are included but of equal importance are references to those who develop artistry later in life. These artists emerge as such for different reasons. They engage in creative practice to develop connectedness and sociality or find a creative energy unlocked through a cognitive disruption. Whatever the reason, the book prefaces the belief that creative energy need not diminish as we age and indeed reinforces the notion that such energy can be encouraged and developed in later life. One can be an emerging artist whatever one's age; it is simply about harnessing creativity and supporting it to develop.

At certain points, evaluation is discussed and its positive and negative aspects considered. The inability of evaluation to adequately grasp the ephemeral yet vital influence of affect in applied theatre with, for and by older adults is considered. Often immeasurable, affect is discussed at various points in the book and its value explored. Not resolved is the question of how the social, affective and connected nature of applied theatre work in this area can be measured and evaluated in terms of impact. This seems to remain a challenge for the field and its practitioners, one which is perhaps inevitable given the links between the applied practice in this area and health and well-being. However, the argument is made by several contributors that the issue can be resolved by trusting the artist to observe and measure the impact of his or her work perhaps using a different language to those already established within other disciplines. Indeed, in his chapter, Parkinson argues, 'Whilst evidence of the impact of arts on health and well-being is growing … our understanding of cultural value might best not be understood through the lens of medicine, but through its own language' (148). As he continues, 'The arts might enable deeper and more engaged conversations around a new philosophy of how we live our lives, and explicitly, end our days; a difficult conversation perhaps, but one that the arts are uniquely placed to address. This, however, will require a significant cultural shift' (154). Thus, the argument is made that applied theatre practitioners need to develop their own language, or at least frame the existing language differently, so as to avoid the need to conform to the medial modules of evaluation.

This new language might offer new ways of thinking about ageing in general. The book therefore considers the need to challenge current thinking around evaluation and encourage more confidence in relation to the artist's and his or her ability to judge the value of his or her practice. The concept of reframing existing established models is reiterated in Basting's contribution which similarly advocates applied theatre practice as a tool to re-imagine care relationships.

By exploring both theory and practice and embracing interdisciplinary connections, this volume addresses a broad readership of practitioners and scholars, along with individuals working in health care who wish to consider adopting a creative ethos in their professional practice. Addressing these interested parties, *Applied Theatre: Creative Ageing* considers the important role applied theatre (along with other arts practices) might play in addressing the needs of older adults, as other interventions (pharmacological, for example) prove ineffective or inappropriate. It analyses the ability of applied theatre to address the complex needs of older adults in ways that promote individuality through a focus on person centred, holistic care over traditional medical models. It also explores how applied theatre, in partnership with other initiatives (age-friendly cities, for example), might assists in rebalancing the position of the older adults in Western society. Thus, the book highlightes the innovative nature of applied theatre practice that acknowledges older members of society as a group with complex, often individualized needs; the political, cultural and social position older adults have in contemporary society; and recent thinking in relation to the care of older adults.

By including national and international practice from Britain, Australia and the United States, the book examines all of the above from a Western context. Perspectives on contemporary practice, interviews with practitioners and contributions from scholars introduce and survey an emerging field. Other publications and voices are needed to expand on this work, addressing further the practice of applied theatre and ageing in other contexts. Gathering these contributions together in one publication has allowed an examination to begin. It provides the first publication that encourages scholarly and critical engagement into the specific needs (social, political, cultural and medical) of older adults and the use of applied theatre to address some of those needs. It is only the beginning, however, more work documenting and analysing this work is needed.

Theoretically, the practice of applied theatre with, for and by old adults is accompanied by strategies of analysis found in social sciences, philosophy and gerontology. It encompasses social, cultural and political elements and acknowledges the heterogeneous nature of older adults. The examples of practice included here exist along a continuum from the public to the private. At points along this continuum, examples have been positioned according to their public or private nature allowing commonalities as well as differences between the states to be explored and analysed. What the book does then is engage a form of theatre practice in broader conversations regarding ageing in contemporary society. What it could never do is provide all the answers as to how society as a whole could age better. It does however attempt some consideration of ageing as is presently experienced and offers some suggestions regarding how that experience might be reconsidered in relation to the challenges ahead.

Notes

Chapter 3

1 Anna Yen, interview 29 June 2015.
2 Australian Research Council Linkage Grant Playful Engagement and Dementia: understanding the efficacy of applied theatre practices for people with dementia in residential aged care facilities (LP120100194). The chief investigators were: Professor Michael Balfour, Associate Professor Julie Dunn (School of Education and Professional Studies, Griffith University), Professor Wendy Moyle, Professor Marie Cooke (Menzies Health Institute and School of Nursing and Midwifery, Griffith University) and Kirsty Martin (Research Associate).

Chapter 6

1 June gave consent for her name to be used although the study did not use her surname. The study is approved by the Institutional Review Board.
2 The first five QoDs were considered pilot and were distributed by Meal Drivers alone. From the sixth question forward, they were delivered to Meal Sites, by Meal Drivers, Interfaith (telephone and in-person) volunteers and home caregivers. Questions two through forty-five were delivered weekly starting in November 2014. We did not deliver QoDs during holidays of Thanksgiving or Christmas, as drivers had other tasks to attend to at those times. An asterisk (*) denotes which QoD yielded a radio segment on WUWM's *Lake Effect*, our Milwaukee-based public radio arts and culture show.
   1. How does water move? (Spring 2013)
   2. If you could go ANYWHERE in Milwaukee right now – where would you go – and why?* (Fall 2014)
   3. What is something you treasure in your home, and why?*
   4. What is something you wish you could learn?*

5. What is something you could teach another person?*
6. Where is a place you would feel comfortable talking to someone you don't know?*
7. What has helped you stay connected to your community? What could make you feel more connected?
8. Is there an intersection you wish you could cross but feel it is too dangerous?*
9. What is the most well worn path in your home?
10. What is a well-worn path for you outside your home?
11. What blocks your path?
12. What are the sounds of your neighbourhood?*
13. What are the sounds of Milwaukee?*
14. What is your safe harbour?
15. Where do you connect with nature?
16. What is the most beautiful sound in your home?*
17. What is the most beautiful sound in the world?*
18. What gift would you give the next generation?
19. What might you like to tell Milwaukee?*
20. How would you start a story?
21. What does courage mean to you?*
22. Let's write a story of courage: Who are the main characters?
23. Let's write a story of courage: Where should our story take place?
24. Let's write a story of courage: What act or situation requires courage?
25. Let's write a story of courage: What should be our hero's strengths? Weaknesses?
26. Let's write a story of courage: Who is our main character's trusty companion?
27. Let's write a story of courage: What obstacles face our main character?
28. Let's write a story of courage: Who or what helps our hero overcome those obstacles?
29. Let's write a story of courage: How should our story end?
30. Let's write a story of courage: What is the moral of our story?
31. Whom do you consider have courage in your own life?
32. How are you courageous in your own life?

33. What is a good citizen?
34. What advice would you give young people today?
35. What advice did your parents or grandparents give you?
36. If you could ask a Question of the Day, what would it be?
37. Have you ever done something secretly kind for someone?
38. How could people be more kind?
39. What is the most valuable thing you've learned?
40. Would you like to be part of the performance/exhibit for this project?
41. What is something beautiful to you?
42. How are you beautiful?
43. How are you creative every day?
44. What are you curious about?
45. Do you like these questions? Why/why not?

3   Outputs from The Islands of Milwaukee Partnership System, Workshops, Training:

1. A partnership system among arts, education, home-care, county and non-profit service providers
2. A system for creating, delivering, gathering, analysing, storing, building upon and re-sharing creative responses to QoD
3. A PowerPoint to introduce arts students to working with older adults
4. Common language and goals for key partners Engagement with Elders
5. Two artist-led workshops at meal sites
6. Ten in-home visits with an artist
7. Ten phone visits with an artist
8. Forty-five Questions of the Day distributed (through five different mechanisms)
9. 3,000 responses to Questions of the Day (through five mechanisms) Communications/Web
10. Ten 'Currents' newsletters
11. Three generations of the IoM website
12. Twenty-one radio segments on WUWM's Lake Effect
13. Performances and exhibits
14. Three Crossings Performances (May 2014)

15. A Crossings guide
16. A Crossings video
17. An exhibit at the UWM Union Gallery (Jan–Feb 2014)
18. Art installation at Milwaukee's City Hall and exhibit guide
19. 'Service Cards' profiling various ageing services in Milwaukee
20. Fourteen brief performances to engage audiences in IoM (Sept 2014)
21. Video of the IoM performance

Chapter 7

1   A critical account of both performances was written by Pearson and published in *Theatre Research International*, volume 20, issue 3 (2015).

References

Introduction

Bennett, J., L. Guangquan, K. Foreman, N. Best, V. Kontis, C. Pearson, P. Hambly and M. Ezzati. (2015), 'The Future of Life Expectancy and Life Expectancy Inequalities in England and Wales: Bayesian Spatiotemporal Forecasting', *Lancet*, 386: 163–170.

De Beauvior, S. (1970), *Old Age*, Middlesex: Penguin.

Gov. UK. (2016), 'NHS Choices: The Top 5 Causes of Premature Death'. Available online: http://www.nhs.uk/livewell/over60s/pages/the-top-five -causes-of-premature-death.aspx (accessed 10 June 2016).

Kirkwood, T. (2001), 'Tom Kirkwood: The End of Age: 2001', The Reith Lecturers, BBC Radio 4. Available online: http://www.bbc.co.uk /programmes/p00ghvdn (accessed 1 April 2005).

NHS England. (2016), 'The Top 5 Causes of Premature Death', NHS Choices. Available online: http://www.nhs.uk/livewell/over60s/pages/the-top-five -causes-of-premature-death.aspx (accessed 12 March 2014).

Public Health England. (2016), 'Recent Trends in Life Expectancy at Older Ages: Update to 2014'. Available online: https://www.gov.uk/government /uploads/system/uploads/attachment_data/file/499252/Recent_trends_in _life_expectancy_at_older_ages_2014_update.pdf (accessed 10 June 2016).

Starratt, V. (2016), *Evolutionary Psychology: How Our Biology Affects What We Think and Do*, California: Green Wood.

Tavernise, S. (2016), 'Disparity in Life Spans of the Rich and the Poor', *New York Times*, 12 February. Available online: http://www.nytimes .com/2016/02/13/health/disparity-in-life-spans-of-the-rich-and-the-poor -is-growing.html?_r=0 (accessed 10 June 2016).

WHO. (2015), 'Life Expectancy at Birth', World Health Organisation. Available online: http://gamapserver.who.int/gho/interactive_charts/mbd/life _expectancy/atlas.html (accessed 10 May 2015).

Chapter 1

Andrews, M. (1999), 'The Seductiveness of Agelessness', *Ageing and Society*, 19 (3): 301–318.

Arber, S. and J. Ginn, eds. (1995), *Connecting Gender and Ageing: A Sociological Approach*, Buckingham and Philadelphia: Oxford University Press.

Atchley, R. C. (1993), 'Continuity Theory and the Evolution of Activity in Later Adulthood', in J. R. Kelly (ed.), *Activity and Aging: Staying Involved in Later Life*, 5–16. Thousand Oakes, CA: Sage.

Bengston, V. L., M. N. Reedy and C. Gordon. (1985), 'Aging and Self-Conceptions, Personality Processes and Social Contexts', in J. E. Birren and K. Warner Schaie (eds.), *Handbook of Psychology and Aging*, 544–593. New York: Van Nostrand Reinhold.

Bytheway, B. (1995), *Ageism*, Buckingham and Philadelphia: Open University Press.

Bowling, A. (1993), 'The Concepts of Successful and Positive Ageing', *Family Practice*, 10 (4): 449–453.

Bowling, A. (2005), *Ageing Well: Quality of Life in Old Age*, Berkshire: Open University Press.

Cohen, G. D. (2006), 'Research on Creativity and Ageing: The Positive Impact of the Arts on Health and Illness', *Generations*, 30 (1): 7–15.

Coleman, P., J. Bond and S. Peace. (1991), *Ageing in Society: An Introduction to Social Gerontology*, London: SAGE Publications.

De Beauvior, S. (1970), *Old Age*, Middlesex: Penguin.

Department of Energy and Climate Change. (2015), 'Annual Fuel Poverty Statistics Report', GOV.UK. Available online: https://www.gov.uk/government/statistics/annual-fuel-poverty-statisticreport-2015 (accessed 7 August 2015).

Ehteth, J. (2003), 'The Global Value of Vaccination', *Vaccine*, 21 (7–8, 30): 596–600.

Eyre, H., K. Richard, R. M. Robertson, C. Clark, C. Doyle, T. Gansler, T. Glynn, Y. Hong, R. A. Smith, K. Taubert and M. J. Thun. (2008), 'Preventing Cancer, Cardiovascular Disease, and Diabetes: A Common Agenda for the American Cancer Society, the American Diabetes Association, and the American Heart Association', *CA: A Cancer Journal for Clinicians*, 54 (4): 190–207.

Ferrano, K. F. (2007), 'Afterword', in K. F. Ferraro and J. Wilmoth (eds.), *Gerontology: Perspectives and Issues*, 325–343, New York: Springer.

Fischer, D. H. (1978), *Growing Old in America*. New York: Oxford University Press.

Healey, S. (1994), 'Growing to Be an Old Woman', in E. P. Stoller and P. G. Gibson (eds.), *Worlds of Difference: Inequality in the Ageing Experience*, 81–83, Thousand Oaks, CA: Pine Forge Press.

Karpf, A. (2014), *How to Age*, London: Macmillan.

Kirkwood, T. (2001), *The End of Age*, London: Profile.

Maddox, G. L. and M. P. Lawton. (1998), 'Varieties of Aging', *Annual Review of Gerontology and Geriatrics*, 8: 37–68.

Manchester Institute for Collaborative Research on Ageing. (2015), 'Older People Join Academics to Research UK's first "age-friendly" city', MICRA. Available online: http://www.micra.manchester.ac.uk/connect/news /press-releases/ (accessed July 2006).

Morgan, L. and S. Kunkel. (2016), *Aging, Society and the Life Course*, New York: Springer Publishing.

Mullan, P. (2002), *The Imaginary Time Bomb*, London: I. B. Tauris.

Nascher, I. L. (1914), *Geriatrics : The Diseases of Old Age and Their Treatment, Including Physiological Old Age, Home and Institutional Care, and Medico-Legal Relations*, Philadelphia, PA: P. Blakiston's Son & Co.

Nicholson, H. (2011), 'Making Home Work: Theatre-Making with Older Adults in Residential Care', *NJ: Drama Australia Journal*, 35 (1): 47–62.

Office for National Statistics. (2015), 'What Are the Top Causes of Death by Age and Gender?' Gov.UK. Available online: http://visual.ons.gov .uk/what-are-the-top-causes-of-death-by-age-and-gender/ (accessed 1 May 2016).

Putney., N, D. E. Alley and V. L. Bengtson. (2005), 'Social Gerontology as Public Sociology in Action', *The American Sociologist*, 36 (3): 88–104.

Riley, J. C. (2001), *Rising Life Expectancy*, Cambridge: Cambridge University Press.

Roos, N. P. and B. Havens. (1991), 'Predictors of Successful Aging: A Twelve-Year Study of Manitoba Elderly', *American Journal of Public Health*, 81 (1): 63–68.

Rowe, J. W. and R. L. Kahn. (1998), *Successful Aging*, New York: Pantheon Books.

Segal, L. (2013), *Out of Time*, New York: Verso.

Strehler, B. (1962), *Time, Cells and Aging*, New York and London: Academic Press.

WHO. (1997), 'WHOQOL: Measuring Quality of Life, Division of Mental Health and Prevention of Substance Abuse', World Health Organisation, WHO/MSA/MNH/PSF/97.4. WHO/MSA/MNH/PSF/97.4, Available online: http://www.who.int/mental_health/media/68.pdf (accessed 7 August 2015).

WHO. (2007), 'Global Age Friendly Cities: A Guide', World Health Organisation. Available online: http://www.who.int/ageing/publications /Global_age_friendly_cities_Guide_English.pdf (accessed 7 June 2016).

WHO. (2016), 'Ageing and Life Course, What Is Active Ageing', World Health Organisation, Available Online: http://www.who.int/ageing/active_ageing/ en/ (accessed 10 June 2016).

Chapter 2

Age and Opportunity. (2016), 'Bealtine Festival', Age and Opportunity. Available online: http://bealtaine.com/ (accessed 16 June 2016).

Age Concern and Help the Aged. (2009), *Response to the National Review of Age Discrimination in Health and Social Care Call for Evidence*. London: Age Concern and Help the Aged.

Age Exchange. (2015a), 'What Is Reminiscence Arts', Age Exchange. Available online: http://www.age-exchange.org.uk/who-we-are/what-is -reminiscence-arts/ (accessed 16 June 2016).

Age Exchange. (2015b), 'RADIQL', Age Exchange. Available online: http:// www.age-exchange.org.uk/what-we-do/care-and-support/radiql/ (accessed 16 June 2016).

Age of Creativity. (n.d.), 'The Case for Arts, Culture and Older People', Age of Creativity. Available online: http://ageofcreativity.co.uk/the_case/ (accessed 27 March 2016).

Arts and Health Australia. (2015), 'Creative Ageing', Arts and Health Australia. Available online: http://www.artsandhealth.org/creative-ageing. html (accessed 1 May 2015).

Atchley, R. (1989), 'The Continuity Theory of Normal Ageing', *The Gerontologist*, 29 (2): 183–190.

Barry, A. (2015a), 'The Elders Company', The Royal Exchange. Available online: http://www.royalexchange.co.uk/616-the-royal-exchange-elders -company-from-pilot-to-intergen-work/file (accessed 1 April 2016).

Barry, A. (2015b), E'lders Company Review', The Royal Exchange, unpublished.

Basting, A. (2006), 'Creative Storytelling and Self-Expression among People with Dementia', in A. Leibing and L. Cohen (eds.), *Thinking about Dementia: Culture, Loss, and the Anthropology of Senility*, 180–194, New Brunswick, NJ: Rutgers University Press.

Bernard, M., D. Amigoni, L. Menro and M. Murrey. (2012), 'Ages and Stages: The Place of Theatre in Representations and Recollections of Ageing', NDA Findings 15, NDA Programme. Available online: http://www.newdynamics.group.shef.ac.uk/assets/files/FINAL%20NDA%20Findings%2015%20(2).pdf (accessed 11 July 2015).

Cohen, G. D., S. Perlstein, J. Chapline, J. Kelly, K. M. Firth and S. Simmens. (2007), 'The Impact of Professionally Conducted Cultural Programs on the Physical Health, Mental Health, and Social Functioning of Older Adults – 2-Year Results', *Journal of Aging, Humanities & the Arts*, 1 (1–2): 5–22.

Department of Health. (2009), *Living Well with Dementia: A National Dementia Strategy*, London: DH Publications.

Dolan, J. (2005), *Utopia in Performance*, Michigan: University of Michigan Press.

Duffy, K. (1995), *Social Exclusion and Human Dignity in Europe*, Strasbourg: Council of Europe.

European Theatre Convention (n.d.), 'About', The Art of Ageing. Available online: http://www.artofageing.eu/about (accessed 28 March 2016).

Goffman, E. (1956), *The Presentation of Self in Everyday Life*, London: Pelican.

Gubrium, J. F. (1995), 'Taking Stock', *Qualitative Health Research*, 5: 267–269.

Harris, B. (2013), 'The Storybox Project Examining the Role of a Theatre and Arts-based Intervention for People with Dementia', University of Manchester. Available online: http://www.humanities.manchester.ac.uk/medialibrary/micra/events/2013/Storybox_Project.pdf (accessed 1 October 2014).

Havinghurst, R. (1963), 'Successful Ageing', in R. H. Williams, C. Tibbits and W. Donohue (eds.), *Process of Ageing*, vol.1, 311–315. Chicago: University of Chicago Press.

Henley, J. (2012), 'The Village Where People Have Dementia and Fun', *The Guardian*, 27 August.

Jenkins, C. and A. Smythe. (2013), 'Reflections on a Visit to a Dementia Care Village', *Nursing Older People*, 25 (6): 14–19.

Johnson, R. (2011), 'On Ageing Case Study: Evaluation Report, Fevered Sleep'. Available online: http://www.feveredsleep.co.uk/wp-content/uploads/2010/10/On-Ageing-Executive-Summary-Report.pdf (accessed 1 April 2012).

Kinney, J. and C. Rentz. (2005), 'Observed Well-being among Individuals with Dementia: Memories in the Making©, an Art Program, versus Other Structured Activity', *American Journal of Alzheimer's Disease and Other Dementias*, 20: 220–227.

Kneale, D. (2012), 'Is Social Exclusion Still Important to Older People', Age UK and The International Longevity Centre. Available online: http://www.ilcuk.org.uk/index.php/publications/publication_details/is_social_exclusion_still_important_for_older_people (accessed 25 October 2015).

Lemon, B. W., V. L. Bretigan and J. A. Peterson. (1972), 'Activity Types and Life Satisfaction in a Retirement Community', *Journal of Gerontology*, 27 (4): 511–523.

Mangan, M. (2011), *Staging Ageing: Theatre, Performance and the Narrative of Decline*, Bristol: Intellect.

Mental Health Foundation. (2011), *An Evidence Review of the Impact of Participatory Arts on Older People*. Available online: https://www.mentalhealth.org.uk/sites/default/files/evidence-review-participatory-arts.pdf (accessed 1 April 2014).

National Centre for Creative Ageing. (2012), 'About NCCA'. Available online: http://www.creativeaging.org/about-ncca-0 (accessed 18 April 2005).

NICE. (2006), 'Dementia: Supporting People with Dementia and Their Carers in Health and Social Care', National Institute for Health and Clinical Excellence. Available online: https://www.nice.org.uk/guidance/cg42/chapter/1-guidance (accessed 18 April 2016).

Nicholson, H. (2011), 'Making Home Work: Theatre-Making with Older Adults in Residential Care', *NJ: Drama Australia Journal*, 35 (1): 47–62.

Ní Léime, A. and S. O'Shea. (2012), 'The impact of the Bealtaine Arts Programme on the Quality of Life, Wellbeing and Social Interaction of Older People in Ireland', *Ageing and Society*, 32 (5): 851–872.

Noice, H. and T. Noice. (2009), 'An Arts Intervention for Older Adults Living in Subsidized Retirement Homes', *Neuropsychology, Development, and Cognition Section B, Aging, Neuropsychology and Cognition*, 16: 56–79.

Organ, K. (2016), 'A New Form of Theatre: Older Peoples' Involvement in Theatre and Drama', The Baring Foundation. Available online:

http://www.baringfoundation.org.uk/wp-content/uploads/2016/03 /OlderPeople'sTheatre.pdf (accessed 1 April 2016).

Philips, J. (2007), *Care*, Cambridge: Polity Press.

Postlethwaite, L. (2014), Personal Interview, 1 August.

Pyman, T. and S. Rugg. (2006), 'Participating in a Community Theatre Production: A Dramatherapeutic Perspective', *International Journal of Therapy & Rehabilitation*, 13 (12): 562–571.

Roe, B., S. McCormick, T. Lucas, W. Gallagher, A. Winn and S. Elkin. (2016), 'Coffee, Cake & Culture: Evaluation of an Art for Health Programme for Older People in the Community', *Dementia*, 15 (4): 539–559.

Small Things Creative Practices. (2015), 'About'. Available online: https:// smallthings.org.uk/ (accessed March 2015).

Thompson, J. (2009), *Performance Affects: Applied Theatre and the End of Effect*, London: Palgrave MacMillan.

Thompson, P., M. Itzin and M. Abendstern. (1990), *I Don't Feel Old: The Experience of Later Life*, Oxford and New York: Oxford University Press.

Thornton, S. (2013), 'The Complexity and Challenges of Participation', in T. Prentki and S. Preston (eds.) *The Applied Theatre Reader*. London: Routledge

Thornton, S. (2015), 'Theatre for Social Change: Collective Encounters on Rediscovering the Radical', *Journal of Arts & Communities*, 7 (1/2): 33–43.

Tronto, J. (1993), *Moral Boundaries: A Political Argument for an Ethics of Care*, New York: Routledge.

University of Arts, London. (2013), 'LCF News: Bloggers, Performers and the Fabulous Fashionistas Contribute to Mirror Mirror', UAL. Available online: http://blogs.arts.ac.uk/fashion/2013/11/01/bloggers-performers -and-the-fabulous-fashionistas-contribute-to-mirror-mirror/ (accessed 25 February 2016).

University of Sheffield. (2016a), 'About the NDA Programme', New Dynamics of Ageing. Available online: http://www.newdynamics.group .shef.ac.uk/about-the-programme.html (accessed 1 March 2016).

University of Sheffield. (2016b), 'Ages and Stages: Read Project Details', Ages and Stages. Available online: http://www.newdynamics.group.shef .ac.uk/ages-and-stages.html (accessed 31 March 2016).

University of Sheffield. (2016c), 'Look at Me! Images of Women and Ageing, News: Now Can You See Me?! Images of Older Women in Sheffield', Available online: http://www.representing-ageing.com/view_news_29.html (accessed 30 March 2016).

Vanderslott, J. (1994), 'Positive Exercise in Damage Limitation: Management of Aggression in Elderly Confused People', *Professional Nurse*, 10 (3): 150, 151.

Victor, C. and M. Evandrou. (1986), 'Does Social Class Matter in Later Life?' in S. Gregorio (ed.), *Social Gerontology New Directions*, 252–267, London: Croom-Helm.

Warren, L. and A. Clarke. (2009), 'Woo – hoo, What a Ride!' *Older People*. Life Stories and Active Ageing', in R. Edmondonson and H. J. Von Kondratwiz (eds.), *Valuing Old People, A Humanist Approach to Ageing*, 233–248, Bristol: Policy Press.

Warren, L., M. Gott, S. Horgan, N. Richards and R. Martin. (2012), 'New Dynamics of Ageing: Representing Self-Representing Ageing Look at Me! Images of Women & Ageing', NDA Findings 10, NDA Programme. Available online: http://www.newdynamics.group.shef.ac.uk/assets/files/NDA%20Findings_10.pdf (accessed 11 July 2015).

Weaver, L. (2013a),'Performing the Issue', *Strategies for Engaging the Public through Performance, Place and The Everyday*. Available online: http://publicaddresssystems.org/projects/performing-as-methodology/ (accessed 23 March 2016).

Weaver, L. (2013b), 'Performing the Persona', *Strategies for Engaging the Public through Performance, Place and The Everyday*. Available online: http://publicaddresssystems.org/projects/performing-the-persona-3/ (accessed 23 March 2016).

Woodword, K. (1991), *Aging and Its Discontents: Freud and Other Fictions*, Indiana: Indiana University Press.

Chapter 3

Barkmann, C., A.K. Siem, N. Wessolowski and M. Schulte-Markwort. (2013), 'Clowning as a Supportive Measure in Paediatrics – A Survey of Clowns, Parents and Nursing Staff', *BMC Pediatrics*, 13 (1): 166.

Basting, A. D. (2006), 'Arts in Dementia Care: "This Is Not the End. It's the End of This Chapter"', *Generations*, 30 (1): 16.

Beard, R. (2011), 'Art Therapies and Dementia Care: A Systematic Review', *Dementia*, 11 (5): 633–656.

Christensen, M. (1999), The Big Apple Circus Clown Care Unit. *The Hospital Clown Newsletter: A Publication for Clowns in Community and World Service*, 1–16.

Cooke, M., W. Moyle, D. Shum, S. Harrison and J. Murfield. (2010), 'A Randomised Control Trial Exploring the Effect of Music on Quality of Life and Depression in Older People with Dementia: A Randomized Control Trial', *Journal of Health Psychology*, 15 (5): 765–776.

Dunn, J., M. Balfour, W. Moyle, M. Cooke, K. Martin, C. Crystal and A. Yen. (2013), 'Playfully Engaging People Living with Dementia: Searching for Yum Cha Moments', *International Journal of Play*, 2 (3): 174–186.

Dunn, J. (2010), 'Video in Drama Research: Formalising the Role of Collaborative Conversations within the Analysis Phase', *RiDE: The Journal of Applied Theatre and Performance*, 15 (2): 193–208.

Etchells, T. (1999), *Certain Fragments: Contemporary Performance and Forced Entertainment*. London: Psychology Press.

Gaulier, P. (2007), *The Tormentor*, Paris: Editions Filmko.

Guzmán-García, A., J.C. Hughes, I.A. James and L. Rochester. (2013), 'Dancing as a Psychosocial Intervention in Care Homes: A Systematic Review of the Literature', *International Journal of Geriatric Psychiatry*, 28 (9): 914–924.

Hendriks, R. (2012), 'Tackling Indifference–Clowning, Dementia, and the Articulation of a Sensitive Body', *Medical Anthropology*, 31 (6): 459–476.

Kerman, J. B. (1992), 'Clown as Social Healer: A Study of the Clown Ministry Movement', *Journal of American Culture*, 15: 9–16.

Killick J. (2003), 'Funny and Sad and Friendly: A Drama Project in Scotland', *Journal of Dementia Care*, 11: 24–26.

Kontos, P., K. L Miller, G. Mitchell and J. Stirling-Twist. (2015), 'Presence Redefined : The Reciprocal Nature of Engagement between Elder-Clowns and Persons with Dementia', *Dementia*, 16 (1): 46–66.

Korr, M. and R. Williams. (2015), 'Not Just Clowning around : Patch Adams, MD, Speaks at URI Honors Colloquium on Humor', *Rhode Island Health Medical Journal*, 98 (10): 67.

Lecoq, J. (2000), *The Moving Body*, trans. David Bradbury, London: Methuen.

Lipsitz, G. (2014), '1 Improvised Listening: Opening Statements', in A. Heble and R. Caines (eds.), *The Improvisation Studies Reader: Spontaneous Acts*, Abingdon: Routledge.

Low, L., B. Goodenough, J. Fletcher, K. Xu, A. N. Casey, L. Chenoweth, R. Fleming, P. Spitzer, J. P. Bell and H. Brodaty. (2014), 'The Effects of Humour Therapy on Nursing Home Residents Measured Using Observational Methods: The SMILE Cluster Randomized Trial', *Journal of the American Medical Directors Association*, 15 (8): 564–569.

Moyle, W., U. Kellett, A. Ballantyne and N. Gracia (2011), 'Dementia and Loneliness: An Australian Perspective', *Journal of Clinical Nursing*, 20: 1445–1453.

Nogueira-Martins, M. F., D. Lima-costa and L. A. Nogueira-Martins. (2014), 'Perceptions of Healthcare Undergraduate Students about a Hospital Clown Training', *Scientific Research* (May): 542–551.

Oppenheim, D., C. Simonds and O. Hartmann. (1997), 'Clowning on Children's Wards', *Lancet*, 350 (9094): 1838–1840.

Peacock, L. (2009), *Serious Play: Modern Clown Performance*, Bristol: Intellect Books.

Raglio, A., G. Bellelli, D. Traficante, M. Gianotti, M. C. Ubezio, S. Gentile, D. Villani and M. Trabucchi. (2010), 'Efficacy of Music Therapy in the Treatment of Behavioral and Psychiatric Symptoms of dementia', *Alzheimer Disease & Associated Disorders*, 22 (2): 158–162.

Ravelin, T., A. Isola and J. Kylmä. (2013), 'Dance Performance as a Method of Intervention as Experienced by Older Persons with Dementia', *International Journal of Older People Nursing*, 8 (1): 10–18.

Schweitzer, P. (2007), *Reminiscence Theatre: Making Theatre from Memories*. London: Jessica Kingsley Publishers.

Svansdottir, H. B. and J. Snaedal. (2006), 'Music Therapy in Moderate and Severe Dementia of Alzheimer's Type: A Case–Control Study.' *International Psychogeriatrics*, 18 (4): 613–621.

Warren, B. and P. Spitzer. (2011), 'Laughing to Longevity – The Work of Elder Clowns', *The Lancet*, 378 (9791): 562–563.

Chapter 4

Bartlett, R. and D. O'Connor. (2010), *Broadening the Dementia Debate: Towards Social Citizenship*, Bristol: Policy Press.

Blunt, A. and R. Dowling. (2006), *Home*, London: Routledge.

Ingold, T. (2011), *BeingAlive: Essays on Movement, Knowledge and Description*, London: Routledge.

Nolan M., S. Davies, T. Ryan and J. Keady. (2008), 'Relationship-Centred Care and the "Senses" Framework', *Journal of Dementia Care*, 16 (1): 26–28.

Pink, S. (2004), *Home Truths: Gender, Domestic Objects and Everyday Life*, Oxford: Berg.

Stewart, K. (2007), *Ordinary Affects*, London: Duke University Press.

Chapter 5

Adriani, G., K. Winfried, T. Karin and J. Beuys. (1979), *Life and Works*, New York: Barron's Educational Series.

Allen, K. (2014), 'Music Therapy in the NICU: Is There Evidence to Support Integration for Procedural Support?', US National Library of Medicine National Institutes of Health, Available online: http://www.ncbi.nlm.nih.gov/pmc/articles/PMC3826794/ (accessed 12 December 2015).

Anonymous. (2015), 'Definition of Tera Electron Volts'. Available online: http://lhc-machine-outreach.web.cern.ch/lhc-machine-outreach/lhc_glossary.htm (accessed 1 January 2016).

Beckett, S. (1973), *Not I*, London: Faber and Faber.

Bygren, L. O., B. B. Konlaan and S. E. Johansson. (1996), 'Attendance at Cultural Events, Reading Books or Periodicals, and Making Music or Singing in a Choir as Determinants for Survival: Swedish Interview Survey of Living Conditions', *British Medical Journal*, 313: 1577–1580.

Bygren, L. O., S. E. Johansson, B. B. Konlaan, A. M. Grjibovski, A. V. Wilkinson and Michael Sjöström. (2009), 'Attending Cultural Events and Cancer Mortality: A Swedish Cohort Study', *Arts & Health*, 1 (1): 64–73.

Cartwright, N. (2007), 'Are RCTs the Gold Standard?' *Bioocieties*, 2: 11–20.

Clapp, S. (2015), 'The Father Review – Touching Journeys in a Shifting Mindscape', *The Guardian*, 11 October, Available online: http://www.theguardian.com/stage/2015/oct/11/the-father-review-kenneth-cranham-florian-zeller (accessed 20 October 2015).

Committee on Environmental Health, American Academy of Paediatrics. (1997), 'Noise: A Hazard for the Foetus and New Born in Paediatrics', *Paediatrics*, 100 (4): 724–727.

Cuypers, K., K. De Ridder, K. Kvaløy, M. Skjei Knudtsen, S. Krokstad, J. Holmen and T. Lingaas Holmen. (2012), 'Leisure Time Activities in Adolescence in the Presence of Susceptibility Genes for Obesity: Risk or

Resilience against Overweight in Adulthood? The HUNT Study', *BMC Public Health*, 12 (820).

Duclow, D. (2003), 'ArsMoriendi', *Encyclopedia of Death & Dying*. Available online: http://www.deathreference.com/A-Bi/Ars-Moriendi.html (accessed 12 November 2015).

Gordon-Nesbitt, R. (2015), *Exploring the Longitudinal Relationship between Arts Participation and Health*, Manchester. Arts for Health.

Gwande, A. (2010), 'Letting Go: What Should Medicine Do When It Can't Save Yourlife?' *The New Yorker*, 2 August. Available online: http://www.newyorker.com/reporting/2010/08/02/100802fa_fact_gawande (accessed 12 December 2015).

Heath, I. (2010), 'What Do We Want to Die From?' *British Medical Journal*, 341. Available online: http://search.proquest.com/openview/2ae3748b1aa c43ee4f76eba081b02bc6/1?pq-origsite=gscholar&cbl=2040978 (accessed 20 February 2017).

Johnson, K. (2015), 'Theatres Are Not Catering for the Working Class Majority', *The Guardian*, 15 September, Available online: http://www.theguardian.com/culture-professionals-network/culture-professionals-blog/2014/sep/15/working-class-people-subsidised-theatre (accessed 5 November 2015).

Kane, S. (2000), *4.48 Psychosis*, London: Methuen Drama.

Kitwood, T. (1997), *Dementia Reconsidered*, London: Open University Press.

Knapp, A. (2012), 'How Much Does It Cost to Find a Higgs Boson?' *Forbes*, 5 July, Available online: http://www.forbes.com/sites/alexknapp/2012/07/05/how-much-does-it-cost-to-find-a-higgs-boson/ (accessed 2 December 2015).

Kouvonen, A., J. A. Swift, M. Stafford, T. Cox, J. Vahtera, A. Väänänen, T. Heponiemi, R. De Vogli, A. Griffiths and M. Kivimäki. (2012), 'Social Participation and Maintaining Recommended Waist Circumference: Prospective Evidence from the English Longitudinal Study of Aging', *Journal of Aging and Health*, 24 (2): 250–268.

Larkin, P. (1964), *The Whitsun Weddings*, London: Faber and Faber.

Lasagna, L. (1964), 'The Modern Version of the Hippocratic Oath', School of Medicine, Tufts University, Available online: http://www.medterms.com/script/main/art.asp?articlekey=20909 (accessed 2 December 2015).

Lajunen, H. R., A. Keski-Rahkonen, L. R. Pulkkinen, J. Richard, A. Rissanen and J. Kaprio. (2009), 'Leisure Activity Patterns and Their Associations with Overweight: A Prospective Study among Adolescents', *Journal of Adolescence*, 32 (5): 1089–1103.

Parliamentary and Health Service Ombudsman. (2015), *Dying without Dignity*, London: HMSO. Available online: http://www.ombudsman.org. uk/reports-and-consultations/reports/health/dying-without-dignity/1 (accessed 20 December 2015)

Philbin, M. K. and P. Klass. (2000), 'Hearing and Behavioural Responses to Sound in Full-Term New-Borns', *Journal of Perinatology*, 20: 68–76.

Sundquist, K., M. Lindström, M. Malmström, S. E. Johansson and J. Sundquist. (2004), 'Social Participation and Coronary Heart Disease: A Follow-up Study of 6900 Women and Men in Sweden', *Social Science & Medicine*, 58: 615–622.

Schaffer, P. (1973), *Equus*, London: Samuel French Ltd.

Smith, R. (2010), 'Medicine's Need for the Humanities', *British Medical Journal*, 30 December. Available online: http://blogs.bmj.com/bmj/2010/12/30/richard-smith-medicines-need-for-the-humanities (accessed 12 November 2015).

'Stichting Ambulance Wens Nederland'. (2015), *Washington Times*, 5 March, Available online: http://www.washingtontimes.com/news/2015/mar/5 /dying-wish-comes-true-dutch-woman-with-als-sees-re/ (accessed 20 January 2016).

Wang, H., A. Karp, B. Winblad and L. Fratiglioni. (2002), 'Late-Life Engagement in Social and Leisure Activities Is Associated with a Decreased Risk of Dementia: A Longitudinal Study from the Kungsholmen Project', *American Journal of Epidemiology*, 155 (12): 1081–1087.

Williams, H. (2015), 'The Father, Tricycle Theatre, Review: A Heartbreaking Portrayal of Old Age', *The Independent*, 13 May, Available online: http:// www.independent.co.uk/arts-entertainment/theatre-dance/the-father -tricycle-theatre-review-a-heartbreaking-portrayal-of-old-age-10248681 .html (accessed 1 January 2016).

Yalden, J., B. McCormack, M. O'Connor and S. Hardy. (2013), 'Transforming End of Life Care Using Practice Development: An Arts-Informed Approach in Residential Aged Care', *International Practice Development Journal*, 3: 2–6.

Zeller, F. (2015), *The Mother & The Father*, London: Faber and Faber.

Chapter 6

Bahlke, L., S. Pericolosi and M. Lehman. (2010), 'Use of TimeSlips to Improve Communication in Persons with Moderate–Late Stage Dementia', *Journal of Aging, Humanities, and the Arts*, 4 (4): 390–405.

Basting, A., M. Towey and E. Rose, eds. (2016), *Playing Penelope: An Arts-based Odyssey to Transform Long-term Care*, Iowa City: University of Iowa Press.

Fritsch, T., J. Kwak, S. Grant, J. Lang, R. R. Montgomery and A. Basting. (2009), 'Impact of TimeSlips, a Creative Expression Intervention Program, on Nursing Home Residents with Dementia and their Caregivers', *Gerontologist*, 49 (1): 117–127.

George, D. and W. Houser. (2014), 'I'm a Storyteller!', *American Journal of Alzheimer's Disease & Other Dementias*, 29 (8): 678–684.

George, D., H. Stuckey, C. Dillon and M. Whitehead. (2011), 'Impact of Participation in TimeSlips, a Creative Group-based Storytelling Program, on Medical Student Attitudes toward Persons with Dementia: A Qualitative Study', *The Gerontologist*, 51 (5): 699–703.

George, D. R., C. Yang, H. L. Stuckey and M. M. Whitehead. (2012), 'Evaluating an Arts-based Intervention to Improve Medical Student Attitudes toward Persons with Dementia using the Dementia Attitudes Scale', *Journal of The American Geriatrics Society*, 60 (8): 1583–1585.

Houser, W., D. George and V. Chinchilli. (2014), 'Impact of TimeSlips Creative Expression Program on Behavioural Symptoms and Psychotropic Medication Use in Persons with Dementia in Long-Term Care: A Cluster-Randomized Pilot Study', *The American Journal of Geriatric Psychiatry: Official Journal of the American Association for Geriatric Psychiatry*, 22 (4): 337–340.

Jackson, S. (2011), *Social Works: Performing Art, Supporting Publics*, New York: Routledge.

Kitwood, T. (1997), *Dementia Reconsidered: The Person Comes First*, Buckingham, UK and Philadelphia, PA: Open University Press.

O'Connor, P. and M. Anderson. (2015), *Applied Theatre: Research: Radical Departures*, London: Bloomsbury.

Phillips, L. J., S. A. Reid-Arndt and Y. Pak. (2010), 'Effects of a Creative Expression Intervention on Emotions, Communication, and Quality of Life in Persons with Dementia', *Nursing Research*, 59 (6): 417–425.

Chapter 8

Alzheimer's Society. (2012), *Coping with Memory Loss*, factsheet 526, London: Alzheimer's Society.

Alzheimer's Society. (2014), *Dementia: Opportunity for Change*, London: Alzheimer's Society.

Ballard, C., J. O'Brien, I. James, P. Mynt, M. Lana, D. Potkins and J. Fossey. (2001), 'Quality of Life for People with Dementia Living in Residential and Nursing Home Care: The Impact of Performance on Activities of Daily Living, Behavioral and Psychological Symptoms, Language Skills, and Psychotropic Drugs', *International Psychogeriatrics*, 13 (1): 93–106.

Bannan, N. and C. Montgomery-Smith. (2008), 'Singing for the Brain': Reflections on the Human Capacity for Music Arising from a Pilot Study of Group Singing with Alzheimer's Patients', *The Journal of the Royal Society for the Promotion of Health*, 128 (2): 73–78.

Beard, R. L. (2011), 'Art Therapies and Dementia Care: A Systematic Review', *Dementia*, 11(5): 1–24.

Clift, S., P. M. Camic, B. Chapman, G. Clayton, N. Daykin, G. Eades, C. Parkinson, J. Secker, T. Stickley and M. White. (2009), 'The State of Arts and Health in England', *Arts & Health*, 1 (1): 6–35.

Csikszentmihalyi, M. (1997), *Finding Flow: The Psychology of Engagement with Everyday Life*, New York: Basic Books.

Department of Health. (2009), *The Use of Antipsychotic Medication for People with Dementia: Time for Action*, London: Department of Health.

Douglas, S., I. James and C. Ballard. (2004), 'Non-Pharmacological Interventions in Dementia', *Advances in Psychiatric Treatment*, 10 (3): 171–177.

Fischer, K. W. (1980), 'A Theory of Cognitive Development: The Control and Construction of Hierarchies of Skills', *Psychological Review*, 87 (6): 477.

Health Innovation Network. (2015), *Peer Support for People with Dementia: A Social Return on Investment (SROI) Study*, London: Health Innovation Network.

Killick, J. and K. Allan. (1999), 'The Arts in Dementia Care: Tapping a Rich Resource', *Journal of Dementia Care*, 7: 35–38.

Kitwood, T. (1997), *Dementia Reconsidered: The Person Comes First*, Buckingham: Open University Press.

Maslow, A. H. (1943), 'A Theory of Human Motivation', *Psychological Review*, 50: 370–396.

McEvoy, P. and R. Plant. (2014), 'Dementia Care: Using Empathic Curiosity to Establish the Common Ground That Is Necessary for Meaningful Communication', *Journal of Psychiatric and Mental Health Nursing*, 21 (6): 477–482.

McShane, R., J. Keene, K. Gedling, C. Fairburn, R. Jacoby and T. Hope. (1997), 'Do Neuroleptic Drugs Hasten Cognitive Decline in Dementia?

Prospective Study with Necropsy Follow-up', *British Medical Journal*, 314: 211, 212.

Merseyside Dance Initiative (MDI). (2014), *Evaluation of Time and Tide, A Dementia Friendly Dance and Movement Programme: 2012–2014*, Liverpool: MDI.

National Institute for Health and Care Excellence. (2012), *Dementia: Supporting People with Dementia and Their Carers in Health and Social Care*, NICE Clinical Guideline 42.

Osman, S. E., V. Tischler and J. Schneider. (2016), "Singing for the Brain': A Qualitative Study Exploring the Health and Well-being Benefits of Singing for People with Dementia and Their Carers', *Dementia*, 15 (6): 1326–1339.

Pink, D. H. (2011), *Drive: The Surprising Truth about What Motivates Us*, London: Canongate Books.

Sacks, O. (1985), *The Man Who Mistook His Wife for a Hat*, London: Picador.

Woods B., E. Aquirre, A. E. Spector and M. Orrell. (2012), 'Cognitive Stimulation to Improve Cognitive Functioning in People with Dementia', *Cochrane Database of Systematic Reviews*, 2, Art No: CD005562.

Index